Critical Wage Theory

The publisher and the University of California Press Foundation gratefully acknowledge the generous support of the Barbara S. Isgur Endowment Fund in Public Affairs.

Critical Wage Theory

WHY WAGE JUSTICE IS RACIAL JUSTICE

Ruben J. Garcia

UNIVERSITY OF CALIFORNIA PRESS

University of California Press
Oakland, California

Library of Congress Cataloging-in-Publication Data

Names: Garcia, Ruben J., author.
Title: Critical wage theory : why wage justice is racial justice / Ruben J.
  Garcia, University of California Press.
Description: Oakland : University of California Press, 2024. | Includes
  bibliographical references and index.
Identifiers: LCCN 2023044866 (print) | LCCN 2023044867 (ebook) |
  ISBN 9780520388017 (hardback) | ISBN 9780520388031 (paperback) |
  ISBN 9780520388048 (ebook)
Subjects: LCSH: Wages—Law and legislation. | Minimum wage—Law and
  legislation. | Critical race theory. | Racial justice.
Classification: LCC K1781 .G35 2024 (print) | LCC K1781 (ebook) |
  DDC 331.2/301—dc23/eng/20231005
LC record available at https://lccn.loc.gov/2023044866
LC ebook record available at https://lccn.loc.gov/2023044867

Manufactured in the United States of America

33 32 31 30 29 28 27 26 25 24
10 9 8 7 6 5 4 3 2 1

Dedicated to the memories of Robert and Emilia Garcia. Eternally loved and in love.

Contents

Acknowledgments   ix

Introduction: The Importance of the Minimum
Wage   1

1. A Critical Race Theory of Wage Justice   13

2. Movements Framing the Minimum Wage as a
    Matter of Racial Justice   29

3. Immigrants, Day Laborers, and Exotic Dancers:
    At Risk for Wage Theft   45

4. Legally Sanctioned Subminimum Wages   64

5. Legacies of Race and Slavery: Sweatshops,
    Prisons, Fields   72

6. The Racial Political Economy: Gig Workers,
    Home Workers, and the State   94

7. Improving the Minimum Wage as a Tool for
   Racial Justice   116

8. The Future of the Minimum Wage in the Global
   Economy   143

   Notes   159

   Bibliography   185

   Index   205

Acknowledgments

If every book is a village, this one was a small city. There are so many people to thank but I have to start with my life partner and inspiration—Victoria Carreón. Tori has been my chief supporter, best editor, and soulmate for 35 years now and I am so looking forward to the next 35 years and more. Thanks, Tori, once again for all of your love, patience, and support.

The faith that the team at the University of California Press had in this project from the beginning was truly awe-inspiring. I hope now that the book is done it all seems worth it. Thank you for your patience with me and my endless questions and revisions. Many thanks go to Senior Editor Maura Roessner for her support of this project and my endless requests for meetings and early morning (7 a.m.) calls. Thank you to Sam Warren for his attention to all of the many details involved in a project like this. Thanks to the anonymous reviewers for their perceptive comments which I have tried mightily to incorporate, but if I have not, it has not been for a lack of respect for their perspectives.

Frank Rudy Cooper deserves special thanks for being able to get me out of the house for coffee once in a while, and for his encouragement and incisive suggestions on the manuscript. Ann McGinley, co-director with me of the Workplace Law Program at the William S. Boyd School of Law, and her husband, Professor Jeff Stempel, were also particularly enouraging.

Associate Dean Jeanne Price, director of Boyd's excellent Weiner-Rogers Law Library, and library professors Jim Rich, Lena Rieke, and Youngwoo Ban were the foundations of so much of the research. Several generations of law students provided excellent research assistance on this book—Melody Rissell, Paloma Guerrero, Alina Krauff. Joey Adamiak, Erika Smolyar, Olive Rothe, Nazo Demirdjian, Servando Martinez, John Regalia, Eric Lundy, Sonia Galan, Tania González Contreras, and Jay Brunner.

Thanks to my mentors in critical race theory at the University of California Los Angeles School of Law, and to the law school for its leadership in that intellectual pursuit. The guidance of Professor Kimberlé Williams Crenshaw is a constant and all-important inspiration in this era of attacks on the freedom to learn. As she has for more than 30 years, Laura Gómez, now back home in Albquerque and working at the University of New Mexico School of Law, has provided steady support and a road map for my academic career. Thanks to all my professors at UCLA, who shaped me in many different ways to become the scholar and teacher that I am today. I especially want to recognize the way that California Supreme Court Justice Cruz Reynoso impacted my life and work. Descanso en paz, Justicia.

My time as a Hastie Fellow at the University of Wisconsin Law School sharpened the focus on race and labor that shaped the book. Two scholars who were key to that process have also broken the bonds of this world since I thanked them in my 2012 book *Marginal Workers*. Rest in peace, Professors Jim Jones and Jane Larson.

As this book is partly a reflection of my practice experience as a labor lawyer in Southern California in 1990s, I owe a great debt to the labor lawyers who "raised me" at the Rothner, Segall, and

Greenstone firm in Pasadena. The partners Glenn Rothner, Tony Segall, Ellen Greenstone, and, in the early part of my time there, Della Bahan, were and are the epitome of what workers' lawyers should be. Their excellent leadership of several of the cases discussed in this book provided a good part of the inspiration for this project.

I have a dedicated community of colleagues at University of Nevada, Las Vegas, who have been been extremely suppportive of this work. Boyd's associate deans for research, Linda Berger, Eve Hanan and Ian Bartrum, and the deans of the Law School, Leah Chan Grinvald and Daniel Hamilton, provided both financial and moral support to complete this project.

I would like to thank the community of Las Vegas for its interest in my work and support over the years. This book has been informed by the context in which I have been fortunate to live for the last 12 years. I think that Las Vegas, for all of its one-of-a-kind glitz and over-the-top-ness, has many of the hallmarks of the future of the workplace. I am so fortunate to be able to live and work in such a dynamic and diverse place. Conversations with several in the Las Vegas community were very helpful in this project, including attorneys Patrick Chapin and Leon Greenberg.

I am also fortunate to be part of an extended community of scholars beyond Las Vegas, who provided moral support and extremely helpful comments and conversations. In 2018, UNLV Law hosted a symposium on the Thirteenth Amendment and Economic Justice, one of the founding meetings of the Thirteenth Amendment Project; symposium participants included Lea VanderVelde, Rebecca Zietlow, Avi Soifer, Jim Pope, Fred Smith, Noah Zatz. and César Rosado Marzán. The ideas that formed some of the foundational work of this book were presented there; my symposium paper was subsequently published in the *Nevada Law Journal*.[1] My presentations of this work to audiences at Brooklyn Law School, the University of Wisconsin Law School, Kline of School of Law at Drexel University, and the University of Haifa Faculty of Law has benefited the work tremendously. I look forward to more engagement with audiences both domestically and internationally about the ideas presented here.

The full staff of the William S. Boyd School of Law supported this work in numerous ways, but Melani Grande Murrieta in the faculty support department deserves special praise for her timely and patient assistance with the manuscript.

Finally, I thank my family for their support. My parents, Robert and Emilia Garcia, will not see the publication of this second book, but their support and pride for my first book and all of my endeavors before their passings in 2014 and 2015 have once again made the impossible possible. Their spirits are imbued in these pages and in the lives of all their children—my six older sisters and one brother—Terry, Patty, Katy, Kathy, Christina, Roberta, and Arnold. Thanks also to my in-laws, Samuel and Argelia Carreón, for their constant support. May Samuel's passion for social justice continue to live long now that he is gone, through his daughter Victoria.

As this book was mostly written during a global pandemic, when so many "essential" workers of color and immigrants were in hazardous zones, especially in food service, transportation, health care, and law enforcement, this book is dedicated to them. While that is of little tangible reward, my humble hope in writing this book is that their struggles will receive more attention and dignity.

Introduction

THE IMPORTANCE OF THE MINIMUM WAGE

For more than a decade, the Fight for $15 movement has called upon the largest corporations in the country and the government to raise the minimum wage for labor in the United States. By many measures, the movement has been very successful. The movement for $15 and a union has put enough pressure on certain employers (mainly fast-food companies) to push wages up at other companies and at state and local government levels.[1] At state and local levels, unions and activists have spearheaded increases to the minimum wage even though the federal minimum wage has remained stagnant at $7.25 per hour since 2009.[2]

Many workers still languish in low-wage labor and struggle to survive. Over the last 50 years, income inequality has widened considerably and the number of workers covered by collective bargaining agreements has dwindled to pre–New Deal levels.[3] At the same time, more statutes have been passed throughout the country to raise minimum standards for labor. This proliferation of legal protections would seem to provide an increase in bargaining power and labor standards. But the data point in a different direction. More and more workers are falling victim to wage theft, and most of them are immigrants and people of color. Wages are too low and must be raised for people of color and immigrants to have greater bargaining power.[4]

Even though there are numerous examples of increases in the minimum wage benefiting workers, there are still claims that the minimum wage disproportionately harms people of color at the bottom of the wage scale. Many economic studies disprove this contention, but this book focuses on justifying higher minimum wages as an essential benefit for marginalized workers by using the postulates of critical race theory, to begin a field of inquiry I call "critical wage theory," abbreviated as CWT.[5]

Critical wage theory, as I use it here, is both descriptive and normative. As the examples in this book show, people of color and immigrants are more likely to suffer wage theft and denial of the minimum wage than other workers. The intersectional nature of the harms inherent in racial and sexual discrimination law that scholars have identified are also present in minimum wage law. The political economic forces that exempt domestic workers, agricultural workers, and gig workers from the protections of federal labor law disproportionately impact people of color and immigrants.[6]

Yet even when the law applies, the protections of the minimum wage fail to lift the most vulnerable out of poverty. In part, this is because the minimum wage is too low to sustain a living in many areas of the country. Also, the system is set up to pay subminimum wages, as in the restaurant industry or sheltered workshops for the disabled. As the stories in this book show, those who are often the victims of wage theft are likely to be people of color and immigrants.

Moreover, some workers are kept from earning the minimum wage by law, including prisoners on work crews doing dangerous work such as fire prevention. The Thirteenth Amendment to the United States Constitution purportedly justifies this exploitation with its allowance for servitude "as punishment for a crime for which the person is duly convicted." Despite this language, there is nothing that prevents inmates from earning a minimum wage, and indeed there is precedent for paying a wage to inmates—but no guarantee that they will earn the minimum wage. Nonetheless, these workers, who lack any political power, are seeking legislation or litigation to get a minimum standard.

The importance of the minimum wage is seen in decades-old litigation involving exotic dancers in clubs. These workers, who dance topless and nude for tips and sometimes earn hundreds of dollars a night, have won several victories in litigation to recover minimum wages and overtime pay. Club owners have reacted to these losses with new legislation and legal devices to avoid paying the minimum wage despite the very protective laws that go back to the New Deal. Even though tipped workers can sometimes earn many times the minimum wage, the failure of employers to pay even a minimal wage represents a kind of affront that has spurred movements for wage justice among strippers as well as restaurant workers.

The normative content of the minimum wage goes back the legal revolutions of the early twentieth century. Here, I write not of the Bolshevik Revolution, but instead the legal revolution that occurred in the American law of the workplace in the 1930s. Before then, workers could be fired for joining a union or refused hiring unless they agreed not to join a union. Under federal law, they could legally be paid nothing for their work. The New Deal legislation revolutionized relations between employers and workers.

The minimum wage was always designed for the bottom of the wage scale—for those who do not have the bargaining power to command higher wages. Thus, the admonition in critical race theory of "looking to the bottom" requires lifting the working conditions and wages of low-wage workers. Critical wage theory requires raising and enforcing the minimum wage to benefit workers of color at the bottom of the scale.

Like critical race theory, critical wage theory is not focused merely on the descriptive nature of statistics that shows people of color and immigrants at the bottom of the wage scale. This book seeks to find structural solutions to some of the persistent problems of low-wage work. Besides reforms like eliminating the exceptions in federal law for large swaths of the workforce, changes to our basic system of hourly wages must occur.

This book tells the stories of workers at or below the minimum wage and the common threads that link their stories. They are all seen as less deserving than other workers of a regulated wage. Denial of minimum wages has far-reaching effects throughout the economy, but it particularly affects workers of color. In the end, this situation emphatically makes the claim that in order to have racial justice, we must have wage justice for workers of color and immigrants. The main way to do this, I argue, is to raise and enforce the minimum wage.

There are many things that can be done to improve the economic conditions of people of color and immigrants. As has been shown in numerous studies, the minimum wage works. But it needs to be raised to a level that supports a minimal standard of living. Yet even those who should be guaranteed a minimum wage under the law are more and more often being denied what they are owed. The systematic denial of the minimum wage to workers needs a wide-scale correction. Legal structures have excluded workers for nearly a century. Legislative action is necessary to protect agricultural and domestic workers at the federal level, as well as state levels. But this book goes further. Here I argue that reforms to the way that we treat work are necessary, including the very idea of hourly wage labor.

The stories in this book of workers laboring at or below the floor of minimum standards point the way toward better enforcement of wage and hour law. They also point toward a more just economy for all workers, but especially workers of color and immigrants.

This story is personal for me as it is for millions of others. Although the minimum wage is sometimes mocked as being only for teenagers, most everyone remembers their first job at minimum wage, and the dignity and entry into the workforce that it represented. It has been a while since I earned the minimum wage. Unfortunately, though, millions of workers still toil at or below this minimal level. Before becoming an academic, I represented workers in Southern California who were trying to organize for better wages and recoup the unpaid wages they were owed. Many of these workers were immigrants and people of color. They utilized New Deal–era laws to try to seek a modicum of justice in the tough landscape of 1990s Los Angeles. Thanks to the assistance of unions, these workers were able to get legal representation to bring their claims. But the legal system did not always work for them, largely because of the transient nature of many of the businesses engaging in theft of their wages.

The goal of this book is to identify the workers most at risk for theft of the minimum wage and the common thread they share— they are people of color and immigrants. Although there are statutes that prevent race discrimination, intersectionality theory shows that these are often ineffective when part of the discrimination is based on economic rather than racial factors.

There are several ways to address this structural discrimination legally. But the limits of the law are evident. While better enforcement is necessary, the only way to ensure that more workers of color get a living wage is to raise the legal minimum wage. This runs counter to the received wisdom of conservative think tanks, but with so many workers of color not getting even the $7.25 they are owed under federal law, the only way to ensure a minimum standard of living is to raise the wage for all.

Raising the minimum wage is also supported by critical race theory. CRT has long expressed the limits of legal remedies. While better legal protections are certainly needed—as critical race theorist Paul Butler once wrote about constitutional criminal procedure protections, "you can't eat rights"—CRT acknowledges the need for minimal rights upon which to build more transformative structures.[7] This book continues the conversation that I and others have been having on the race/class divide in legal theory. It aims to bridge the gaps between race and class. It highlights the structural features that keep low-wage workers poor and that hold back racial progress throughout the United States.

BLACK LIVES MATTER

Black Lives Matter—these three words spawned a movement and then a backlash against racial progress. They are thought of as primarily focused on protecting Black men from being arbitrarily injured and killed by law enforcement. That is an understandable conclusion from, for example, the George Floyd murder that propelled global protests in 2020. But the Black Lives Matter movement was and is about several additional goals central to progress. One of these is economic progress and forward movement.

This book explores the many ways that Black workers and other workers of color have organized for higher wages, whether through collective bargaining, litigation, or legislation. All these efforts are intended to build power for greater economic development in society. The fight for a minimum wage has been a Black Lives Matter struggle from the beginning, all the way back to nineteenth century slavery. To recognize the importance of Black labor, the floor must be raised for all workers.

But that is not enough. When the minimum wage is increased, the state has a responsibility to ensure that it is enforced on an even-handed basis. Unfortunately, the evidence from the civil rights era suggests otherwise.[8] Workers who have multiple claims are generally disadvantaged, according to data showing that bringing more than one claim of discrimination more likely results in the plaintiff losing both claims compared to a plaintiff who claims only sex discrimination (often a white woman) or the Black man who claims racial discrimination. This is a central paradox of intersectionality that Professor Kimberlé Williams Crenshaw, my teacher and mentor, identified and first developed in 1980s. The thesis has been confirmed by more recent empirical studies.

Further, the worker who brings only a minimum wage claim is more likely to be a white man or woman. But the worker who is denied the minimum wage and who is also the victim of race discrimination or sex discrimination has multiple intersecting claims that limit the success of each. As this book shows, the law does not fully account for the intersectional nature of discrimination.

It should be made clear that this book is not about the economics of the minimum wage. Most studies of the minimum wage start from an economic analysis of its effects and then move on to a normative conclusion about whether the minimum wage should be increased. This book goes in the opposite direction. It starts with the minimum wage as a measure of the way we value workers and the work they do. Then it shows the effects on their communities of increasing the minimum wage.

There is mounting evidence that the effects of minimum wage increases are positive within minority communities.[9] Nonetheless, there are still numerous well-funded think tanks arrayed against any increases in the minimum wage. Their studies have shaped public opinion about the *negative* effects of the minimum wage on people of color and immigrants.

The litigation and the mass mobilization around the minimum wage shows its importance. In this book, I describe the campaigns of so many workers of color and immigrants for whom the minimum wage is an important component of the dignity of their work. When a living wage is denied by employers, who are enabled to do this by local and state governments, the result is borne disproportionately on workers of color and immigrants.

In Chapter 1, I describe the theoretical foundations of this book and the application of critical race theory (CRT) to the law of the minimum wage. It is revealing that CRT has become a political football recently, as some politicians have tried to use it as shorthand for any honest conversation about race.

Nonetheless, I argue that race and immigration status must be at the center of setting wage policy, both in establishing livable wages and, once set, in their enforcement. The move for higher wages and the end of the tipped minimum wage already is being framed as a social justice issue by social movements. The Fight for $15 has put fast-food workers of color in the forefront of the campaign for a higher minimum wage. These workers and their struggles have shown the legacy of race and racism embedded in practices like tipping. These historical insights provide important frames.

In Chapter 2, I apply the insights of critical race theory to wage theft issues that confront workers of color and immigrants every day. Although many people assume that undocumented workers are unable to bring wage claims, in fact they do often bring wage claims. I know. As a lawyer, I represented some of them in the 1990s. But even when the documented workers or citizens are owed a legal wage, such as a prevailing wage, they still have trouble securing the wages they are owed because many employers consider it possible to compensate "brown collar" labor for less. They assume that such workers will not complain—the subservience thesis. In fact, there are several examples of such workers organizing for justice.

Even after a global pandemic and soaring inflation, the minimum wage has not budged for nearly 15 years. In addition to the obvious buying power workers lack today, the dignity deficit may be even greater for many who toil at or near the minimum wage. The minimum wage will eventually go up, but it is unlikely to catch up to productivity and inflation. For example, if the minimum wage were indexed to these vital factors, it would be $25 an hour.[10] Yet even an increase to the hourly minimum wage is not enough. The entire structure of the hourly wage discussion must change. Legislation must focus not on a minimum hourly wage, but on a minimum salary, as I detail in Chapter 7.

THE IMPORTANCE OF FRAMES

Why is it important to see the minimum wage, usually understood in terms of class, through a CRT lens? There are several reasons: The first is to grasp the world as it is. The second is that policy efforts ought to be targeted toward those who would benefit most from enhanced enforcement efforts. Finally, social movements use frames to mobilize action, as several have done using the minimum wage. As Chapters 3 and 4 detail, the minimum wage is an important organizing principle for achieving other rights. Chapter 5 discusses legal theories such as using the Thirteenth Amendment to the United States Constitution to challenge unequal wage systems. Even in this time of regressive decisions by the Supreme Court, movements have been putting wage justice in the context of the legacies of United States racial history.

Like many of its New Deal counterparts, the federal minimum wage was transformative to the relationship between workers and employers.[11] In 1938, when the minimum wage was set at 25 cents, over 300,000 workers got a raise for the first time: this proved life-changing for those workers finally allowed to work only an eight-hour day. As one retail clerk put it, for the first time in his working life, he could walk out of work when it was still daylight; he noted that "people were amazed, almost felt guilty to leave after only eight hours, I couldn't believe it."[12]

WHY A MINIMUM WAGE INCREASE IS NEEDED NOW

This book makes the case that substantially increasing the federal minimum wage is essential now. In 2020, racial and economic justice issues dominated the headlines, from the growing economic inequality exacerbated by the COVID-19 pandemic to the worldwide protests against racism in the wake of the murder of George Floyd. By 2023, however, the media and many Americans have become obsessed with inflation and the loss of democratic norms. The importance of the minimum wage has receded significantly. But the economic losses of the pandemic have devastated minority and immigrant communities particularly, though wages now exceed the minimum wage in several industries.

But other industries lag far behind. In the hospitality industry, for example, many jobs were lost and may never return.[13] For years, the argument by pundits and tech moguls was that labor could not get too expensive or it would price itself out of the market. In the meantime, while wages have generally remained stagnant since 2009, technology has rocketed forward to produce several labor-saving mechanisms, such as self-service checkouts and apps—a trend only accelerated during the pandemic.

The other key trend spawned by the pandemic is the categorization of some jobs as "essential." In other words, these jobs can only be done in a physical workplace. Once again, many of these job categories track the racial stratification in society. Workers at meatpacking plants, grocery stores, and in agriculture tend to be people of color and mostly immigrants. Although there was talk about hazard pay at the beginning of the pandemic, most "essential" workers are still earning at or near the minimum wage unless they have a union, and few are represented by unions. Without the market adequately compensating for the essential nature of these jobs, as well as for the risks involved, there is a classic market failure of precisely the sort that the minimum wage is intended to remedy.

FAILURES OF ENFORCEMENT AND POLITICAL ECONOMY

Few economists would debate whether the United States economy includes the constraints of structural discrimination. Structural discrimination is the idea that certain factors will drive the market despite legal attempts to change behavior. Race has been identified as a factor in everything from property values to health outcomes. Wage disparities between men and women have existed between and among racial groups for centuries. Individual bargaining power is even more illusory in a negotiating environment marked by race. Once again, default rules such as the minimum wage are intended to reduce market failures caused by racism. If these baselines are too low, the discrimination will "ripple up" and distort wages for workers of color and immigrants throughout the economy.

Workers of color and immigrants are often denied the minimum wage, whether through non-enforcement of the law or through structural margins in the law that leave workers unprotected. I discuss many examples of workers who fought for their right to a minimum wage through either private enforcement or government action. When these workers are successful in recovering the back wages they are owed, the penalty is simply the unpaid wages, plus an equal amount as liquidated damages. If the minimum wage is low, however, even when the law is fully enforced, the threat of deterrence is also low and often can be considered simply as the employer's cost of doing business. In Chapter 6, I introduce a concept called racial political economy. Even when the law on the books is protective for workers, the law often fails to protect workers because of the politics surrounding the minimum wage.

THE LOST PROMISE OF MINIMUM WAGE LAW

In Chapter 7, I discuss several reforms that will lead to a more just minimum wage. The most important example is to get away from the hourly wage and instead to base all compensation on a minimum salary. Chapter 7 also analyzes several other reforms already in the works in several states and localities that will bring relief to many low-wage workers if implemented on a national scale, and particularly to immigrants and people of color.

There are many factors that have gone into the economic and racial inequality that afflicts the United States today. These forces, however, also work on a global scale. The definition of what a "living wage" should be is continually contingent on many factors. In Chapter 8, I address this debate on a global and human rights scale, and I commit to continuing the conversation with two principles in mind—a living wage is a human right and it should not be denied on the basis of race, nationality, or immigration status. The policy path going forward, however, must proceed from the principle that wage justice is needed for racial justice in the United States and abroad.

This book examines three different groups of workers. First, there are the workers of color and immigrants, who are most likely to be the victims of misclassification and wage theft, including guest workers, day laborers, and sex workers. Whether they get the minimum wage or not depends on private and public enforcement. For several reasons, enforcement is woefully uneven.

Then there is the category of legally sanctioned wage theft—exemptions that affect workers outside the legal regimen that extends minimum wage, overtime, and a host of other protections. This category includes agricultural workers, domestic workers, and prisoners. And, finally, there is the category of workers the law allows to be paid a subminimum wage: these are tipped workers and those with disabilities.

The book takes the view that *all* people who work deserve a livable wage. Currently, the law's protection is rife with holes that need to be plugged: workers of color and immigrants are those who work and yet most often fall through these holes. Fixing these holes will require society to confront the structures of racism and xenophobia operating within attempts to deny wages to those who do the work that is required to keep our society running. In the process, all who work will benefit.

1 A Critical Race Theory of Wage Justice

In 2020, critical race theory (CRT) suddenly became a trending topic on social media and Fox News. Once an academic theory born in law schools and then adopted by several other academic disciplines, the new attention it garnered from politicians and right-wing zealots was uninformed and unwelcome. The Trump administration in its waning days targeted CRT as well as anti-racist education and accurate historical information about the legacy of race and racism in the United States. The Trump administration's scattershot approach included an executive order that directed federal agencies not to use CRT, though that order was blocked by a federal appeals court, and the policy was soon scrapped by the incoming Biden administration. President Trump's acolytes saw an opportunity to rally their base with dog whistles about a new and presumed anti-American way of teaching history, law, and numerous other disciplines, through the lens of race. For them, "critical race theory" has become shorthand for any frank or honest conversation about race.

Now, some witnesses testifying in Congress are effectively asked, "Do you support, or have you ever supported, CRT?"

CRT has been taught in higher education for decades, and has influenced numerous disciplines and students, including me. At UCLA's law school in the early 1990s, I learned CRT from the person who helped create the field ten years earlier—Professor Kimberlé Williams Crenshaw. In Professor Crenshaw's CRT seminar, I was able to connect my lived experience growing up on the border in El Paso, Texas, with the fault lines of race and racism that were present from the founding of the country. My seminar paper for that class was published as a critical race analysis of California's Proposition 187 in 1995 in UCLA's *Chicano-Latino Law Review*.[1]

One of the core tenets of CRT is that purportedly race-neutral laws and policies, such as immigration law, have racialized impacts. CRT also showed that the dialectics of racial history tend to repeat and reframe in the present, and this echoed my experience growing up on the border. The theory perfectly fit the reality of California in 1994, when proponents pitched Proposition 187 as an attempt to conserve the state's resources but instead seemed to be an effort to preserve white racial identity in the state. In the realm of immigration law and policy, the life cycle of Proposition 187 has been repeated many times, from racially loaded political campaigns to official actions and litigation—though changing demographics may entirely obviate the perceived need for such a measure.

Even after leaving California to complete a William H. Hastie Fellowship at the University of Wisconsin Law School (thanks to the inspiration and pathfinding by Professor Crenshaw, herself a previous Hastie Fellow), I continued to use CRT to examine the field of labor and employment law and the issues of wage inequalities. In my LLM thesis at Wisconsin, I looked at the interaction of race and gender identity within labor unions and discussed how workers organized into identity groups within majoritarian labor unions. I published that work as "New Voices at Work: Race and Gender Identity Caucuses within the U.S. Labor Movement," which illustrated how CRT informed my research with union members who were in Black, Latino, Asian, and other identity groups. In my subsequent writing and teaching, CRT has deepened my perspective and the perspectives of my students.

While CRT has been applied in several different genres and areas of law, it has been utilized only in limited ways in labor and employment law. Several authors have criticized New Deal legislation for leaving out minorities and women, which undoubtedly it did.[3] There are key racial elements in the Fair Labor Standards Act and the National Labor Relations Act, such as the exclusion of domestic workers and agricultural workers. Another line of scholarly analysis is critical of the racial origins in protective labor laws, and critiques the existence of the law as doing ongoing harm to minorities—claiming that the laws intended to improve working conditions still operate to exclude African Americans from the job market. Proponents of this theory include law professors David Bernstein and Harry Hutchinson.[4] In *Only One Place of Redress*, Professor Bernstein argues against prevailing wage laws because they originated as a way to protect white union members by raising wages to such a high level that employers would not be willing to pay them to Black workers.[5] Effectively, employers would never hire Black workers to do high-wage work, because employers associated Black workers with low wages.

Professor Harry Hutchinson criticizes New Deal minimum wage legislation for essentially the same reason—by requiring employers to pay higher wages, the legislation priced Black labor out of the market, thus benefiting white workers but increasing Black unemployment.[6] The arguments by Bernstein and Hutchinson are well known in the economic literature but are they part of "critical race theory"? Both authors probably would bristle at the label. Upon further examination, though, their economic arguments merely restate what is already known about employer behavior: in an unregulated market, employers will tend to devalue the labor of people of color and immigrants and compensate workers accordingly.

The historical record shows unmistakably that racism was baked into the passage of New Deal measures, but it does not show the value of such legislation to the lives of people of color and immigrants. Here, I outline a new approach to minimum wage law and policy through the lens of CRT that acknowledges the racial origins of past legislation, but also discusses what low-wage workers need right now. My focus on how to improve the lives of those "at the bottom" is a central tenet of CRT, as Professor Mari Matsuda has argued.[7]

Indeed, legislative history shows that the National Labor Relations Act and the Fair Labor Standards Act clearly meant to exclude people of color and women by exempting agricultural and domestic workers. The difference between the critical histories of these laws and this book is my focus on what needs to happen for these laws to work for racial minorities. Of course, the laws could be more protective if Congress would simply remove the exemptions. Current politics make that unlikely. As in my previous book, *Marginal Workers*, I argue here for reforms within the current system that are more likely to advance the interests of marginal workers. The higher the minimum wage, I argue, the more benefit for people of color and immigrants. The minimum wage is necessary for greater racial justice.

THE FAILURE OF THE ENFORCEMENT REGIME

In an unregulated market, in theory, the law can prevent the operation of racism in setting wages. Yet CRT clearly tells us that law often fails those it intends to protect. This book, as did my previous book, offers leading examples of how law fails marginal workers. Certainly, better enforcement of the law would go a significant way toward ensuring racial justice. In the end, however, the clearest path toward racial justice is to raise wages for all workers. I argue here that increasing wages, rather than eliminating all minimum wages, is the essence of critical wage theory.

Critical race theory (CRT) originated in Madison, Wisconsin, at a conference challenging the emergent critical legal studies (CLS) movement.[8] One of the main divides between CLS and the new movement was the question of whether there would be a reform agenda for the law or whether there would be a deconstructionist project aimed at delegitimizing the authority of the then-current laws that were dominated by conservative economic ideals. The tension between a liberal reformist agenda and a transformative agenda was evident in the pages of a special symposium in the *Harvard Civil Rights–Civil Liberties Law Review.*

CRT thus began as a theory both to explain the law's subordination of people of color and to identify potential remedies. The theory has been applied to several different areas of law—ranging from criminal law to civil rights law. In general, CRT has shown how law has a negative impact on people of color and immigrants, and also how laws are structured to make it very hard for those workers to improve their station within the law. That is the principle of structural determinism—that the structure of law determines its content. These overlapping structures of antidiscrimination law and collective bargaining law have operated to disadvantage workers of color in unions, as evidenced, for example, by the Supreme Court's 1975 decision in *Emporium Capwell v. Western Addition Community Organization.* I interviewed leaders of many of the identity groups in unions to understand why they supported the doctrine of exclusive representation despite these structural obstacles. The resulting article was published in the 2002 *Hastings Law Journal* as "New Voices at Work: Race and Gender Identity Caucuses within the U.S. Labor Movement," and it showed me how using the tools of CRT can sometimes lead to results that support liberal reforms.[9]

MARGINAL WORKERS

In my 2012 book *Marginal Workers,* I applied CRT to a central paradox facing workers today—how the proliferation of individual employment laws often leaves workers less protected than ever. I argued that the structures of labor and employment law intersect to the disadvantage of people of color and immigrants. This is true both for the workers who are formally covered by the law and for those who are excluded from the law. Because of the diffusion of worker political power, workers are unable to improve their protections at the federal level. This is one of the reasons that the federal minimum wage has stagnated while local minimum wages have increased in many cities and states during the same period.

The minimum wage is a great example of how, even when there are increases, those gains are often illusory. There are often explicit exemptions written into protective labor laws that disproportionately affect workers of color and immigrants. It is not enough to end these exemptions. It is important to increase the minimum wage and to enforce it. Proportionally more workers of color and immigrants will benefit in this way.

WAGES AND COMMODIFICATION IN A MARKET ECONOMY

In the workplace, the primary way that people are valued is through their compensation. In modern society, labor is commodified in exactly the way that Karl Marx wrote about in the nineteenth century. In the 150 years since Marx, examples of commodification have proliferated—intellectual labor is now firmly established as legal property, emotional labor may be compensated but often not adequately or not at all, and much art is now valued as commerce. In a society where everything has a monetary value, the value of a human being is tied to the value that the market places on their labor. Throughout our society, such messages are everywhere, and became even more clear during the pandemic: for example, immigrants working in meatpacking, people of color in warehouses and indeed, all low-wage occupations deemed "essential," were not paid anything like essential wages.[10]

Classical market theory posits that the less employers value workers, the less those workers will be compensated. Multiple studies have shown that workers of color and women are paid less for the same jobs than white men, reflecting the relative value employers place on their labor and on them as individuals. The wage gap has grown over many years. While the pay gap between men and women narrowed recently to 79 cents on the dollar, the gap between women of color and white men is even larger. Between Black women and white men, the gap is 63 cents on the dollar. Between Latinas and white men, the gap is 58 cents on the dollar.

When the minimum wage is kept low, as it has been for the last 12 years, this policy sends a message to workers of all colors about the value of their work and, by extension, their worth. That is why we need a higher minimum wage. In the post-COVID-19 world, the minimum wage debate may have receded from the top of the agenda due to several additional factors. The need to survive the working day has been a priority for many workers, particularly "essential" workers forced to work on the front lines. Business closures also have made many workers increasingly concerned about having a job at all.

At the same time, employers desperate for workers were forced to raise their wages even higher than the minimum wage in many states and cities. Employers have made much about the labor shortage, and some larger employers have attempted to deal with the shortage by raising wages. During such a period of labor scarcity the question arises as to whether a minimum wage is still needed.

Data from the pandemic tend to show that while the wage per hour has gone up, the number of hours available to workers has gone down. During the pandemic, employers were able to get by with fewer workers, and this pattern has become the new normal. In Chapter 7, I address the lack of hours that many workers must endure, and I propose changes to the structure of how work is compensated to help ameliorate this problem. This phenomenon shows, however, that the answer is hardly a more laissez-faire approach to the labor market.

THE REJECTION OF CLASSICAL LAW
AND ECONOMICS

The objection to minimum wage laws by some economists is that such laws reduce employment. This classical approach was once accepted as gospel. However, now there is a significant and growing body of scholarship that challenges this conventional wisdom. For example, economist David Card did the pioneering study of the relationship between raising the minimum wage and jobs in the fast-food industry in Pennsylvania and New Jersey. Card found that raising the minimum wage in Pennsylvania did not adversely affect fast-food employment in neighboring New Jersey. Card received the Nobel Prize in economics in 2021 for his work on the minimum wage.[11]

But at what level the minimum wage is set is only part of the story. Workers of color and immigrants are most at risk for wage theft, for example. If there is a lack of enforcement of the labor rights of low-wage workers, immigrants and workers of color are most likely to be disproportionately hurt. These disparities reflect the systemic racism that is part of the labor market at all levels. The data also reflect the deficit in bargaining power that people of color and women face. Classical economics fails to consider adequately (or ignores entirely) these asymmetries in favor of a frictionless market that sets wages according to each worker's merit or talent. In the 1980s, the intersection of law and economics became a dominant study, first in law schools, and then in government, generating a great deal of legal analysis. But both the data and the lived experience of people of color show that systemic racism has a significant impact on the setting of wages. There are countless examples of lawsuits over unequal pay in both federal and state courts. Most of these cases involve workers of color and immigrants.

CLS and CRT originated as explicit counterpoints to the law and economics movement. Instead of prizing the efficiency of legal regimes, the test for critical race theorists is normative—whether laws and policies benefit or harm people of color. This is where racial realism focuses—that is, looking at the material conditions of people of color and immigrants and how these conditions might be improved, or how these workers are harmed, through the lens of law and policy.[12]

LOOKING TO THE BOTTOM

Another aspect of critical race theory is its recentering from the dominant perspective to the perspective of outsiders. "Looking to the bottom," Matsuda wrote in her foundational article, "can lead to concepts of law radically different from those generated from the top."[13] Matsuda discusses reparations as a remedy for racial justice and argues that a top-down approach, by contrast, favors litigation remedies or other solutions better suited for the elite.

An orientation which looks to the bottom does not mean that there are not racial disparities all through the wage scale that must be addressed. There are ways in which raising the floor of the minimum wage will benefit all workers throughout the economy. As I discuss in the latter part of the book, new legal strategies may improve the working conditions of all workers. The first step is recognizing the interactions between race discrimination and wage discrimination throughout the economy. Unfortunately, as I show, these interactions fall most heavily on low-wage workers of color and immigrant workers.

DISPARATE IMPACTS IN CERTAIN INDUSTRIES

The data on who would benefit from an increase in the minimum wage are mostly in the aggregate. Many would be women, and most of them women of color. Industries in which minimum wage workers are concentrated are demographically dominated by people of color and immigrants.

According to the Bureau of Labor Statistics, for example, home health care workers average $14.87 an hour. These workers are often considered legally to be independent contractors and many of their employers are governmental agencies. Nonetheless, these workers tend to be near or below the minimum wage. When workers have tried to unionize their home care workplaces, the U.S. Supreme Court classified them as "partial public employees," thus making their rights to collective bargaining negligible at best, particularly as compared to other employees. This has significantly affected the wages these workers are allowed to bargain for, even when they are in unions. When workers are precluded by law from bargaining, as is also the case with domestic workers, the minimum wage becomes even more important for their dignity and well-being, beyond what they may earn. As discussed above, though, the federal minimum wage does not apply to domestic workers, so collective bargaining or state law remain the only avenues for greater domestic worker power.

CRT AND THE FUSION OF RACE AND CLASS

The long dialectic of race and class in history and law has vexed so many movements for greater social and racial justice. The fusion of the two has been a central focus of my research from the beginning. But the scholarship on the minimum wage has focused solely on class as the *sine qua non* of the discussion. Race and class are inextricably linked, however.

From the beginning, CRT has theorized the intersections of various marginalized identities. In "Mapping the Margins," Crenshaw showed the ways that intersecting bodies of law negatively affect Black women.[14] Her article also uses an intersectionality lens on the minimum wage to show both the racialized impacts of a low minimum wage, and how workers of color and immigrants would chiefly benefit from a higher minimum wage and enforcement of existing laws. For decades, law in general has made it difficult for marginalized workers to bring claims when different forces are at work in the same situation. As Crenshaw has shown, claims by Black women are treated differently from claims by Black men or white women.

Similarly, workers of color are often the victims of multiple sources of legal violations. Low-wage workers of color frequently are victimized by wage theft, but they are also likely to be illegally prevented from forming a union and likely to be the victims of racial discrimination as well. This book demonstrates how workers of color and immigrants are often victims of multiple axes of oppression.

Besides a higher minimum wage, this book also proposes improvements in the enforcement and design of minimum wage laws to benefit workers of color, and ultimately all workers. The key remaining question is strategic: whether the message about the benefits of raising the minimum wage for people of color will help or hurt the cause of enacting higher minimum wage laws. In this regard, the work of CRT scholar Ian Haney López is very instructive. In the last three election cycles, Professor López did extensive work on the racial dynamics of support for various policy positions or candidates. Through that research, it has become clear that a racial justice message did not resonate with all groups, but a fusion of race and class did.[15]

López's empirical and survey research tells a great deal about the continuing "third rail" status of race in American society. In politics, law, and the workplace, raising race as an issue has tended to ratchet the debate up to another level, because of its historical sensitivity. López's research shows that there are ways to tell the stories of racial inequities that can garner white support along class lines.

These considerations offer pragmatic ways to try to gain popular support, but they also represent an accurate depiction of the complexity of human life: it is not and has never been only about class or race. A core problem for many of the arguments about the minimum wage is that they focus only on the class aspect of low-wage work while ignoring the racial dimensions. In the end, I believe that seeing justice in wages as a racial movement is more accurate and more effective.

CONNECTING THEORY TO SOCIAL MOVEMENTS

One of the other hallmarks of CRT and its progeny, such as Latina and Latino critical legal (LatCrit) theory, is the possible connection to social movements—such as movements for immigrant rights or Black Lives Matter—which is sometimes called "critical race praxis" in LatCrit literature.[16] These connections illustrate that scholars seek not only to explain the world, but also to make it more just. Their normative commitments involve greater human flourishing through justice at the workplace, in human rights, and racial justice. These goals overlap with the goals of Congress in passing legislation such as the Fair Labor Standards Act and the Civil Rights Act. It is therefore hard to argue that seeking to make these laws better and more protective is somehow inconsistent with the role of a scholar.

That is why this book looks to the social movements for what they want. Social movements have prioritized stories of race in their campaigns for higher wages. For one example, the movement for $15 has changed the conversation about economic justice. These social movements have also been led largely by people of color and immigrants. In the effort to end the tipped wage in some states, which allows a minimum wage of as little as $2.13 an hour, the Restaurant Opportunity Council (ROC United) traced the practice of tipping to slavery and the Jim Crow era. This book details these campaigns and what they mean for the current legal policy towards tipping and wages.

THE IMPORTANCE OF THEORY

When the material conditions of workers are so close to the edge, some may question whether a race or class frame is dominant, or even necessary. Why should CRT matter at all if, in the end, workers can get the wages they are owed and deserve? The answer has to do with the importance of telling the real story of race and the minimum wage.

This racial realism, as Derrick Bell called it, brings us back to the manufactured controversy over CRT.[17] As I argue above, the goal of federal executive orders during the Trump presidency as well as legislation in various states was literally to "whitewash" the reality of racism in this country. In fact, the reality of racism *is* central to the history of this country. There is no separating the two. The murder of George Floyd in May 2020 reminded the world that racism continues in many aspects of society, and not simply in the criminal justice system. Black Lives Matter movements have further illuminated inequities in the workplace, the educational system, and government. These movements will continue to broaden and enrich the lessons that CRT and LatCrit theory brought to the forefront decades earlier. In the chapters that follow, I bring the lens of these theories to bear directly on the debate about raising the minimum wage.

A DEONTOLOGICAL APPROACH TO THE MINIMUM WAGE

Critical race theory is not the only theoretical frame I employ in this book. My approach is completely agnostic to the actual economics of the minimum wage, though it seems clear that the weight of economic opinion bears out the conclusion that higher minimum wages do not cost jobs. Even if this were the case, the point of my approach is to show the need for minimum wages to maintain the dignity of work. The costs imposed by a completely unregulated market for labor long have and still do fall disproportionately on workers of color and immigrants.

In the chapters that follow, I describe several types of workers on the edges of the economy, and why many of them tend to be workers of color and immigrants. For labor law to be truly responsive, it must take these workers into account. A higher minimum wage is needed to guard against racism in the workplace. This is because of the clear inadequacy of legal remedies that are supposed to guard against wage theft and unequal pay but most often disproportionately fail to protect people of color and immigrants.

I take at face value, however, that other scholars have a genuine concern for the protection of the interest of African Americans in their arguments for the end of the minimum wage. Yet this does not mean that legislators and courts consistently share the same motives. There is a current use of history that is meant to justify a blatantly regressive direction in social policy. Nowhere is this more disingenuous than within the abortion debate.

It is well documented that many eugenicists and white supremacists of the nineteenth and early twentieth centuries sought to provide access to abortion to women of color to limit the procreation of races they considered "inferior." Despite their efforts, abortion remained illegal for decades in many states until the Supreme Court decided *Roe v. Wade*. In its 2022 opinion overturning *Roe v. Wade*, the Supreme Court referred to the efforts of eugenicist racists and invoked this racial history as a reason to overturn *Roe*. This disingenuous use of race seeks to soften the blow of *Dobbs* and other regressive measures. Similarly, in the debate over minimum wage, racial history is sometimes deployed by those who seek to keep the minimum wage low. Whatever the motivation, this ought to be called out and rejected.

THE NEED FOR AN INTERSECTIONAL APPROACH

In most surveys, Americans express broad support for maintaining or raising the minimum wage. Similarly, most surveys show a strong support for antidiscrimination laws. Racism remains virulent, however, and the denial of the minimum wage is also rampant. Thus, the need for intersectional approaches.

For too long, we have looked at the minimum wage and civil rights as separate spheres. The purpose of critical wage theory is to show how legal structures determine outcomes. As Crenshaw has shown regarding the ways that Title VII marginalizes women of color, the interaction of antidiscrimination laws and minimum wage law operates to the disadvantage of the very workers these policies and commitments are intended to protect.

The goal of this book is to show that by increasing and enforcing the minimum wage, we can address the devastating ripple effects of a low minimum wage throughout the economy. To deal with wage disparities throughout the chain, we must start with the bottom.

A separation between economic rights and civil rights has not always been the dominant trend, however. After the formation of the U.S. Justice Department Civil Rights Division in the 1940s, the new division sought to use the Thirteenth Amendment to bring a modicum of economic justice to a segregated society.

THE FAILURE OF CIVIL RIGHTS LAW TO ADDRESS SYSTEMIC UNDERPAYMENT BY RACE

Just as some fields dominated by women are dubbed "pink collar" occupations, occupational segregation by race has led some jobs to be considered "brown collar." Professor Leticia Saucedo has explained cogently that employers sometimes prefer Latino immigrant workers for certain jobs in order to exploit them, though occupational segregation is already banned by Title VII of the Civil Rights Act. However, these claims are difficult to win. In most cases, employers do not leave overt evidence that they intend to discriminate. Rather, several factors tend to contribute to people of color and immigrants getting the lowest wage jobs.

Claims based on Title VII of the 1964 Civil Rights Act have not been particularly successful in addressing job segregation and its impact on keeping wages low for workers of color. An alternative theory would be to claim that an employer's wage-setting practices have a disparate impact on people of color in the workplace, which might gain some legal traction

And yet, when these claims have been brought to the courts, they have generally failed. This is because an employer can simply point to nondiscriminatory factors to avoid liability. Several large class actions show this. As the chapters that follow describe in detail, law as it now stands hardly begins to capture the scope of the problem faced by underpaid workers of color and immigrants. As can be seen in a number of fields such as domestic labor, hospitality work, and sex work, the predominance of women in those work contexts leads to intersectional discrimination and, in certain cases, sexual harassment.

FUSING RACE AND CLASS

The fusion of race and class is even more important in this period of backlash. As more attempts to limit the use of critical race theory are put into effect, coalitions that include all low-wage workers will need to be formed to raise working standards for all workers of color and immigrants. This is especially true in a period of backlash against immigrants. Workers of color and immigrants are systematically underpaid and denied the wages they are owed often *because* of their race and immigration status. Like its critical race theory anteced-ents, critical wage theory seeks not only to critique the status quo, but also to find ways to improve the situation of the most marginal-ized workers. The following chapters tell the specific stories of work-ers trying to achieve both racial and economic justice through a higher minimum wage. Their advocacy points to the path forward.

2 Movements Framing the Minimum Wage as a Matter of Racial Justice

Three years after the 1992 riots, Los Angeles continued to see high levels of racial and economic inequality. It was at this time that groups began to form to explore a "living wage ordinance" (LWO) in the city as one way to blunt that inequality. While the federal minimum wage at the time was still $5.25 an hour, these activists argued that the minimum wage for living in an expensive city like Los Angeles needed to be much closer to $10 or $12 an hour.[1]

The fight in Los Angeles moved to the beach city of Santa Monica after passage of the LWO in the City of Los Angeles in 1997. At that time, I had begun practicing law at the union-side labor firm Rothner, Segall, and Greenstone and had been involved with groups trying to enact the Pasadena Living Wage Ordinance. The Pasadena City Council ultimately passed an LWO similar to the Los Angeles ordinance, which I had assisted with, and then the cause moved to Santa Monica, brought by Santa Monicans Allied for Responsible Tourism (SMART).

The typical idea behind LWOs was that since local governments were the purchasers of services, they could set the contract terms for wages. This led to several cities enacting "responsible contractor" ordinances and ensuring that workers on city contracts earned enough to live on in these increasingly expensive cities. This makes sense if the city is spending its own dollars. These LWOs were also supported by organized labor.

The Santa Monica LWO was designed differently than previous living wage ordinances. Rather than tying the minimum wage only to those employers who contract with the city, the Santa Monica living wage was designed to cover all workers in the "Coastal Zone," a two-mile-long area next to the beach where most of the tourist attractions and amenities are sited.[2] The minimum wage proposed for that area in 1999 was $10.69 an hour plus benefits, while the California State minimum wage at the time was $5.75 an hour. The location of several large hotels in the Coastal Zone was not coincidental. Local 814 of the Hotel Employees and Restaurant Employees (HERE) union was interested in organizing some of these Coastal Zone hotels (the union already represented employees at hotels in the City of Santa Monica). I became involved with a group of volunteer lawyers working on some of the legal issues that the campaign would face, such as federal preemption, the interaction with collective bargaining agreements, and equal protection challenges.[3]

Of course, most of the objections to the Santa Monica LWO were framed in economic terms. How could businesses afford the increased wages with their thin profit margins? Would there have to be layoffs or a reduction in hiring? Would a hamburger cost $12? (Twenty-five years later the price of a hamburger in the Santa Monica Coastal Zone has risen to well over the federal minimum wage.) After I left California in 2000 to complete a Hastie fellowship at the University of Wisconsin Law School, the fate of the ordinance would not lie in the courts, but instead in the political world. The Santa Monica City Council passed it in 2001, but the business community put the ordinance to referendum in 2002 and the voters repealed the ordinance.

The repeal of the Santa Monica LWO was certainly a localized setback for the living wage movement at the beginning of the 2000s, but the fact that there was an explicit move to tie wage standards to a part of the economy was an innovation that would be repeated in subsequent campaigns. Because the campaigns were connected to hotel worker organizing and low-wage workers in the hospitality industry, immigrant workers and workers of color stood to benefit most from a higher minimum wage.[4] Data from 1999 show that 77.8 percent of all workers earning $5.75 to $10.75 were either non-white or Hispanic, and 59.5 percent were Hispanic.

And the defeat of the Santa Monica LWO provided the groundwork for the next wave of organizing the Fight for $15 in the years that followed. But the repealed Santa Monica LWO was also not the end of the story. The coalition would eventually return with a new Santa Monica LWO that focused on the hospitality industry.[5] Some years later, the SMART coalition enacted a living wage ordinance that was focused on the hotel industry as a whole rather than within a specific zone. This method of setting wage standards by employment sector has become the norm in several jurisdictions.

RACIAL FRAMING

The framing of the minimum wage as an issue of racial justice is not new. Every display of people power in the halls of power, whether it be in Los Angeles City Hall or at the Santa Monica Pier, has shown the full spectrum of diversity from native born to immigrants, from African Americans to Asians to Latinos and Latinas. As described by Marblestone and Erskine in their research on the Santa Monica LWO, the attempt was to show, through large demonstrations, the impact an adequate minimum wage would have on workers of color and immigrants.

As described in Professor Scott Cummings's book, *An Equal Place*, a significant number of workers of color joined these movements. Cummings described the 1990s campaign by the garment workers union UNITE! against Guess? Inc., during the time I was working as a lawyer in Los Angeles, including in that campaign. As I observed, and as Cummings confirms, the campaign was driven largely by Latino immigrants working in downtown LA garment shops. The union's messaging was clearly targeted at other Latino immigrants (as well as the public): "The campaigns targeted industries that, in general, were disproportionately comprised of Latino immigrants' workers, thus the theme of immigrant worker organizing features prominently." Cummings continues, "Low-wage work cut across race and the campaigns themselves aspired to be self-consciously cross-racial, attending to the different racial compositions of different industries."[6]

This framing is also present in the fight against the tipped wage. The Restaurant Opportunity Council's (ROC) fight to end the tipped wage had traced the issue to its origins in the 1938 passage of the minimum wage, which was accomplished in part by installing a tipped minimum wage to appease Southern Democrats who did not want the largely African American and female workers in the service industry to earn a living wage. The groups that now are focused on ending the minimum wage have highlighted the racist origins of the tipped minimum wage as a route to get one fair wage for all.[7]

The vital question facing social movements is strategic and stems directly from the theoretical frameworks discussed in Chapter 1. If, as critical race theory posits, American society is intrinsically racially stratified, does it make sense to make a call for a higher minimum wage only about race? The lesson, as demonstrated by Lopez's research, is not to exclude either race or class from the narrative but strategically to fuse the two for the benefit of all groups.

Research can often confirm empirical and lived realities. As individuals, we are the product of multiple identities at the same time. We toggle between our sexual orientation, disability, class, race. This is the lesson of labor law over the last 30 years. Labor organizing has never been completely successful when focused only along class lines. From the earliest days of the labor movement the organizing took place by necessity along racial and gender lines. Just a few examples are the Brotherhood of Sleeping Car Porters, the International Ladies Garment Workers Union, and the Dodge Revolutionary Union Movement. A singular focus on class as an organizing principle hindered the labor movement's progress for years and may have contributed to its decline. But other factors may have also contributed to the decline of the labor movement. Some point to the growing number of laws that provide many of the same benefits that are available in a union contract. The question of whether labor's lobbying for protective labor laws hastened the demise of the labor movement has occupied scholars for some years.

LABOR'S MOVEMENT FOR A LIVING WAGE

The labor movement's successful support for minimum wage increases and other minimum labor standards law dates to the beginning of the Fair Labor Standards Act of 1938. Three years earlier, Congress had enacted the National Labor Relations Act because of years of sustained activism and agitation by the labor movement; President Franklin D. Roosevelt signed the law in 1935, which was intended to make minimum standards a matter of union contract rather than legislation. Soon after, Secretary of Labor Frances Perkins began lobbying President Roosevelt for the first federal minimum wage law. Secretary Perkins had the support of several partners in the labor movement, such as the Women's Trade Union League (WTUL). The WTUL had been advocating for several legislative reforms such as the eight-hour day and the end of child labor.[8]

The WTUL was not a labor union, but had a number of allies in the labor movement, particularly in the textile unions, such as the Amalgamated Clothing and Textile Workers Union (ACTWU) and the International Ladies Garment Workers Union (ILGWU). But not all unions were supportive of the effort to legislate labor standards. Samuel Gompers, as the head of the AFL, famously said, "More, more, more." But he also said, "Why would they pay for something they can get for free."

THE CIVIL RIGHTS MOVEMENT

In the 1950s, two factors changed the labor movement's approach to external legislation, First was the merger of the American Federation of Labor (AFL) and the Congress of Industrial Organizations (CIO). The more conservative, craft-focused AFL was less diverse than the CIO, which was committed to organizing all the workers in a workplace, "wall to wall." This commitment led to growing coalitions with groups of color and the unions in the Los Angeles area. According to María Elena Durazo, interviewed in the early 1990s, that was part of the plan the whole time.[9] Then, in the 1950s and 1960s, labor had to reckon with the emergent civil rights movement and its call for greater equality, both with employers and among labor's own ranks.[10] CIO unions like the United Auto Workers (UAW) and the United Steelworkers (USW) pushed for legislation such as the Civil Rights Act of 1964 and the Voting Rights Act of 1965.[11]

After passage of the landmark 1960s legislation, unions became more active in other minimum standards legislation, helping to pass occupational safety and employee benefits laws in the early 1970s.[12] From then on, labor has consistently advocated for a higher minimum wage.

At the same time, the racial composition of labor was changing. This became very clear in Los Angeles in the late 1980s and early 1990s. The Service Employees International Union's (SEIU) Justice for Janitors movement was in full swing in the early 1990s when Los Angeles was riven with racialized conflicts. The first of these was the

Los Angeles Police Department's (LAPD) beating of dozens of janitors in Century City on June 16, 1990. The LAPD's tactics in breaking the strike harkened back to the 1930s when Pinkertons hired by coal companies engaged with impunity in violence toward strikers. The result of the melee in Century City was several janitors sent to the hospital with injuries and a settlement in the millions of dollars with the City of Los Angeles.

The Century City melee was dwarfed by what happened on April 29, 1992, when four white officers were acquitted of brutally beating Rodney King, a citizen who had been pulled over for a traffic stop. The resulting rebellion engulfed the city's neighborhoods of color, south and west of downtown LA. The conflagration ultimately took the lives of 63 people and resulted in thousands of injuries and more than one billion dollars in property damage. But the acquittal of the officers coupled with the need for rebuilding LA focused new attention on the problem of race and economics.

THE LIVING WAGE MOVEMENT

The Los Angeles Alliance for a New Economy (LAANE) was born out of this ferment.[13] Forged by a coalition between organized labor and South Los Angeles community organizations, the movement's main backers were Miguel Contreras and María Elena Durazo. They represented the new faces of Los Angeles labor, which is what the rest of the labor movement would look like 25 years later. Contreras was the head of the Los Angeles County Federation of Labor, consisting of all AFL-CIO affiliated unions in the county. And Durazo was president of the Hotel Employees and Restaurant Employees Union Local 11.

Local 11 was and is an extraordinarily diverse labor union that I was privileged to represent as an attorney.[14] Just as the hotel workforce is very diverse, so is the union. What was interesting was the cross-racial nature of the organizing. Asians made up a large share of the guest room attendants. Latinos were a large part of the kitchen staff. African Americans were well represented at the bell desk. The question remained why the union would be interested in legislation on wages. But there was another piece of legislation that the union was interested in to begin with. And that was the worker retention ordinance.

The worker retention ordinance (WRO) had its genesis in hotels changing hands and leaving behind collective bargaining obligations. The WRO was the first move in Local 11's strategy to legislate local working conditions. The ordinance stated that when a company changed hands, it had to retain the workers for at least 90 days and could only fire employees for just cause. The WRO passed the Los Angeles City Council in 1995 and affected several properties. As Cummings has detailed in *An Equal Place*, the worker retention ordinance eventually made its way from covering only city contractors to covering other retail establishments. This move to minimum standards was again led by a multiracial coalition of workers, both in unions and without.

THE FIGHT FOR $15

In 2008, the economy was in the tank. Wall Street had collapsed, taking Main Street with it. Unemployment reached levels not seen since the Great Depression. It may have seemed an inopportune time to seek a higher minimum wage, but this was when the Service Employees International Union decided to create its Fight for $15 movement.

The impression that fast-food workers are all teenagers is a strong one. It is not borne out by reality, though. Most fast-food workers are breadwinners for their family, and most are people of color. Workers such as Karesha Manns, a McDonald's worker in Memphis who is part of the Fight for $15 movement, linked her participation in a strike with the legacy of Martin Luther King, Jr., as part of "Dr. King's vision of racial and economic justice which means that every working person has a living wage and has a job with dignity."[15]

THE "FARM" SYSTEM OF COLLEGE SPORTS

For decades, college athletes have "played" for their education. In the age of college sports as big business, money has poured into colleges and universities and enriched salaries for head coaches. For more than 150 years, the rules of the National Collegiate Athletic Association (NCAA) have prevented college athletes from earning wages or profiting from their name and likeness. The racial structures developed over the years were not lost on the players. Coaches make millions of dollars, and 80 percent of the coaches are white. This racial disparity, and the hard luck of some college athletes in various court cases, caused the players to go to state legislatures to get relief.

California was the first domino to fall. The California legislature put through the first "name and likeness" statute. This law was supposed to level the playing field by allowing the players to earn money for sponsorship deals as well as receive compensation. After California passed its law, many other states around the country looked to pass similar laws. At the same time, the Supreme Court took up the case of *NCAA v. Alston*, which challenged on antitrust grounds the rule that college athletes cannot earn compensation during their playing career. In June 2021, the Court agreed with the challengers and held that the NCAA's no-pay rule had to be struck down. Then, the NCAA lifted its rule, allowing states to seek legislation authorizing compensation, as the Nevada legislative did in its 2021 session.[16]

SEX WORKERS, GIG DRIVERS, AND BATTLES OVER CLASSIFICATION

Like college athletics, another job that is assumed to be play, not work, is "sex work." Sex work, as defined by University of Nevada Las Vegas sociology professor Barb Brents, can encompass several fields, including topless or nude dancing, escort services, and prostitution.

The industry has been structured to avoid the obligations of employees to pay the minimum wage. Strip clubs have long incorrectly classified their workers. Sex workers of color especially have faced monumental challenges in getting the wages they are due.[17]

Like the sex work industry, the gig economy is built upon a model that seeks to avoid the rights available to many employees, such as earning a minimum wage, overtime, and workers' compensation.

From the beginning, the model for gig jobs has been to "casualize" employment. The result is that many gig workers clear $4 or $5 an hour. As courts have found through the many cases brought by drivers against companies such as Uber, Door Dash and Instacart, the companies do exercise a significant degree of control over their workers, making them employees.

Litigation against these companies faces enormous challenges. First, the gig companies can afford to pay large law firms almost unlimited sums to defend against lawsuits. But through the work of innovative plaintiffs' lawyers like Shannon Liss-Riordan, plaintiffs have been able to score several victories against the companies.

The law firms that pumped out defenses in California state courts, Florida unemployment tribunals, and London tribunals have been only partially successful. The reason for these partial victories is that the many courts act as if they do not understand the new technologies. But for decades, the law has favored employee status for workers. The gig employers know this and have tried to change the law.

In 2018, the California Supreme Court decided *Dynamex v. Superior Court*, confirming this pro-worker bias in the law.[18] The court looked at the language of the California Labor Code and the court precedents and concluded that California's rule was much closer to the "ABC test" that exists in the statutes of many states. The ABC test has three factors:

A. Is the worker independent from the business's control?

B. Is the worker doing work the business does not usually do?

C. Is the worker a separate business entity from the employer?

If the answer to any of the above questions is no, the worker should be considered an employee.

The most important factor for the ride-hail drivers of the world was B, which asks whether the worker and the supposed employer are in the "same business." Uber and others argued that they were not in the same business as the drivers, claiming they are "software companies" and not transportation companies or delivery companies. Clearly, Uber's whole reason for being is to provide transportation—their app is simply the "vehicle" that is used to accomplish that job. The ABC test looks to the reality of the situation.

After the California Supreme Court's decision in *Dynamex*, the California legislature moved to codify it in the form of Assembly Bill 5 (AB 5), which ensured that gig companies would be liable for paying a minimum wage plus all the other attendant responsibilities of being an employer, including workers' compensation for injuries, health and safety protections, and unemployment insurance.

The primary sponsor of AB 5 was Assemblywoman Lorena Gonzalez. Gonzalez, a Latina lawyer from San Diego County, was a member of the labor council and interested in providing a means for employee rights, and possibly union rights. Gonzalez championed the rights of Latino farmworkers and likened the gig workers' denial of labor rights to the situation of farmworkers in San Diego. She engaged in Twitter wars with detractors, who often used racist and sexist epithets, but AB 5 ultimately prevailed when Governor Gavin Newsom signed it on September 18, 2019.[19]

For their part, the gig-economy companies went in search of a new angle. Proposition 22 was a California ballot initiative that was intended to reverse AB 5. The companies sought to create a legal category of workers who wouldn't be owed either the federal or state minimum wage, which in California is approaching $15 an hour. The companies tried to argue that there was a minimum wage that gig workers could get outside of the usual rules of being an employee. In the end, much of the battle revolved around which side was friendlier to the gig workers. Both sides highlighted how many gig workers were women and people of color.

THE MINIMUM WAGE AS A CIVIL RIGHT

On August 28, 1963, Rev. Dr. Martin Luther King, Jr., spoke on the steps of the Lincoln Memorial as part of the March on Washington. In his legendary speech, Dr. King specifically called for a $5 minimum wage, which in today's dollars would be over $15 an hour. His words about racial justice were also couched in economic justice. He talked about the fact that he was standing in front of the statue of Lincoln, who at Gettysburg 100 years before had talked about a new nation, "born in freedom." But 100 years after Lincoln's oration, Dr. King stated that freedom for Blacks did not translate into material progress: "One hundred years later, the Negro lies on a lonely island of poverty in the midst of a vast ocean of material prosperity."[20]

As large and important as it was, the 1963 March on Washington did not by itself lead to changes in law, such as the Civil Rights Act, Voting Rights Act, or the Fair Housing Act. Those were the product of years of struggle. As King stated in his speech, nondiscrimination in employment, housing, and voting were key to so much else. But a higher minimum wage or other labor law reforms were not a primary part of the legislative agenda; that fight was left to the labor movement. This split between "civil rights law" and "labor law" is certainly understandable and long standing. And the reasons for the schism have been well documented. But in the last 20 years, that chasm has lessened. Labor unions have been uniformly supportive of minimum wage campaigns.

The minimum wage as an accommodation and a civil right has come up in the work of some academics, most notably Professor Noah Zatz, who has discussed the minimum wage as a civil rights accommodation, much like those available under another civil rights statute, the Americans with Disabilities Act.[21] Professor Brishen Rogers also describes the minimum wage as a civil rights measure.[22]

The argument I make here is that the minimum wage and civil rights laws should be fused in the same way that social movements have been doing for years. The paradigm of labor rights as civil rights was also present in the work leading to the enactment of the National Labor Relations Act of the 1930s and Title VII of the Civil Rights Act of the 1960s.[23]

EQUAL PAY AND THE STORY OF LILLY LEDBETTER

Women of color not only have to struggle to get the minimum wages they are owed, they also have to make sure they are getting equal pay. The data tell us that pay inequities are greater between men and women of color and white workers. Yet, the symbol of unequal pay in the last 20 years is a white woman from an Alabama named Lilly Ledbetter. Ledbetter worked at Goodyear Tire for 19 years, moving her way up through a variety of jobs to a supervisory position. It was at that point she found an anonymous note in her mailbox listing the salaries of all the managers. Thus she found out that she was being paid less than other supervisors for the same job. With this seemingly slam-dunk evidence, Ledbetter sued under the Equal Pay Act of 1963 and Title VII of the Civil Rights Act of 1964.

Although the pay disparity had started years before, Ledbetter did not know that until the salary sheet appeared in her mailbox years later. Nonetheless, her lawsuit could have been brought much earlier, according to the federal court in Alabama that heard her claims. The suit invoked two different statutes, both of which dealt with the two aspects of her identity—her status as white and a woman. Title VII prohibits discrimination in terms and conditions such as rates of pay based on race and sex. The Equal Pay Act of 1963 protects against pay disparities based on sex.

The Equal Pay Act used the enforcement structure of minimum wage and overtime claims in the 1938 Fair Labor Standards Act (FLSA). This states that when the employee knew or should have known that they had a claim, the clock started ticking. The rule for accrual of the statute of limitations in some courts under the FLSA had been "the paycheck rule." In short, every time a new paycheck is issued, that marked the onset of a new statute of limitations. The question raised by Ledbetter's lawsuit was whether the paycheck rule should apply to Title VII claims. The lower courts held that the paycheck rule should not be used in Title VII claims, which teed up the issue before the U.S. Supreme Court.

The Court, in a majority opinion written by Justice Samuel Alito, dispatched Ledbetter's lawsuit. The Court apparently wanted Ms. Ledbetter to predict the list of salaries in her mailbox six years before it happened, when the pay inequities began. The blistering dissent by Justice Ginsburg is the stuff of legend, especially her direct call to Congress to fix the situation as it had done with the Civil Rights Act of 1991, reversing parts of three Supreme Court decisions that had limited antidiscrimination law. "Once again," Justice Ginsburg wrote, "the ball is in Congress's court. As in 1991, the Legislature may act to correct this Court's parsimonious reading of Title VII." After the 2008 elections, the newly elected Congress and President Barack Obama heeded the call. In 2009, the first bill that President Obama signed was the Lilly Ledbetter Fair Pay Act.

While the Lilly Ledbetter Act is no doubt critical to many Title VII claims that would otherwise be lost, much will continue to depend on the other factors that make all claims difficult to bring. These obstacles include the lack of information about what other employees make and, as research has shown, the relative lack of success for claimants who have multiple intersecting claims and identities. These factors are likely to continue to present obstacles for the low-wage workers who are the focus of this book.

INTERSECTIONALITY

The Ledbetter legislation codified the paycheck rule as the baseline for claims under Title VII of the Civil Rights Act. These claims mostly benefit white women, however, which Crenshaw wrote about in 1989, coining the term "intersectionality." Even though most wage theft also involves race discrimination, plaintiffs are notoriously unsuccessful in claims that raise both Title VII claims and FLSA claims.

A few illustrative cases underscore the point. Zhengfeng Liang was a dishwasher at Spice Restaurant in New York City. She was denied pay rates equal to male dishwashers. Her boss, Williams, made remarks that suggested bias against Chinese people. Liang was fired. She sued in federal court in Manhattan. The court dismissed her Equal Pay Act and Title VII claims. The court's rationale was that the boss did not just fail to offer decent pay to ethnic Chinese, the evidence was that he poorly paid a lot of his workers. Of course, almost all the workers who weren't getting paid were "of color," but the court said that did not matter in terms of Title VII doctrine, nor for the FLSA.

The question posed by intersectionality is not just a matter of which statute will provide the most favorable statute of limitations. This is consistent with empirical research. When plaintiffs aggregate different kinds of claims, they tend to be less successful than when they choose just one claim (such as race or sex). The empirical realities bear out the theory of the problem of legal intersectionality.[24]

While many of the movements for a living wage discussed in this chapter share much in common, all have had to make choices about the framing of their struggle and the extent to which to frame their specific struggle in terms of racial identities. The point here is not to draw conclusions about which framing is successful or strategic. Instead, the point is to show the inexorable connection between racial justice and wage justice that so many movements have begun to realize. This comes from the lived experience of workers—people of color and immigrants who are victims of wage theft often *because* they are people of color and immigrants. It is these struggles that lead many of them to join movements for a higher minimum wage even as they have had to face a wall of organized resistance from lawyers and economists.

Immigrants, Day Laborers, and
Exotic Dancers

AT RISK FOR WAGE THEFT

When I was a lawyer in Southern California, I was proud and honored
to represent unions and individual employees in matters ranging
from wrongful terminations and union organizing drives, to actions
for unpaid wages. At the Pasadena labor law firm I worked for in the
late 1990s, my clients included unionized bakery workers, graphic
designers, and undocumented immigrant painters. It was work that I
loved and continue to draw upon as a law teacher and scholar.

Besides regular union clients, the firm regularly took individual
employment cases. In 1998, Ellen Greenstone, a brilliant, longtime
labor lawyer originally with the United Farm Workers, and one of
the firm's partners, asked me to help her with a case that was going
to trial on behalf of some individual employees who had not been
paid the minimum wage or overtime pay. I excitedly agreed and
looked forward to the experience. Then she let me know that we
were representing two "exotic" (i.e., topless) dancers in a case against
their former club. Although I am no prude, I cannot I say that I had
expected to represent such workers when I started my career. And

45

why would they want minimum wage and overtime pay—when they can make so much more than that in tips on a nightly basis? The answers revealed much about the importance of a minimum wage requirement even for supposedly well-compensated workers.

I soon learned that the scheme that the club used to pay the dancers nothing at all for their work is one that nearly all the clubs in the industry use. Such employers use these schemes to evade the requirements of the law, as well as other statutes designed to provide minimum working conditions. An employer's classification of a worker as an "independent contractor," whether mistakenly or fraudulently, deprives that worker of any wage and hour protection; the right to bargain collectively; and the right to be protected from employment discrimination or harassment. The law defines employment status very broadly—yet from the beginning employers have tried mightily to reduce their liability for everything from minimum wages to workers' compensation.

Although this case was the only topless dancer case that I ever worked on, there are strong parallels between it and the minimum wage cases on which I worked for immigrants. In both, the workers seeking minimum wages are expected to work for their actual employers for free or well below the wage level that other workers, usually white citizens, earned. Although in both instances, the law clearly protected the workers' rights to earn the minimum wage, society has assigned these marginalized groups of workers an air of criminality, as somehow less worthy of the protections other workers take for granted. And in both instances, racial hierarchy compounds these legal disadvantages. This chapter is about all such workers.

THE DENIAL OF THE MINIMUM WAGE
TO EXOTIC DANCERS

Courts have been nearly uniform in finding exotic dancers to be employees and entitled to the protection of minimum wage and overtime laws.[1] Both liberal and conservative judges alike have reached the same proper result in such cases. Consider the source of this quote in a federal court of appeals opinion affirming a trial court finding that exotic dancers were owed minimum wages and overtime by the defendant clubs:

> We must be mindful in the end that we are applying a statute which Congress thought was necessary to provide "fair labor standards" for employees, including those marginalized workers unable to exert sufficient leverage or bargaining power to achieve adequate wages in the absence of statutory protections. To rule for the clubs under the circumstances here would run too great a risk of undercutting the Act's basic aim.[2]

This opinion's author was not a crusading labor lawyer planted on the bench by progressives but instead was President Ronald Reagan–appointed conservative jurist J. Harvie Wilkinson of the Fourth Circuit Court of Appeals based in Richmond, Virginia. Judge Wilkinson's opinion for the panel clearly comprehended what the Fair Labor Standards Act was intended to do—to reward work, especially for marginal workers without bargaining power.[3]

But often it is the identity of who is doing the work that seems to disqualify the worker from payment. Exotic dancers are nearly all women, and there is a long history of underpayment and nonpayment for women's labor. Unfortunately, the issue is even more acute for women of color.[4]

The earliest records of prostitution in the State of Nevada, unearthed by researchers at the University of Nevada, Las Vegas, reveal that in the 1910 census, four of the eight prostitutes listed in Las Vegas were Black and one was Hispanic.[5] At the time, the population of Las Vegas was 90 percent white. The city aimed vagrancy laws at Black prostitutes to enforce segregation. The sex workers of that era, as well as those today, would be unlikely to expect government officials to be sympathetic to their claims.[6]

Nonetheless, government agencies at the federal and state levels have brought several enforcement actions against exotic dance clubs for these schemes. During President Bill Clinton's administration, Secretary of Labor Robert Reich initiated several such actions, including *Reich v. Circle C Investments*. That case involved a club in Dallas, Texas, that called its dancers "independent contractors" yet subjected them to a set of mandatory rules and discipline for failing to follow onerous rules. Instead of paying their workers, the club "rented" the stage to them for a stage fee, between $10 and $15 a night. This meant that if the tips were bad on a particular night, the worker might not make enough money to cover the stage fees. Anyone who has worked for tips is familiar with the phenomenon of a "bad night." But unlike the tipped workers discussed in Chapter 4, these workers are not even earning the tipped minimum wage of $2.13 an hour from the club.[7]

At the insistence of the defendants, the case described above went to trial by jury in California state court. The defendants reasoned that the "sex work" of the plaintiffs would lead to a favorable defense verdict because the jury would not respect the work that the plaintiffs do, even though the defendants were in the same business. But the resulting judgment for the plaintiffs and the awarding of back wages in the amount of six figures serve as a microcosm of the public's attitudes toward schemes to avoid paying the minimum wage— these schemes are generally not going to be popular with most people, other than the employers who benefit from them.

"Sex work" remains a contested term for a wide range of occupations both legal and illegal.[8] There is a wide range of activities sometimes encompassed in the term, ranging from sex for sale to commercial transactions online to nude dancing in private clubs. In this book, my focus is on the types of activities that have been the subject of litigation thus far, usually termed "exotic dancing." I am not making a claim here about whether all who engage in sex-related transactions for money are doing "sex work" and thus are owed a minimum wage. There are many ways to analyze prostitution and sex work, as my late mentor Jane Larson and her co-author Berta Herandez-Truyol have superbly documented.[9] My focus here is on the exotic dancing cases for minimum wage, such as the jury trial that I participated in during the late 1990s in San Bernardino County, California.

Any jury of 12 men or women may have a range of opinions about different types of work and the people doing it. This trial was only one of many cases brought by exotic dancers throughout the country over the last 30 years. In nearly in all cases, the dancers were found to be employees. Meanwhile, sex workers have been successfully asserting their workplace rights outside of the courts as well. A group of dancers at the North Hollywood, California, Star Garden club sought to unionize because of concerns which included a mandatory share of the dancers' tips returned to the club (plus the customary fees charged simply to work) and an end to "racist hiring and firing practices." The workers at the club engaged in collective action and won an NLRB election in December 2022 to be certified as an independent union representing dancers.[10]

It became evident to me that attitudes about sex workers seeking a minimum wage often match the attitudes about immigrant workers, who are also seeking what is owed to them. Yet, immigrant workers getting pay for the work they do may be complicated by several other attitudes that people have about immigrants or immigration. That is why the law protects the right of *all* immigrants to receive the wages due for the work they have done. Unfortunately, that is not the experience of many immigrant workers of color.

IMMIGRANT WORKERS BELOW THE LINE

Exotic dancers certainly were not the only workers I have represented who were seeking unpaid minimum wages. Like sex workers, the undocumented are frequently the victims of wage theft. One area in which this has been a particular issue is in the construction industry. In the 1990s, Michael's Painting, a small-time painting contractor in Southern California, had successfully bid on several contracts to paint public schools and other government buildings. Michael's employees were primarily Spanish-speaking immigrants from Mexico and other countries in Latin America. Ordinarily, public jobs require the employer to pay workers not just the minimum wage, but a prevailing wage, which would have been over $20 an hour. Companies that successfully bid with local and state governments as the "lowest responsible bidder" often do so by underbidding what it would cost to pay workers properly.[11] The result is that many workers are subjected to scams to prevent them from earning legally owed wages.

Employers subject to federal prevailing wage laws are also required to submit to the Department of Labor certified payroll records attesting that they have paid employees correctly and are keeping documentation of the checks their employees received.[12] One of the ways that an employer can cheat is to hand over checks for the legitimate amount to the workers and require the worker to sign them over to the employer and then take the check back, handing the worker a smaller amount of cash. Think about it as a check cashing service, except that no worker asked for this "service." Of course, the submission of false certified payroll records would also be a federal crime.[13]

Alejandro Dueñas certainly did not ask for cash pay at less than half of what he was legally owed per hour. Dueñas was an employee of Michael's Painting in the late 1990s in Southern California. Like his fellow employees at Michael's Painting, he generally earned $10 an hour, even though the regular wage should have been $23 to $28 an hour. This is because unionized workers generally received those higher amounts, and these immigrant workers were not yet represented by a union.

After meeting with the local Painters Union representatives, Dueñas learned that he was been shorted more than $10 an hour. In March 1998, he proceeded to the offices of Michael's Painting and demanded prevailing wages from one of its principals, Michael

Abikasis; instead, he was summarily fired.[14] But the message that Michael's was cheating its workers had already been received by Dueñas and his co-workers. Soon, they began signing cards to authorize the Painters Union to represent them in negotiations with Michael's Painting. By March 24, the employees had signed up more than 50 percent of the workers to be represented by the union, and they sought to bargain.[15]

On March 27, 1998, the workers and their union protested the failure to pay prevailing wages at the offices of Michael's Painting in Van Nuys, California, with picket signs reading: "We need a Union," "Michael's fired me for asking for the legal wage," and "Michael's doesn't pay prevailing wage."[16] I was privileged to play a role representing these workers in their efforts to organize a union and obtain the wages they were owed by their employers. The union drive resulted in most of the workers at Michael's signing authorization cards, and ultimately in an order issued by the National Labor Relations Board requiring Michael's Painting, and its successors, to bargain with the Painters Union.

The prevailing wage is the minimum wage on public works construction contracts. These laws were first passed in the 1930s to try to maintain a higher standard of living for construction workers, whose work can often be episodic. But these laws have been criticized for decades as discriminatory toward people of color in the workplace.[17] Professor David Bernstein, in his book *Only One Place of Redress*, argues that prevailing wage laws negatively impact African Americans and should be repealed. The argument is that these laws were intended to exclude Blacks from the labor market and lead to high Black unemployment because employers are less likely to hire Black workers.[18]

If the experience of the employees of Michael's Painting is any guide, the problem is not the existence of prevailing wage laws, but the evasion of them. The Davis Bacon Act, a federal statute passed in 1931, was intended to ensure that government contractors did not pay poverty wages.[19] While there were certainly racial motivations present at the creation of the Davis Bacon Act, it is important to see the positive impact it is having on workers today. Michael's Painting was undoubtedly not the only employer to be vehemently anti-union, but the combination of that and the scheme to defraud workers was especially egregious.

The failure to pay prevailing wage resulted in a separate proceeding. The workers filed a federal lawsuit against the company and its principals, Michael Abikasis and his wife, Laurie Abikasis, alleging violations of the federal Fair Labor Standards Act, the Davis Bacon Act, and the California Labor Code. Soon after filing the case, the defendants summoned the plaintiffs to a deposition and were surprised when they all appeared. It seems the usual modus operandi was to cheat and then assume that the immigrant workers would be too afraid to enforce their rights. Obviously, the employer did not count on the bravery of the workers, or on a union getting involved.

The union's organizing and minimum wage cases continued for years in different tribunals. Eventually, Michael's Painting ceased doing business as Michael's Painting, and re-opened as Painting L.A., the initials of the other principal, Laurie Abikasis. Although it purported to be a new business with a different mission and clientele, that did not deter the federal labor board from alleging that the new business was merely an "alter ego" of the old one, launched to evade the requirements of federal labor law to bargain with the elected representatives of the workers. The NLRB's finding was affirmed by both the board in Washington and the federal Court of Appeals for the Ninth Circuit.[20]

The workers at Michael's Painting are not alone in their struggle for the prevailing wage—which is the minimum wage on public construction contracts. Many other workers have also sought prevailing wages, often with the help of unions. These cases often involve immigrant workers, not just from Mexico but many other countries.

The battles over the prevailing wage may seem to be specific to a particular industry or type of workers, but they mirror the battle over the minimum wage writ large. There are those who argue that minimum wages negatively impact people of color by reducing the employment levels of the lowest paid workers.[21] Nonetheless, public opinion polls routinely place support for raising the federal minimum wage above 70 percent.[22] Minimum wage laws remain very popular public policies for legislators and voters at the state and local levels.

Many other workers, like the painters at Michael's, must do battle to obtain the wages that they are owed. Their experience also shows a dynamic that is present in many wage disputes—employers systematically undervalue the labor of immigrants and people of color, whether that is through paying workers of color less than their white counterparts, or not paying them the minimum wage, also known as "wage theft."

The Michael's Painting case tells us two important things about the minimum wage. First, many undocumented immigrants are paid some wage, even when it is below the legal wage. This tells us that the higher the legal wage, the higher amount even those who are denied the minimum wage will make. Second, while the actions of the employers invariably had an air of contempt for the workers because of their immigration status and race ("the jobs are gone," "finito"), the case was brought both as a wage case and a union organizing case.[23] The denial of these rights is all too often linked to the race of the workers.

This chapter explores the racial dynamics of underpayment and nonpayment of wages. I argue that the racial dynamics of the minimum wage requires a higher wage than is currently in place at the federal level and many state levels. The movements that have fought for "$15 and a union" will continue even after the minimum wage is reached in many states or at the federal level.[24]

IMMIGRANTS EXPLOITING OTHER IMMIGRANTS

Immigrant workers are especially at risk for exploitation, but their exploiters are often immigrants themselves. They often have come to the United States in a previous generation or even only a few years earlier, but they own small businesses that rely on network hiring which results in many employees of the same ethnicity or national origin. Sometimes they are recent European immigrants, such as from Greece or Russia. Other times they rely on ethnic affinities to justify subminimum wages and to keep enforcement agencies from investigating. In a recent example, the U.S. Department of Labor (DOL) sued a nail salon in Rhode Island run by ethnic Chinese that also subjected its Chinese immigrant workers to unsafe working conditions in violation of the Occupational Safety and Health Act (OSHA). An employee named Wing Ting Wong raised claims with the DOL, and an investigation into these complaints revealed numerous minimum wage and overtime violations.

The owner of the salon, Steven Xingri Cao, did not appreciate the attention from enforcement agencies and lashed out at Wong, according to the retaliation complaint filed by the DOL, accusing Wong of biting "the hand that feeds her." Cao called Wong a "white-eyed wolf" and told the DOL that the Chinese phrase meant that Cao was an ungrateful person.[25]

This case is one of many examples of immigrants exploiting other immigrants. Often the exploiters are immigrants from the same country or ethnicity who believe that they are doing a favor for later-arriving immigrants by employing them regardless of whether the employers are following the minimum wage or overtime laws. Some might ask how this could be racially motivated since the worker and the employer are often of the same "race." As many critical race scholars have pointed out, there are racial and hierarchical components to the immigration system.[26]

IMMIGRANT WORKERS STRUGGLING FOR THE MINIMUM WAGE

Although some of the workers at Michael's Painting were not authorized to work in the United States, all were legally entitled to the minimum wage. The workers were all under the control of Michael's Painting—they were told to report to work before their shift started and do various jobs around the shop, like washing Michael's cars. During this time, the law in California was clear— time spent under the employer's control is working time.

The U.S. Supreme Court has held since 1984 that when protective labor laws use the term "employee" to denote who is covered by federal law, that term includes workers regardless of immigration status. In *Sure-Tan v. NLRB*, the workers of Surak Leather Factory near Chicago organized a union in 1983. The employer called in the INS (Immigration and Naturalization Service) to raid the factory, and several of the workers were found to be undocumented and deported to Mexico. The union filed charges in the National Labor Relations Board alleging that the employer retaliated against the workers for the protected concerted activities.

The Court held that the workers were statutory employees despite their immigration status, and thus could bring unfair labor practice charges to the NLRB for denial of their right to organize unions. The rub was that the workers had already been deported to Mexico and thus were unable to collect the back pay owed to them by the employer.

The *Sure-Tan* decision left an ambiguity in the law about whether the undocumented workers in that case were not entitled to back pay simply because they were in Mexico. Unfortunately, the Supreme Court clarified this issue 18 years later in *Hoffman Plastic Compounds, Inc. v. NLRB*, which held that undocumented workers were not entitled to back pay at all because of their immigration status. In doing so, the Court ignored that statute's plain language that treats all employees the same regardless of their immigration status. Instead, the Court found that the back pay remedy "trenched upon" the federal law on immigration.[27]

The *Hoffman* decision was a blow to all immigrant workers seeking justice through organizing with their fellow workers. The decision did not change the rights of undocumented workers to the minimum wage law that the Court's decision in *Sure-Tan* directed, however. In the years that followed *Sure-Tan*, several cases were brought on behalf of undocumented workers. One of the first to reach the federal appellate court level was *Patel v. Quality Inn South.*[28] Rajni Patel came to the United States from India on a tourist visa in June 1982, but he overstayed his visa. Despite his immigration status (this was before federal law required employers to verify immigration status), he found work at a Quality Inn South in Birmingham, Alabama, doing janitorial and maintenance work. His employer refused to pay him minimum wage and overtime, so he sued the parent company of the hotel in federal court in Alabama. The trial court granted summary judgment to the employer, reasoning that Patel's undocumented status precluded him from receiving minimum wage and overtime. The Second Circuit Court of Appeals reversed the decision of the trial court. In its decision, the court focused on the plain language of the definition of employee in the law, "an employee is a person employed by an employer." It says nothing about immigration status.

IMMIGRANT WORKERS AND THE GIG ECONOMY

Immigrant workers also form a significant part of the gig economy. Even in the 100-degree-plus heat of Las Vegas in the summer, one can drive the streets and see a gathering of workers on corners and parking lots near Home Depots or other big box stores. These scenes play out in every American city. Las Vegas, because of its explosive growth in the last 30 years and its large number of immigrants, provides a ready environment for day labor, and, unfortunately, for exploitation.

The laws that are supposed to protect these workers are woefully inadequate for the job. And because many of the workers are noncitizens, they lack political power to ensure that they can seek and obtain work under fair conditions. Despite these structural barriers, activists at nonprofit worker support centers such as Make the Road Walking and Arriba Las Vegas Workers Center have been able to change the equation. In her book *Suburban Sweatshops*, Jennifer Gordon explains that workers lobbied local governments and state legislators to get better protections in New York.[29] But this is an uphill battle in many parts of the country. In this environment, immigrants are unwelcome and have a very difficult time advocating for their interests. Their lack of citizenship gives them virtually no regular political power compared to other workers. Nonetheless, immigrant workers can make change, as thousands did in LA in 2006.

PROPER WAGES ONLY FOR CERTAIN PEOPLE

A study of racial political economy would ask the question, Why does law include, or more to the point, why does law exclude certain individuals from protection? The answer has much to do with political power—and in the United States, lower political power is closely correlated with race and immigration status. Let us start with race. Studies by the Brennan Center for Justice at New York University School of Law show that people of color are more likely to face voter suppression. Voter participation by people of color is lower than for whites. Chapter 1 discusses the exclusion of agricultural workers and domestic workers from the New Deal legislation. Here, we look at the modern legacies of those exclusions.

IMMIGRANT WORKERS AND BARGAINING POWER

Not all immigrants are people of color. But a large share of undocumented workers come from Latin America and Asia. Sixty-seven percent are from Central America and Mexico, and 15 percent are from Asia, according to the Migration Policy Institute. Even apart from the language or economic barriers they face in a new country, these workers are often trapped in a labyrinth of immigration regulations.

Despite the conflation of immigration status and race, the lack of bargaining power is not limited to the undocumented. Many workers of color who are on temporary visas are also denied the minimum wage and overtime.

These examples of the denial of wages defy traditional economic sense. Employers in need of seasonal labor continually petition the federal government for expansions of the temporary labor visa programs. Employers who use this program are required to pay a prevailing wage for labor and to ensure that there are not American workers who can do the job. In theory, this would lead to the workers having bargaining power to demand even higher wages than the prevailing wage. In many instances, however, there is rampant wage theft and violations of overtime laws.

One such example involves the Allied Signal Shipyard in Louisiana in the years after the September 11, 2001, attack, when shipyard workers were being called into military service. As the war ramped up in Iraq and Afghanistan, more shipbuilding was needed. The Allied Signal company claimed it could not find enough workers to meet the government's demand for military hardware.

The guest workers that Allied Signal recruited to fill its labor needs were largely from India. Ordinarily, work on a federal government contract would be subject to prevailing wage requirements. In the name of military readiness, however, President George W. Bush suspended the requirements of the Service Contracts Act, which mandates prevailing wages for contracts.[30]

Far from getting prevailing wages for their work, the guest workers of Allied Signal did not even get the minimum wages or overtime they were due. They organized a strike and started litigation. The post-Katrina environment in Louisiana after 2005 was a challenging one for all workers. But guest workers and other immigrants faced the brunt of the wage theft.

The experience of the workers at Allied Signal is not unique among guest workers. As many times before, guest workers have been denied the minimum wage.[31] There have been numerous lawsuits brought by guest workers against the companies that hired them for denial of minimum wage and numerous other employment rights.

WORKERS OF COLOR AND IMMIGRANTS CAUGHT IN THE FISSURES OF THE WORKPLACE

Professor David Weil, the former administrator of the Department of Labor's Wage and Hour Division, coined the term the "fissured workplace," in his 2014 book of the same name. This definition focuses on the atomization of supply chains that creates a pool of contractors that often makes it very hard to hold an "employer" responsible for wage violations.[32] Workers in the construction industry have been familiar with this interlocking system of contracts for years, but the janitorial industry has seen much more growth in recent years. Within this industry, fissurization has fallen most heavily on immigrants and people of color.

The best examples of this disproportionate burden are the numerous Jan-Pro cases. Jan-Pro is a company that markets the idea of running an independent business to low-wage workers toiling in the janitorial industry for other companies. The idea is to use the Jan-Pro brand to market the workers as independent businesses. Unfortunately, these "independent businesses" often look very much like employment relationships, and that has led to number of lawsuits against Jan-Pro in several states.

In *Depianti v. Jan-Pro*, for example, the plaintiffs were a racial cross-section of janitors in Massachusetts: Giovanni Depianti, Hyun Ki Kim, Kyu Jin Roh, Gerardo Vasquez, Gloria Roman, Juan Aguilar, Nicole Rhodes, Mateo Garduno, Chiara Harris, and Todor Sinapov. Although the scheme applied to all, workers of color and many immigrants have long been disproportionately represented in the ranks of janitorial workers. Many of them are likely to be undocumented. In *Depianti*, the plaintiffs argued that their employment conditions were dictated by Jan-Pro.

In *Becerra v. Expert Janitorial*, a case in Washington State, the plaintiffs were night janitors at the Fred Meyer grocery stores who worked more than 40 hours a week without being paid minimum wage and overtime.[33] Here, the workers were Carolina Becerra, Julio Cesar Martinez, Orlando Ventura Reyes, Alma Becerra, Adelene Mendoza Solorio, Heriberto Bentura Santurnino, José Luis Coronado, and Moises Santos. The names of the plaintiffs are all Latino, and like the workers at Michael's Painting, they probably represented different countries and varied immigration statuses.

The Jan-Pro model of subcontracting and the fissured workplace applied here too. In this case it was Expert Janitorial that was the intermediary between the workers and the Fred Meyer chain. Once again, the legal questions centered on who should be responsible for the wages of the workers. They undisputedly worked for Expert Janitorial, but the responsibility of Fred Meyer under the joint employer doctrine was a key issue. At the same time, Expert had at least nine different second-tier subcontracts with other entities. The joint employer doctrine holds that an employee can have more than one employer if other entities exercise direct or indirect control over the working conditions of an employee. The workers in *Becerra* did all janitorial work when the stores were closed at night, but none of the workers had a contract with Fred Meyer or Expert. Although their work was governed by a web of contracts in English, "it appears that neither contractor hired janitors who were fluent in English."[34]

The basis for this interlocking system of contracts is to avoid paying these immigrants the minimum wage. The owner of the company, Sergey Chaban, testified to this directly: "We ran the numbers and the amount we were getting paid, we couldn't, we would be, we would go negative if we would treat them as employees." The workers made between $7.36 and $7.75 during a time when the minimum wage in Washington State ranged from $7.93 to $8.55 per hour. Of course, the misclassified employees did not get overtime, Social Security, or workers' compensation. Nonetheless, the trial court dismissed several defendants from the lawsuit, finding that their lawyers had not proven the joint employer theory. Because there was copious other evidence that the workers were subject to the control of those defendants, the Washington State Supreme Court reinstated their claims.

The *Becerra* case is a good example of how the fissured workplace disproportionately ensnares workers of color and immigrants in a web of interlocking contracts. Within the Department of Labor, Weil did what he could do increase enforcement of the federal joint employer rule, but the rule has been a political football. As soon as the Trump administration took over, the joint employer rule that had been used to cover situations of direct and indirect control was sidelined entirely.

Although the federal rule may be reinstated by the Biden administration, it will likely be challenged in court or rolled back by a future administration. Thus, federal law is inadequate to ensure that workers do not fall through the cracks. State law will have to supplement. Fortunately, there are movements to try to establish joint employer liability at the state level. In the meantime, activism by workers' centers is badly needed.

WORKERS' CENTERS

One of the things that unions did during the last century was to help workers receive minimum wages by enforcing collective bargaining agreements. With the loss of union representation in much of the country, workers' centers have played an increasing representational role in getting wages.

This is what happened in Las Vegas with Arriba Workers Center. Las Vegas is a city that is particularly ripe for the exploitation of immigrant workers, as there are many recent immigrants and a lot of construction and hospitality. Suburban homeowners need jobs done, and they often go to street corners and the parking lots of home improvement stores, looking to hire day laborers. Laborers also may hire other workers in subcontractor relationships.[35]

MISCLASSIFICATION TASK FORCES

As immigrant workers are most often the victims of wage theft, they stand to benefit the most from government enforcement to recover the minimum wage. Unfortunately, enforcement of the minimum wage has not been consistent and has often been dependent on politics. The administrator of the Wage and Hour Division (WHD), the role that David Weil held from 2009 to 2016, is appointed by the president subject to the consent of the Senate. The WHD administrator has the authority to investigate wage and hour violations and to issue interpretive rules and regulations. The administrator also has the authority to issue partial exemptions to minimum wages for workers who are bona fide apprentices, trainees, disabled persons, and students.

The WHD administrator can also prioritize certain enforcement actions. In 2011, the Department of Labor began a major enforcement initiative focused on employee misclassification, in conjunction with the Internal Revenue Service and several cooperating state agencies. Weil notes that these efforts are aimed at stopping forms of "fissuring that are not only illegal, but have the secondary effect of creating conditions that undercut legitimate competition in an industry.[36] During Weil's tenure, the budget for DOL enforcement increased from approximately $550 million to $856 million.[37] In inflation-adjusted dollars, this was considerably flatter over this period, but it still increased about $100 million to $378 million in constant dollars.[38]

During the Bush administration, from 2001 to 2009, the number of WHD investigators decreased from 945 at the end of 2000 to 732 in 2007. The total number of enforcement actions decreased from 47,000 in 1997 to under 30,000 in 2007. The Government Accountability Office (GAO) in 2008 and 2009 released reports finding that the WHD under President Bush and Secretary of Labor Elaine Chao continually failed to enforce wage and hour laws.[39] Enforcement improved during the Obama administration from 2009 to 2017, but the attitude of the Trump administration against regulation of business meant an even greater decrease in funding.[40]

Immigrants and people of color, who have a harder time accessing legal services, repeatedly bear the brunt of these cuts. Access to justice is a problem for many individuals who need legal services, and particularly in "red states." Only robust federal public enforcement will reach the many workers of color and immigrants who suffer wage theft. There is very good reason to think that enforcement is still falling far short of the need for wage justice.[41]

THROUGH DIFFERENCE, OPPORTUNITIES
FOR COALITION

No one would deny that there are many differences between the plight of sex workers and immigrants, whether documented or not. Of course, there may also be sex workers who are immigrants and thus the victims of wage theft for several different reasons. And yet even with their differences, both groups are seen as less morally deserving of full payment of wages. When there is a confluence of race, immigration status, gender, and work that is seen as morally objectionable by some, it is even more likely that those workers will be the victims of wage theft.

4 Legally Sanctioned Subminimum Wages

The servers at a high-end restaurant on the Las Vegas Strip often earn much more than the minimum wage on a good night. At some high-end restaurants, servers can earn as much or more in a year as many professional workers. Of course, on some nights and in most restaurants, servers may earn far less than a middle-class salary. Like tipped workers throughout the country—bartenders, door attendants, taxi drivers—restaurant servers too can have bad nights. But in Nevada and five other states, tipped workers must be paid the minimum wage, and they get to keep their tips as well. In the other 44 states and the District of Columbia, however, employers need only pay tipped workers $2.13 per hour. If tips from customers do not make up the difference between this subminimum wage and the federal minimum wage, the employer must do so. Many studies show that this rarely happens.[1]

Federal minimum wage law has legally sanctioned subminimum wages for tipped workers since 1961. The employer is responsible for paying their tipped workers $2.13 per hour. The rest of the minimum wage, theoretically, is made up through tips.[2] The employer is required to, but seldom does, make up any difference to reach the minimum wage. The fact is that, despite this "tip credit" rule, many workers do not receive the minimum wage on bad nights, and this has led to calls to end the tipped minimum wage.[3]

Although these practices hurt all workers, there is evidence that the brunt of the tipped minimum wage especially affects women and people of color. The One Fair Wage movement to end the tipped wage has mobilized shame about the racial legacies of tipping, which go back to the Reconstruction era. These racial legacies both past and present certainly call for the end of the subminimum wage for tipped workers, but they also call into question other subminimum wage regimes, such as the subminimum wage for disabled workers. All these exemptions communicate the message to the people who fall within them that they are not worthy of minimum labor standards. This is why many of these exemptions should be repealed. But they also raise larger questions about who is responsible for the wages of workers—governments, customers, or employers. This chapter explores what the impact will be for people of color and immigrants, particularly in the hospitality industry.[4] Tipping as we know it should be reformed in ways that encourage a more equitable distribution among tipped workers.

THE TIPPED MINIMUM WAGE

The tipped minimum wage was put into the law at the behest of the restaurant industry to lessen the responsibility of employers, particularly for the wages of women and people of color. The legislative history shows a clear racial intent of the industry to avoid responsibility for these employees who already occupied a significant portion of the service ranks—from dishwasher to server to hostess.[5] "The employer needs the flexibility to pay certain workers less."[6] The other justification employers often make is that tipped workers do not need the minimum wage because their tips add up to at least the minimum wage per hour anyway.

The litigation that I was involved in was one of numerous similar lawsuits against exotic dance clubs throughout the country seeking minimum wage and overtime for dancers, who often earned hundreds of dollars per night. The reason I think that these lawsuits were filed, and continue to be filed, goes to the fundamental responsibility of the employer for the minimum wage. This concept is firmly rooted in our private contract model of employment, and it is now one of the driving reasons behind the movement to end the practice in the 44 states and the District of Columbia that rely on customers' tips to supply the minimum wage to tipped employees.

THE CHAIN OF SERVICE

One of the complications of organizing the hospitality industry is the stratification that exists in the chain of service. The hierarchy generally starts at the top with the front-of-the-house servers and the hosts, including those known in the past as the maître d', generally a man and generally the supervisor of the waitpersons and busboys. Those at the top of the chain of service are generally white, and those at the back of the house—the bus boys—are often immigrants and disproportionately people of color.[7]

The informal norm in the industry is for front-of-the-house staff to share tips with back-of-the-house staff. But informal norms only go so far, especially when the employer manages the tip pool. Supervisor involvement in tip pools, though illegal, happens because of the slippery nature of defining who is a supervisor. A significant recent example arose in Las Vegas.[8]

THE WYNN DEALERS

The table game dealers of the Wynn Hotel and Casino in Las Vegas can earn much more than minimum wage on good nights, sometimes as much as $1,000 a night. Of course, some nights they earn significantly less than that. Since the hotel opened in 2004, it has greeted millions of high rollers seeking to part with their money at gaming tables. Even in situations where gamblers lose hundreds of dollars, they often generously tip their dealers. But the casino required dealers to pool their tips with so-called "floor persons," whom the dealers alleged were in fact supervisors disguised under a different name. Under Nevada statute, supervisors are prohibited from sharing in tip pools. This led dealers to organize a union and take their allegations of violations of law to the Nevada courts.[9] The Nevada Supreme Court ruled against the dealers.[10] Although the statute is clear that supervisors cannot share in tips, the question is whether the floor persons are supervisors. The court decided that the floor persons were not supervisors.[11]

THE DOL AWAKENS

But that was not the end of the story. Because even though the dealers might not be supervisors, there was still the possibility that the tip pools included supervisors. But even if the dealers participated in a tip pool, the question remained whether they should also get the minimum wage in states that did not allow a tip credit. Although the dealers can make many dollars per hour above the minimum wage, they believed that they were still entitled to the minimum wage. The issue in the litigation, *Cezarz v. Wynn*, was whether the courts should defer to the Department of Labor's return to the interpretation that the minimum wage was owed even to those workers who participated in a tip pool.[12]

PROGRESSIVE FEDERALISM

The reason the DOL must opine on the minimum wage for workers who participate in a tip pool is because of the patchwork of rules that

Congress has allowed states to maintain. In the Fair Labor Standards Act, Congress allows states to require a minimum wage of $2.13 per hour if the employer makes up the difference in tips. There are numerous ways in which the tipped minimum wage is exploitative, which is discussed later. In *Cezarz*, the question was whether employees who participated in tip pools in states where there is no minimum wage were entitled to a minimum wage.

The court upheld the DOL's interpretation as not inconsistent with federal minimum wage law. Thus, the dealers of the Wynn Hotel and Casino were owed the minimum wage plus their tips.

LEGACY OF RACISM AND SEXISM

The tipped minimum wage has called into question the entire system of tipping. From the beginning, tipping was a way to absolve employers from having to pay anything to the people of color they employ. Then, customers could choose to tip based on their own biases and decisions about what the worker's service was worth.[13]

These tipping schemes predate the Fair Labor Standards Act, but even after a minimum hourly wage law was passed in 1938, employers could pay nothing to their employees and force them to work only for tips. This was the case until 1948, when Congress amended the FLSA to require employers to pay at least $2.13 per hour.[14]

The racial roots of tipping continue today. Several studies have documented that servers of color experience discrimination in the number of tips they receive. As is mentioned earlier, when tip credits are allowed, the employer may be able to avoid paying the minimum wage per hour because the tips might not add up to minimum wage.[15]

But the practice of tipping raises other equity issues. Often, women are forced to subjugate themselves to the whims of men to get higher tips. And there clearly is a gap in tips received between employees who are people of color and those who are white. Even when the minimum wage is met, there is such extensive inequity in the minimum wage that some have called for the end of tipping.[16]

There is a good case to be made to end the tip credit. There may be good reasons to end tipping as well. Instead, service charges would ensure more predictability in compensation. Some hospitality workers, however, have been able to regulate tips more equitably through collective bargaining.

THE CULINARY UNION SOLUTION

Culinary Workers Union Local 226 is one of the most powerful labor unions in the country. The union represents more than 60,000 workers on the Las Vegas Strip in some of the busiest, wealthiest resorts in the country.[17] Almost all the employees in the union are tipped workers throughout the chain of service. You arrive at the hotel; you tip the valet. You go to the front desk; you tip the staff there. You go to your room; you tip the bellman. It goes on from there throughout the rest of the casino. If you are a gambler, you tip the dealers. Go to a restaurant or bar, more tips.

The union found a way to regularize the tipping system into pools that are monitored by the union. One of the problems with a tip pool is the way that the entire resort is racially stratified. The front of the house is predominantly white and male. They tend to make the higher tips. But in Nevada and other states where the service industry is strong, the minimum wage is the base. Thus, from the front of the house to the back of the house, everyone starts at the same foundation—currently $12 an hour. The front of the house will be getting more of those tips and then be distributing them to the back of the house. Incentives to discriminate—either consciously or unconsciously—abound. The union-bargained tip pool is policed by the union to avoid favoritism. This solution works well for the workers who have collective bargaining agreements. But only a small percentage (less than 10 percent) of all hospitality workers are subject to a collective bargaining agreement.

In the end, as is discussed in Chapter 7, a rule that encourages employers to move to evenly distributed service charges would be preferable to one that encourages tips. For the foreseeable future, the legacies of racism and sexism make tipping systems inherently unfair. But service charge systems run by the employer can suffer from many of the same problems. The best alternative is collective bargaining agreements, but until that option is more universally in place, tipping should be closely scrutinized and discouraged by policy.[18]

DISABLED WORKERS

Restaurant workers are not the only workers whose exploitation is written into statutes. An unequal floor for wage labor goes against the spirit and intent of the Thirteenth Amendment. As the above discussion shows, there are several exemptions to the minimum wage under the FLSA.[19] Some of these disparities have been implemented in different ways.[20] What happens when Congress or the Department of Labor allows for some workers to be paid less than the minimum wage? In certain instances, the federal government has sanctioned subminimum wages for disabled and tipped workers.[21] For disabled workers, the rationale is that employers might be less inclined to hire disabled workers if they have to pay them the same as nondisabled workers under U.S. Code 29, section 214(c).[22] Some of the workers in sheltered workshops—workplaces for disabled workers that are segregated from the rest of the workplace— may be earning less than $1 an hour.[23] This disparity occurs even when disabled workers have made great strides in other areas of law. For example, even with the passage of the Americans with Disabilities Act of 1990, which required employers to offer reasonable accommodations to people with disabilities, disabled employees are still subjected to disparate wage treatment because they earn less than the minimum wage in sheltered workshops.[24]

The benefits of the sheltered workshops provision of the FLSA will continue to be debated, but a question remains whether Congress should have legislated subminimum wages, considering the Thirteenth Amendment. Does the exemption for sheltered workshops rise to the level of involuntary servitude? Again, a broad interpretation of the Thirteenth Amendment suggests yes, but even without broad interpretation the creation of classes of labor seems counter to the universal nature of the Thirteenth Amendment.[25]

THE SERVICE CHARGE SOLUTION

Tipping should be discouraged in favor of service charges that go directly to the employees, and not to the employer. Hawai'i has already legislated to ensure that service charges are not the property of the employer: "Any hotel or restaurant that applies a service charge for the sale of food or beverage services shall distribute the service charge directly to its employees as tip income or clearly disclose to the purchaser of the services that the service charge is being used to pay costs or expenses other than wages and tips of employees." Massachusetts has similar legislation, but it applies to all service workers, not just those in the food and beverage industry.[26]

The service charge system will not work for all employees, nor all businesses. Those businesses which have used it tend to be high-end restaurants whose patrons are less likely to be concerned about an automatic percentage levied on top of other charges. Moreover, there can be issues similar to the tip pooling issues that led to litigation in Nevada and other states. This is why the optimal solution remains to increase the minimum wage and end the tipped minimum wage, as several groups have argued, to improve the lives of those who work both in front of and behind the curtain of the service "performances" that take place every day.

5 Legacies of Race and Slavery

SWEATSHOPS, PRISONS, FIELDS

The lead story in the *Los Angeles Times* on August 3, 1995, was shocking. Seventy-two Thai workers were being held captive, sewing garments for contractors; the garments eventually made their way to the shelves of major retailers' stores. The raid on the sweatshop in El Monte, California, freed the workers, and also at least briefly prompted the realization that while such sweatshops might be hidden, they were common throughout Southern California and indeed in much of the world. The operators of the El Monte sweatshop were prosecuted under federal criminal law, but the retailers who received and benefited from the "hot" goods were not criminally liable. These retailers were, however, subject to a civil lawsuit in federal court.

Upon finally gaining their freedom, the Thai plaintiffs sued both their captors and the clothing manufacturers and retailers who received the goods produced in the sweatshop. Besides making state and federal claims for lost wages, the plaintiffs asserted that the defendants had violated their Thirteenth Amendment right to be free of involuntary servitude. Although the case ultimately settled, the vigorous litigation resulted in federal court decisions that made damages a possibility under the Thirteenth Amendment. It was an early attempt to use the amendment against private parties. As a new lawyer, I worked at one of the law firms in Pasadena which brought the Thai worker case, but primarily I was an observer. The story of that litigation has been told best by those who were involved in it from the beginning and saw the case through to the conclusion.[1]

This Thai worker case sadly was a high-profile example of what occurs every day in the United States—immigrants and people of color are denied the wages they have earned, and some, like the Thai workers at the El Monte sweatshop, are directly subjected to force and threats of violence. In May 2021, federal authorities discovered a group of 200 Indian workers brought to New Jersey in captivity. They worked 13 hours a day constructing a Hindu temple, earned less than $1.20 an hour, and had their passports confiscated.[2] Although these high-profile cases attract brief media attention, statistics show that everyday wage theft is rampant among people of color and immigrants. Most wage theft cases do not involve threats of violent coercion. The legacy of depriving people of color and immigrants of their dignity and wages has a long pedigree, however. This is not only a twenty-first-century phenomenon—it goes back to the legacy of slavery, the Civil War, and Reconstruction.

RACE, CLASS, AND THE THIRTEENTH AMENDMENT

The Thirteenth Amendment to the U.S. Constitution provides that "Neither slavery nor involuntary servitude . . . shall exist in the United States, or any place subject to their jurisdiction." The broad, encompassing language in Section 1 of the amendment is supplemented by the grant of future power in Section 2, that "Congress shall have the power to enforce this article by appropriate legislation." Thus, the Thirteenth Amendment can be used as a basis for much more than simply the elimination of chattel slavery. Scholars have invoked it as the basis for the right to unionize and for the minimum wage. Both policies have protected people of color and immigrants for generations.

The Thirteenth Amendment is as famous for its emancipatory intentions as it is infamous for making an exception for "punishment for a crime for which the person has been duly convicted" from its sweeping definition of servitude. As shown by numerous historians and the popular 2016 film *13TH*, the exception clause has played a key role in the five-fold incarceration rate increase over the last 50 years. There is increasing awareness that the exception clause needs to be reinterpreted or amended.

Thirteenth Amendment jurisprudence is not as well developed as jurisprudence of the Fourteenth Amendment. This is largely because after the Thirteenth Amendment's passage in 1865, the Supreme Court severely limited the reach of Congressional power under the Thirteenth Amendment. Later, however, the Court acknowledged that the Amendment was not simply about the end of slavery, but also the kind of onerous employment arrangements that remained after the end of slavery—debt bondage and peonage. As this chapter shows, Thirteenth Amendment legal doctrine can and should be further developed in support of minimum wage legislation and enforcement.

I argue here that the Thirteenth Amendment can challenge instances of modern unequal applications of minimum wage laws. This is because the history, text, and structure of the amendment support the passage of minimum wage legislation. Further, in conjunction with the Fourteenth Amendment, the Thirteenth Amendment imposes obligations on states to enforce minimum labor standards. These obligations, coupled with the racial and nativist history of exclusions and exemptions to minimum wage laws, now render such exemptions for certain kinds of workers and employees vulnerable to constitutional challenge.

In the new and growing literature of government obligations under the Constitution, the existing possibilities under the Thirteenth Amendment remain to be developed further.[3] The

Fourteenth Amendment is generally considered to provide rights against government interference, but not positive obligations. Attempts to locate responsibility by the government to provide education, housing, and health care under the Fourteenth Amendment have generally been unsuccessful. But there is a now a growing literature about the Thirteenth Amendment. In keeping with my past work on new sources of worker protections in an era of political gridlock, the question this chapter addresses is whether the structure, text, and history of the Thirteenth Amendment illustrate how the amendment anchors a positive government obligation. This would put on government a duty to regulate abusive employment relationships.

Several scholars have applied the Thirteenth Amendment to labor problems, including James Gray Pope, Aviam Soifer, Lea VanderVelde, and Rebecca Zietlow.[4] This chapter applies their insights, as well as my own, to several contemporary problems involving the minimum wage. While there are several reasons to focus on the Thirteenth Amendment as an independent basis for minimum labor standards, in this chapter I argue that the Thirteenth and Fourteenth Amendments in conjunction provide a powerful case for equally applied minimum wages for all those who work.

In the American constitutional system, it is usually assumed that the Constitution sets up a system of negative rights, dictating what the government must refrain from doing.[5] But this vision of the Constitution stems largely from the Supreme Court's pinched interpretations of the Bill of Rights and the Fourteenth Amendment.[6] The Thirteenth Amendment was meant to be and still can become a positive basis for the establishment of labor standards, including the minimum wage.[7] This would honor the history and purpose of the amendment as well as later interpretations. I argue that the Thirteenth Amendment places obligations on governments to provide and enforce minimum labor standards.[8] The remaining question is what those standards should be. The government's obligation to legislate a minimum wage seems to be a core obligation under the free labor system mandated by the Thirteenth Amendment.[9] In combination with the Fourteenth Amendment, there is a compelling case that governments have a duty to enforce minimum labor standards.

Further, recent decisions by the Supreme Court raise questions about the durability of the Commerce Clause as the constitutional authority for the federal minimum wage.[10] In 2012, the Supreme Court agreed that the constitutionality of minimum wage legislation under the Commerce Clause has been settled since 1936. Yet, placing the constitutional basis for minimum wage on Congress's authority to regulate interstate commerce is at the very least normatively unsatisfying. At worst, this basis could be destabilized by future changes in doctrine.

PLAIN TEXT AND HISTORY

Section 1 of the Thirteenth Amendment to the U.S. Constitution reads:

> Neither slavery nor involuntary servitude, except as punishment for a crime whereupon the party shall have been duly convicted, shall exist in the United States, or any place subject to their jurisdiction.

Section 2 of the amendment gives Congress the power to enforce the amendment through "appropriate legislation." Since its enactment in 1865, the Thirteenth Amendment has become the basis for several federal statutes, including the Civil Rights Act of 1866 and the Peonage Act of 1867.[11]

Congress during Reconstruction intended a fundamental change in the state-federal relationship.[12] The 39th Congress wanted to encourage states to enact legislation to remove the badges and incidents of slavery. The Radical Republicans established the Freedmen's Bureau, for example, to require and implement fair contracts for former slaves and to set minimum wages.[13] There was a clear Reconstruction plan to tie wage rates to the effort to reconstruct the union and also to eliminate the "badges and incidents" of slavery and servitude.

THE LEGAL INFRASTRUCTURE OF
THE MINIMUM WAGE

One might ask why the Thirteenth Amendment should be a constitutional basis for minimum labor standards, when the Fourteenth Amendment is capacious and could and should sustain several theories to support workers' rights.[14] As Pope develops in his 1997 article, there are several reasons why the Thirteenth Amendment should be the basis for arguments about enhanced labor rights. First, it is the only constitutional text to address labor directly. Second, the courts have interpreted it more broadly than the Fourteenth Amendment. Third, the fact that the Thirteenth Amendment applies to private action as well as to government action is also a source of interpretive power.

Under the Fourteenth Amendment, fundamental rights such as the right to travel, the right to procreate, and the right to marry can only be abridged if and when a government can present a compelling government interest accomplished through the least restrictive means.[15] But what if government fails to act to protect the dignity of workers? The current fundamental rights analysis is inapplicable here.[16] Until labor rights are viewed as fundamental rights, substantive due process will likely not apply to minimum wage laws, leaving immense discretion to government decision-makers.[17]

The Fourteenth Amendment and the Commerce Clause are not necessarily the only constitutional basis for the minimum wage.[18] The Thirteenth Amendment is another basis for minimum standards legislation.[19] What should be the responsibility of government— whether federal, state, or local—for minimum labor standards? The Thirteenth Amendment is clearly directly relevant. In our system of negative constitutional rights, the government's obligations are generally considered to be minimal under the Fourteenth Amendment.[20]

Little attention is paid to the Thirteenth Amendment as a source of positive obligations.

The text of the Thirteenth Amendment is a command to both private and public actors: "Neither slavery nor involuntary servitude, except as punishment for a crime that whereof the party shall have been duly convicted, *shall exist* within the United States or any place subject to their jurisdiction." This text contrasts with the Equal Protection Clause of the Fourteenth Amendment, which reads: "No state shall . . . deny to any person within its jurisdiction the equal protection of the laws." The language of the Thirteenth Amendment is more expansive than the language in the Fourteenth Amendment. In both cases, Congress has the power to enforce the amendments through appropriate legislation.

The long journey to the end of slavery in the United States culminated in the passage of the Thirteenth Amendment to the U.S. Constitution.[21] Besides the formal ending of the most obvious and brutal forms of subjugation, the amendment proactively prohibited future forms of involuntary servitude.

The other central interpretive question that arises is the term "involuntary servitude."[22] Several cases make it clear that even arrangements that are voluntary, such as debt bondage, can violate the law.[23] Many states and the federal government have laws that prohibit debt bondage and peonage.[24] Many of these laws were passed[25] as the United States moved from an agricultural economy to an urban industrial economy, with factory labor gradually replacing sharecropping and other debt bondage schemes.[26] As the textile mills in Lowell, Fall River, and other Massachusetts towns teemed with workers in the late 1800s and early 1900s, the State of Massachusetts began to look for ways to keep both the children and adults working in the factories from facing abject poverty.[27] The legislative response was the first state minimum wage.[28] Reconstruction had brought wage peonage and other forms of subordination that had the "impact of servitude that the Amendment intended to prohibit."[29] The Thirteenth Amendment is also unique in that it applies to private conduct as well as state action.[30]

There were several additional efforts to establish more humane working conditions during Reconstruction.[31] In 1868, for example, Congress mandated eight-hour workdays for federal employees.[32] Over the next 40 years, many states and the federal government made several attempts to regulate minimum wages and maximum hours. The line of Supreme Court interventions associated with *Lochner v. New York* proved to be a major stumbling block.[33] Finally, after the "switch in time that saved nine," the Supreme Court began to uphold New Deal legislation designed to regulate the workplace under the Commerce Clause.[34]

The Thirteenth Amendment provided a floor for free labor but did not define what the terms and conditions of that labor should be.[35] Its text gave Congress the authority to enforce its provisions through "appropriate legislation."[36]

It would be nearly 50 years after the ratification of the Thirteenth Amendment before states began to legislate work conditions.[37] Massachusetts passed the first minimum wage law in 1912.[38] Simultaneously, other aspects of the employment relationship began to be regulated. In 1911, for example, Wisconsin became the first state to pass a workers' compensation law, instigated by progressive reformers.[39] Despite the Haymarket protestors in Chicago calling for an eight-hour day as early as 1887, however, Illinois did not pass its first minimum wage law until 1939.[40] The focus of the labor movement in the early part of the twentieth century was the right to organize and bargain collectively.[41] Nonetheless, organized labor was deeply involved in lobbying to try to increase wages through state and federal laws.[42]

MODERN LITIGATION USING THE THIRTEENTH AMENDMENT

The 1990s Thai worker case is a high-profile example of the kind of exploitation that continues in the United States as well as throughout the rest of the world. Congress legislated federal criminal protections pursuant to the Thirteenth Amendment to protect victims of sexual and labor trafficking in the Trafficking Victims Protection Act (TVPA).

But there are many other contexts in which the Thirteenth Amendment should be used to challenge domestic labor conditions. In the Thai worker case, for example, the workers alleged that the *retailers* themselves were liable for the sweatshop conditions. The Thirteenth Amendment applies both to government action and private action. The idea, then, is that private companies can be liable for slavery or involuntary servitude. This was the theory presented to the federal court in Los Angeles in *Bureerong v. Uvawas.*

The retailers moved to dismiss the Thai plaintiffs' complaint on several grounds, but their primary strategy was to sever their responsibility for the servitude of the Thai workers from the defendants' contracts to receive garments and components for retail. This generally proved to be unsuccessful. First, a retailer may be responsible for the actions of its contractors if the retailer is involved in the working conditions of the employees. And second, retailers may be liable in tort for their failings in hiring and supervising their contractors, as in the *Bureerong* case itself.

And even governments can be liable through the Thirteenth Amendment. Though state obligations under the Fourteenth Amendment are generally thin,[43] states may have positive obligations under the Thirteenth Amendment, based on its capacious language and its text and history.[44] The amendment was intended to end slavery, but it was also intended to set a floor for free labor. In this regard, I focus on three questions. First, what are the ramifications of no minimum wage in some states?[45] Second, if states do have obligations, do cities and localities also have obligations?[46] Third, if there is a constitutional right to a minimum wage, does the state meet its obligation by setting the minimum wage at a level that does not qualify as a living wage?[47] Additionally, some states have a low tipped minimum wage plus a subminimum wage for the disabled, which I discuss below.

A key question remains: when is a wage-floor so low that it qualifies as "involuntary servitude"?[48] The anti-peonage cases provide some assistance in addressing this question.[49] Courts have deemed many formally voluntary arrangements to be nonetheless so exploitative as to violate the Thirteenth Amendment.[50] And, if minimum wages were to be considered an entitlement, what are the elements of the minimum floor? That is, what is a constitutionally appropriate living wage? Clearly, the definition of a living wage has had to change over time. Nonetheless, it seems beyond debate that the minimum wage of 25 cents per hour in 1938 would not provide a living wage today.[51] The fact that the Constitution does not mention a living wage does not undermine the need, and there is a possible constitutional obligation for governments to try to set a basic living standard.

Finally, what is the effect if there is no state minimum wage? Many states simply tie their state minimum wage to the federal law.[52] In most cases, this is not a legal problem if there is federal jurisdiction. Yet there are three problems with this assumption.[53] First, there will be some small employers who are not subject to the FLSA, and thus federal law will not apply to them.[54] Second, state minimum wage laws are often more favorable in their remedial options than is the FLSA.[55] Finally, *Wal-Mart v. Dukes* raises the issue of whether federal collective action provisions will be as effective as state law when class actions arise.[56]

The rest of this chapter describes five areas in which the Thirteenth Amendment offers a useful framework for untangling and challenging substandard wages: (1) prison and detained labor; (2) the gig economy; (3) states without minimum wage laws; (4) subminimum wages for disabled workers in sheltered workshops; and (5) state preemption of minimum wage laws.

DETAINED AND BONDED LABOR

Despite the Thirteenth Amendment's exception clause, prison labor paid below the minimum wage may still be problematic under this amendment. The exception clause in the amendment exempts work that is "punishment for a crime whereof the party has been duly convicted" from the amendment's prohibition against involuntary servitude.[57] Additionally, the FLSA applies only to employees under the control of an employer.[58] Some courts have held that prisoners who work for the government are categorically not employees, while others have suggested that prisoners ought to be considered employees.[59]

In states that have no state minimum wage, there often has been no legal recourse for exploited workers. The rights of prisoners to receive wages has been contested in several cases, however. In *Alexander v. Sara, Inc.*, the District Court held that Louisiana prisoners making FLSA claims were not employees. Thus, the judge dismissed their arguments.[60]

As is discussed above, the Thirteenth Amendment's exception clause allows for servitude as punishment for a crime. Yet, several immigration detention centers have been sued for violating anti-trafficking laws enacted pursuant to the Thirteenth Amendment as well as for other labor violations.[61] So far, the Thirteenth Amendment claims have survived motions to dismiss.[62]

Litigation challenging conditions in immigration detention centers is another important contemporary use of the Thirteenth Amendment. The need for the Thirteenth Amendment's exception clause itself strongly suggests that the amendment was intended to deal with exploitative labor conditions. Unfortunately, the growing number of detention centers for immigrants means that detainees now are performing labor for considerably less than minimum wage. Leading contractors who have operated facilities that exploited immigrants, at times including immigrant children, were the GEO Group and CoreCivic (previously known as Corrections Corporation

of America, CCA) and both have often been sued, such as in a series
of federal lawsuits in California and Colorado. In *Sylvester Owino
and Jonathan Gomez v. CoreCivic*, the plaintiffs represented a class of
former civil immigration detainees in the Otay Mesa detention center
outside San Diego. Their tasks included cleaning bathrooms, performing barber services for other detainees, and doing clerical work—
all for $1 a day. Plaintiffs allegedly did other work for "no pay at all"
upon threat of "confinement, physical restraint, substantial sustained
restriction, deprivation, and violation of their liberty and solitary confinement." CoreCivic responded by claiming a civic duty exception to
the Thirteenth Amendment. The District Court rejected the argument, stating that any civic duty exception would not apply to a contractor such as CoreCivic. Discovery in this case continues.

In *Menocal v. GEO Group*, immigrants in a Colorado detention
center in Colorado filed suit against the private contractor that
ran the facility. They claimed forced labor and unpaid wages, based
on the Thirteenth Amendment. The District Court dismissed
the case for failure to state a claim and the plaintiffs appealed. As in
the *Owino* case, the defendants raised innovative defenses, but the
Tenth Circuit reversed, holding that the plaintiffs had stated a viable
claim for subminimum wages, and sent the case back to the trial court.

In states in which there is no state minimum wage whatsoever,
guest workers suffer many of the worst abuses—they are often paid
far below the minimum wage.[63] Some have sued with the help of the
Southern Poverty Law Center.[64] Recently, for example, workers in
South Carolina who entered the United States legally through the
H2-B program to work at Professional Golf Association tourna-
ments alleged violations of even the low federal minimum wage as
well as other minimal labor standards.[65]

These cases represent the leading edge of a growing challenge to
detained and bonded labor. These immigrant detainees clearly
are not being held for any crime for which they have been "duly
convicted" but are being badly exploited, and their employers cannot
be shielded by the exception clause of the Thirteenth Amendment.

THE THIRTEENTH AMENDMENT AND
THE GIG ECONOMY

The Thirteenth Amendment also should provide a framework for challenges to federal, state, and local government actions that facilitate paying subminimum wages in the gig economy. The Fourteenth Amendment has not been held to require the government to enforce federal law in this context.[66] Further, the Thirteenth Amendment has not been utilized to support better enforcement of state laws. Yet individual states are responsible for ensuring that chattel slavery is not reintroduced in the United States "or in any place subject to their jurisdiction."

Particularly if one considers the Thirteenth and the Fourteenth Amendments together, the obligation of states to enforce minimum labor standards is clear. When states support or foster exploitative "independent contractor" arrangements, that also might be a Thirteenth Amendment violation. And numerous specific issues raised by the new on-demand economy implicate Thirteenth Amendment concerns. Many cities and local governments are in contractual relationships with companies, like Uber and Lyft, for example, for data sharing and services.[67] Such governmental entities thus become complicit in the exploitation of workers by allowing subminimum wages to exist.[68]

Recently, workers sued companies such as Uber, Lyft and Homejoy for minimum wage and overtime violations on the theory that these workers are misclassified as independent contractors rather than as employees. Their lawsuits are proceeding in federal court in California under both the Fair Labor Standards Act and California law. Some have been settled, but these cases raise serious questions about whether these arrangements can be legally structured as contractor relationships.

Uber drivers are given the opportunity to lien their cars over to the company.[69] These labor arrangements look very similar to arrangements the Supreme Court struck down under the Thirteenth Amendment.[70] Liability under statutes may be premised on employee status, but the Thirteenth Amendment does not and should not depend on whether a worker is an employee or an independent contractor.

Even if they are not classified as employees, legal arrangements for ride-hail drivers share characteristics with situations that run afoul of anti-peonage statutes.[71] In essence, these arrangements require workers to work off their debt. The ability to sue under the Thirteenth Amendment is limited to the instances where Congress has provided for a cause of action under Section 2 of the amendment, however. Another option is for victimized individuals to successfully get federal prosecutors to bring criminal charges under U.S. Code 18, section 241,[72] which prohibits conspiracy to deny a person's right to be free from "involuntary servitude," or under U.S. Code 18, section 1584, which makes it a crime to "knowingly and willfully hold another person to voluntary servitude."[73]

In our legal system, criminal statutes require proof beyond a reasonable doubt because the risk of error in depriving someone of their life or liberty is severe. Because the bar for criminal statutes thus understandably remains high, the need for some affirmative obligation on states and localities to police involuntary servitude within its borders is evident.[74] Further, the high degree of prosecutorial discretion is another reason why affirmative obligations on the states are important.[75]

Given these concerns, states must be very careful not to endorse or sanction employment arrangements that approach "involuntary servitude."[76] When new employment arrangements are tantamount to involuntary servitude, states should join with private attorneys who are already suing these companies to ensure that involuntary servitude does not exist within their borders.[77]

STATES WITHOUT A MINIMUM WAGE

The Thirteenth Amendment may also provide a basis to legislate minimum wage laws at state government levels. Forty-five states and

the District of Columbia have minimum wage laws.[78] Five states—
Alabama, Louisiana, Mississippi, South Carolina, and Tennessee—
have no minimum wage law for work that is not covered by the Fair
Labor Standards Act.[79] This means that if workers are not covered
through the criteria for federal FLSA jurisdiction, they will not have
any remedy even for egregiously poor employment conditions.[80]
Generally, if the employer is engaged in interstate commerce or is
part of an enterprise with a gross volume of more than $500,000
per year, however, the employer will be subject to the FLSA.[81] Stark
recent examples include guest workers in Florida who were held in
slavery and workers on J-1 visas at the Hershey plant in Pennsylvania. Such situations might also involve criminal violations of trafficking laws, but this requires prosecutors to bring charge,[82] and they
might not involve any minimum wage remedy.[83]

In many states, there have been rampant wage abuses, particularly in the aftermath of Hurricane Katrina in 2005.[84] Several years
earlier, guest workers brought in to do shipbuilding were also badly
mistreated, and they sued to recover back wages.[85] Because there is
no state minimum wage in Louisiana and Alabama, however, the
federal Department of Labor is not be able to police the working
conditions for such workers.[86]

SUBMINIMUM WAGES: DISABLED
AND TIPPED WORKERS

An unequal floor for wage labor goes against the spirit and intent of
the Thirteenth Amendment. As the above discussion shows, there
are several exemptions to the minimum wage under the FLSA.[87]
Some of these disparities have been implemented in different ways.[88]
What happens when Congress or the Department of Labor allows
for some workers to be paid less than the minimum wage? In certain
instances, the federal government has allowed subminimum wages
for disabled and tipped workers.[89] For disabled workers, the ration-

ale is that employers might be less inclined to hire disabled workers if these workers have to be paid the same as nondisabled workers under U.S. Code 29, section 214(c).[90] Yet some of the workers in sheltered workshops—workplaces for disabled workers that are segregated from the rest of the workplace—may be earning less than $1 an hour.[91] This disparity occurs even when disabled workers have made great strides in other areas of law. For example, even with the passage of the Americans with Disabilities Act in 1990, which required employers to offer reasonable accommodations to people with disabilities, disabled employees are still often subjected to disparate wage treatment, earning less than the minimum wage in sheltered workshops.[92]

The benefits of the sheltered workshops provision of the FLSA will continue to be debated, but the question remains whether Congress should have legislated subminimum wages, considering the Thirteenth Amendment.[93] Does the exemption for sheltered workshops rise to the level of involuntary servitude? Again, a broad interpretation of the Thirteenth Amendment suggests yes, but even without such a broad interpretation, the creation of classes of labor seems counter to the universal nature of the Thirteenth Amendment and the oft-stated promise made through its supporters to eliminate caste.[94]

The justification for a lower wage for tipped workers is even more elusive, that the amount they receive from customers will remedy any deficiencies in the minimum wage.[95] Tipped workers can be paid as low as $2.13 per hour in states (currently 47 of them).[96] There are many instances where employees cannot live on the subminimum wage.[97] The Restaurant Opportunity Council (ROC) took the lead in arguing for an end to the tipped minimum wage.[98] They catalogued the many instances where workers have made less than the federal minimum wage because of "off nights" or "off shifts."[99]

One might look at a restaurant worker's entire day's or week's wage and see a higher minimum wage.[100] Once again, however, the underlying problem is applying unequal minimum wages to certain classes of workers.[101] The idea that exemptions are just part of the legislative process should not mean that some vulnerable workers fall below the floor for minimally decent working conditions.[102] Thus, even if it is hard to fit the practices of tipped employment into the phrase "involuntary servitude," the practice of paying a class of workers below the minimum wage runs counter to the spirit of a floor for all workers.

Also, the tipped minimum wage allows employers to shift responsibility for payment of wages to the beliefs and whims of consumers.[103] This runs counter to the employer's final responsibility for wages. Some states do not allow the employer to take a credit against the minimum wage for employer tips, but 45 states do allow a tip credit.[104] This means that the employer's responsibility is as little as $2.13 per hour, and the difference between that and the minimum wage (which can vary between $7.25 and $15 per hour) is theoretically made up by tips received by the employee.[105]

There are strong policy reasons why the FLSA should be amended to abolish the tipped minimum wage. The race and gender legacies of significant differences provide further reason why the tipped minimum wage should be eliminated. The tipped minimum wage was created to pay women and minority servers less.[106] Under "the equal floor" theory embodied in the labor standards engrained in the Thirteenth and Fourteenth Amendments, the tipped minimum wage should not continue.

STATE PREEMPTION AS A CONSTITUTIONAL PROBLEM

The Eleventh Circuit Court of Appeals offers a good example of the constitutional litigation strategy described above. In 2016, the city council of Birmingham, Alabama, passed a minimum wage act which increased the city minimum wage to $10.10, from the federally mandated $7.25 an hour. The Alabama legislature responded by preventing local governments from enacting a higher minimum wage level than the state minimum. In *Lewis v. the Governor of Alabama*, the NAACP and the plaintiffs challenged the preemption in federal court, alleging violations of (1) the Thirteenth Amendment, (2) the Fourteenth Amendment, and (3) the Voting Rights Act.

The District Court dismissed the lawsuit on the grounds that there was no standing and that the complaint raised no plausible theory upon which relief could be granted. The Eleventh Circuit reversed, holding that the plaintiffs stated a claim and that several precedents had found that seemingly neutral municipal actions could include discriminatory purposes.[107] In 2014, the U.S. Supreme Court examined these issues in *Schutte v. Coalition to Defend Affirmative Action*.[108] There, the Court held that the State of Michigan did not violate the Equal Protection Clause by passing a law that repealed affirmative action.[109]

On remand, however, the *Lewis* court held that the political process theory remained, and the repeal of the minimum wage laws could be an equal protection violation. Despite *Schutte*, the Eleventh Circuit court found that there still could be a discriminatory purpose. As Judge Anne Conway noted for the majority, one day the residents of Birmingham had a raise; the next day they did not. The court then remanded the case to the District Court for a discovery process as to whether there was discriminatory intent in passing the law.

A litigation strategy to bring the Thirteenth Amendment into public constitutional dialogue has begun, but it will be a long discussion for several reasons. First, the amendment is not self-enforcing but instead requires congressional action as a basis for litigation. Congress has done this before in the antipeonage, hate crimes, and human trafficking statutes.[110] With Congress in 2024 very unlikely to enact new legislation enforcing the Thirteenth Amendment, a litigation campaign very similar to the welfare rights movement under the Fourteenth Amendment is necessary.[111] There are formidable conceptual obstacles to judges thinking differently about the

Thirteenth Amendment.[112] For one, there is much less litigation and case law under the Thirteenth Amendment. Further, parties have been hesitant to utilize it because it has been seen simply as the amendment that ended the Civil War.

The question for advocates of better labor standards is how to change the thinking of the public about the Thirteenth Amendment.[113] The most often used example of popular constitutionalism is the gun-rights movement and its elevation of the Second Amendment from the constitutional wilderness to an individual right that the public frequently invokes.[114]

Several scholars have argued for the Thirteenth Amendment to become a kind of Second Amendment for the labor movement. However, several important distinctions should be noted.[115] First, for much of its history, the gun-rights movement did not utilize the Second Amendment as a reason to resist gun regulation.[116] Then, in 1968, Congress passed comprehensive federal gun legislation.[117] According to Adam Winkler in *Gunfight*, it took a public campaign of nearly 40 years before the Supreme Court's 2008 decision in *District of Columbia v. Heller* articulated the Second Amendment as an individual right.[118] This tells us that the road to constitutionalizing labor rights will have to start with significant inroads made on the domestic statutory front. Fortunately, as Professor Kate Andrias argues, there is a new constitutionalism at work in the labor movement.[119] This includes a growing interest in a range of state and local measures that provide the minimum wage standards that federal statutes have failed to provide. The Thirteenth Amendment is part of the new constitutionalism for the labor movement of the future.

The buying power of wages has stalled over the last three decades. The federal minimum wage has not risen since 2009 and is currently 37 percent of the average wage. As such, many states and localities have increased their minimum wage in recent years. In Seattle, for example, the wage went up to $13 per hour, and then to $15 per hour by 2021.[120] Cities such as Seattle and Tacoma were among the first to raise their minimum wage.[121] In July 2016, several more localities raised their wage.[122] Other states, such as California, will be moving their minimum wage up in the years to come.[123] By January 1, 2017, 19 states had raised their minimum wage laws, continuing a trend that has been increasing for some years.[124]

States and localities pass increases to the minimum wage through their police power.[125] Seattle has led the way in this regard.[126] Even so, Seattle legislation has faced several challenges.[127] The Seattle Chamber of Commerce sued to block the minimum wage law on grounds that it was preempted by the federal Employee Retirement Income Security Act (ERISA) and the Commerce Clause.[128] While that litigation has been unsuccessful, it raises the concern that an alternate basis for minimum wage laws may be needed. Current data show that a person working full time at the federal minimum wage of $7.25 makes $15,089 a year, or approximately $4,000 below the federal poverty line for a family of three.[129] In five states, however, there is no minimum wage for work not covered by the Fair Labor Standards Act.[130]

In some states, state legislatures have prevented local jurisdictions from raising the minimum wage.[131] For example, when the City of Birmingham passed a higher minimum wage than the State of Alabama, the legislature responded by preventing cities from enacting their own wage levels. A coalition of civil rights groups and unions challenged the law on several grounds, including the Thirteenth and Fourteenth Amendments.[132] These challenges raise the question of how firmly minimum wage provisions are rooted in our law. As with any statute, the FLSA can be repealed by the president and Congress.[133] This is why the Thirteenth Amendment is an important new basis for minimum and equal labor standards.

REMEMBERING THE THIRTEENTH

The Reconstruction amendments fundamentally changed the balance between the federal and state governments. It has long been accepted that the ratification of the Thirteenth Amendment over 150 years ago did more than simply end the institution of slavery in the United States. The Supreme Court has stated repeatedly that the amendment was intended to protect a system of free labor and to prohibit arrangements that prevent the right to quit, oppressive work arrangements, and the "badges and incidents" of slavery.[134] The amendment is also the only one to formally breach the public/private wall that dominates the rest of constitutional law.[135] Of course, slavery was not predicated only on the lack of payment but was a system of violence and economic oppression organized around white supremacy. But vestiges of that system have been continued through the practices of low wages, racially based pay disparities, and unequal employer-employee power relations. And that is exactly the point—the work of the Thirteenth Amendment is not complete if there are systems of economic subordination like subminimum wages, tipped wages, and employee misclassification schemes. The promise of the Thirteenth Amendment to provide for a fair system of free labor, including both the right and *the ability* to quit, is jeopardized when some workers are working for less than the minimum wage. For this reason, states should be constitutionally obligated to legislate and enforce a minimum wage that protects the dignity of workers and the work that they do.

The current debate about prison labor raises the issue of wages for work done in yet another venue. If the amendment is not about wages, why is prison labor for no wages justified by the exception clause of the Thirteenth Amendment? The ongoing debate over the meaning of "slavery" and "involuntary servitude" is certain to continue. If these issues are contested, examples of subminimum wages and denial of the minimum wage to low-wage workers will continue. There is much to do, and if this debate continues, minimum wage laws will remain a crucial part of the floor for free labor envisioned by the Thirteenth Amendment.

While the debate about what the minimum wage should be will continue, there are several reasons to conclude that both states and private parties have obligations to ensure that workers receive at least a minimum standard for their labor. These duties may not always be through the hourly wage. The different ways that these obligations can be discharged is the subject of the next chapter.

6 The Racial Political Economy

GIG WORKERS, HOME WORKERS, AND
THE STATE

The fight over California Proposition 22 in 2020 was one of the most expensive elections in history, with over $200 million expended to sway voters on a technical issue of law—whether so-called gig workers should be employees or independent contractors.[1] The initiative aimed to ensure that most gig workers would be classified as contractors—meaning that they would have none of the protections that employees have—workers' compensation, unemployment insurance, and a minimum wage. The initiative passed by a comfortable margin, handing gig companies like Uber, Lyft, and Door Dash a political victory after several defeats in court.[2]

The battle in California showed the lengths to which many companies will go to prevent the application of minimum wage and wage theft laws to their employees. These companies embrace a vision of an unregulated labor market that allows them often to pay far less than a living wage for labor, even when the workers' out-of-pocket expenses may completely wipe out all remuneration from the job. This is at odds with the New Deal philosophy, which required

employers to provide a minimum wage for "employees."[3] If employers in the gig economy can successfully convince courts—and the
public—that they do not really have "employees," they can avoid all
responsibility for minimum labor standards. This battle has implications for both gig workers and other workers who receive no pay for
their labor, including college athletes.[4]

This chapter describes the political economy of employers evad-
ing their responsibility, and how it impacts racial minorities. It
examines how powerful interests have used the political and legal
system to avoid obligations to their workers. The legal exemptions
and rules that they have pushed for have led to millions of workers
laboring under the line, including many immigrants and people
of color. I describe this political economy in three industries—
meatpacking, the tech industry, and college athletics. In these cases,
and others which I discuss in less detail, the deck is stacked against
workers through structural features and political power. This political economy makes it very hard for workers to improve their lot
through legislation and regulations. This is part of the reason why
the federal minimum wage remains $7.25 per hour. I also describe
the ways in which the law can be reformed to make the system fairer
for all workers.[5]

THE RACIALIZED GIG ECONOMY

In the modern economy, many gig workers are workers of color and
immigrants.[6] This is not surprising, particularly given the higher
unemployment rates for African Americans and other people of
color.[7] The gig economy is often the last resort for immigrants who
have suffered discrimination in the rest of the labor market, regardless of whether they are documented or not. Even if not a full majority, African Americans, Latinos, and Asians make up the heart of
the on-demand economy. Nail salons offer a strong case in point,
and many Asian women work as independent contractors in this

business. Nail salon workers are often paid a fixed amount rather than an hourly wage. A 2015 *New York Times* story documented that many nail salon workers in New York City were paid less than minimum wage, or not paid at all.[8] Some could be paid as little as $30 per day with most averaging between $40 and $70 per day. This led to tips being a crucial part of the workers' compensation. Tips could range from $50 to $2,000 per day, but in some salons, tips are pooled and can be docked in some instances when the employer takes deductions directly from the tip pools. A recent survey also found wage theft pervasive in immigrant-heavy businesses in New York City, Chicago, and Los Angeles.[9] Eighty-two percent of workers experienced some degree of wage theft.[10] In many of these instances, the workers who were exploited were immigrants from a single country, such as Korean women in nail salons in New York City.

Nail salons are just one example of the way that the negative consequences of the gig economy fall disproportionately on workers of color and immigrants. Such situations have led many workers to fight against the gig economy, even though the media may offer an appealing picture of the gig economy as the epitome of freedom.

The architects of the gig economy did not count on California wage and hour law to complicate their methods to avoid paying the minimum wage. The delivery drivers of the Dynamex Company were working 60 to 80 hours a week, sometimes for less than the California minimum wage. The drivers sued in California state court, because of the favorable state law for wage claims in California. The plaintiffs won at the trial court and the defendants appealed to the California Supreme Court.[11]

In *Dynamex*, the California Supreme Court considered the meaning of the category "employee" under California law.[12] The court considered a variety of approaches to how to find a worker to be an employee, and settled on the ABC test, a standard three-part test used by several states. The test creates a presumption of employment and places the burden on the employer to establish that the worker is an independent contractor. The employer must prove:[13]

A. the worker is free from control or direction in the performance of the work;

B. the work is done "outside the usual course" of the firm's business and is done off the premises of the business; and

C. the worker is customarily engaged in the independent trade, occupation, profession, or business.

The California Supreme Court in *Dynamex* adopted this test and found the delivery drivers to be employees, which caused a fundamental change in how the legality of the gig economy was viewed in California.[14] The ABC test has been touted by many advocates as a way to deal with misclassification and to ensure more workers are employees. However, there has been a great deal of resistance to the test, and organized groups have sought to overturn it.

In the wake of *Dynamex*, the California legislature quickly moved into action. In Assembly Bill 5, the California legislature adopted the ABC test for unemployment insurance and for the state's Labor Code, subject to a list of exceptions for certain professions.[15] The bill's primary target, of course, was protection for Uber drivers. Although Uber litigated the question, the bill passed and made Uber drivers employees for the purpose of California employment laws. After threatening to leave the state, Uber instead responded by mounting a campaign to countermand much of the legislation through Proposition 22, which passed with 58.6 percent and defined "app-based transportation . . . and delivery drivers as independent contractors."[16] The initiative set other standards instead of a minimum wage for drivers. Studies show, however, that the minimum wage mandated by the initiative does not begin to equal the state's minimum wage when the out-of-pocket expenses of Uber drivers are taken into account.[17]

On the surface, the debate over Proposition 22 was not about whether the drivers should get a minimum wage, but rather the calculations about what the hourly rate was per hour. Proposition 22 promised to pay the drivers 120 percent of the minimum wage, assumed to be $15.60 per hour in California in 2021. That calculation does not take into account the amount of time that drivers spend waiting to be hired. If the workers were employees, they would be paid for the time waiting for a call requesting a ride. As it is, though, various estimates put the amount workers would earn under Proposition 22 to be between $5.64 and $6.63 per hour.[18]

Yet the passage of Proposition 22 was not the end of the story. Workers and unions challenged the law as a violation of the California Constitution. Proposition 22 was founded on the idea that the legislature could not change the initiative, itself a violation of the principle that, in a republican form of government, the legislature's authority is primary. In August 2021, a state court in Los Angeles enjoined implementation of the law. Although there will be future appeals, there are several doctrines that might be deployed against future Proposition 22s.[19]

Nonetheless, it is worth noting that employer attempts to avoid responsibility for payment of wages has been going on since the first minimum wage laws were finally enacted after long struggles. From the very beginning, employers organized themselves politically and sought exemptions to the laws that were supposed to protect all workers. The history of the minimum wage is, at its core, a struggle by workers and unions seeking the broadest possible coverage within the "sausage making" of exemptions in the legislative process. This chapter details a few of those struggles.

THE NEW OLD GIG ECONOMY

The gig economy is not a new phenomenon. In fact, its negative effects have been consistently and disproportionately borne by people of color and immigrants. For centuries, workers have endured "shape-up" hiring practices at loading docks, kill floors, and construction sites. In these settings, the workers who often are at the bottom of that competition are people of color and immigrants. This chapter shows the disproportionate burden of stagnant and even nonexistent wages that people of color and immigrants face in the gig economy.[20]

The stated goal of Proposition 22 was for companies like Uber and Lyft to be able to pick and choose the rules they would follow. This is the exactly the kind of regulatory arbitrage covered within the broad mandates of the Fair Labor Standards Act in its goal to protect individual "employees." And yet, there has been a plethora of exemptions and gaps from years of special interest legislation that prevents workers from obtaining practical protection.

The goal of the gig companies is to avoid being considered the employer, with all its attendant responsibilities. This has also been the goal for some time of the National Collegiate Athletics Association. The NCAA has argued that the association is not an employer because the nature of the enterprise is educational. While the college experience for athletes involves academics, there are many for whom the athletic experience is more like work than education.

In both the gig economy and college athletics, legislative choices construct a political economy in which a typical employer-employee relationship is idealized as something else. One typical tool for balancing economic power in a marketplace is antitrust law. But antitrust law has historically been constructed to make bargaining power difficult for individual employees to gain. Like gig workers, college athletes have also begun organizing and recreating their own political economy to increase their bargaining power, with some success even in the U.S. Supreme Court.

THE GIG INDUSTRIAL COMPLEX

Silicon Valley is awash in money. Venture capital is everywhere. But the goal is creating self-driving cars and robotics, not increasing employment at a living wage. Nonetheless, in the heart of this rarefied universe, tech companies are looking for ways to make labor obsolete. Until their labor-free nirvana arrives, they are creating ways to use technology to get "microwork" out of people all over the world. Sometimes, these "ghost workers" can make as little as a dollar an hour for doing repetitive tasks.

The regulatory landscape favors outsourcing into other countries. But much of this outsourcing is now occurring within the United States of America. Amazon, Facebook, and a host of other tech companies rely heavily on U.S. workers doing minimal, repetitive tasks. These workers are often single parents or caregivers who need a flexible job that provides at least some income. Like agricultural and garment workers, these workers are paid by the piece, and sometimes they do not make minimum wage. And yet, because like Uber drivers, they need money and are atomized from their fellow workers, they lack the capacity to organize.

Some workers are fighting back. The documentary *The Gig Is Up* shows workers confronting the tech moguls who control their working lives.[21] Companies such as Amazon employ workers in the so-called "Turk economy," on platforms such as Amazon Mechanical Turk, do not recompense them at levels that amount to minimum wage, and make them wait for payment of the meager wages they have earned.[22]

THE COLLEGE ATHLETIC INDUSTRIAL COMPLEX

Once a Saturday pastime between Ivy League schools, college athletics have become a multimillion-dollar industry. Television broadcasts, licensing, and ticket sales make billions for universities. Athletes are not the beneficiaries of this largesse because of their "amateur" status. The "student player as amateur" thesis was tested in the recent Supreme Court case, *NCAA v. Alston*. This decision merits exploration because of what it says about the reality that college athletes are living in today.

In *Alston*, college athletes challenged the prohibition on their ability to earn income from sponsors and advertisers during their period of eligibility. Their argument was that the rules operated as an illegal restraint of trade in violation of the Sherman Antitrust Act of 1893.[23] The Sherman Act, the trustbuster law originally levied against Standard Oil, has morphed in so many ways that its drafters would not recognize it. But the initial goal remains the same, to stop economic concentration. Many researchers are finding that economic concentration has a downward pull on wages.[24]

The Court held in *Alston* that the NCAA could be considered a monopoly per se under the Sherman Act, which essentially made the NCAA rule against compensation to college athletes, which it imposed on all college teams, an antitrust violation.[25]

ECONOMIC CONCENTRATION AND
THE MINIMUM WAGE

Minimum wages can raise the floor against concentration. But there is also a broader, and vital, narrative. Some huge companies are raising wages to higher than $15 an hour. In 2019, Target raised its starting wages to $15 an hour and, during the COVID-19 pandemic, Amazon raised its starting wage to over $16 an hour in 2021.[26] The supposition that large companies might have become more beneficent to their workers is belied by the multiple union organizing drives mounted at Amazon warehouses. In 2020, workers at an Amazon warehouse in Bessemer, Alabama organized a union. They petitioned the National Labor Relations Board (NLRB) for an election to be certified as the exclusive bargaining representative at the warehouse. Unfortunately, the union lost that election in 2020, but the company's conduct during the election caused a rerun of the election, that the union also lost. But there is another recount going on, as well as claims of labor law violations, that could tie up the results for years.[27]

A more successful example of a union election drive occurred at the Amazon warehouse in Staten Island, New York. At this warehouse during the pandemic there was a great deal of worker concern about COVID-19 safety precautions that the company apparently was not taking. There were some walkouts over safety in mid-2020, leading to the firing of an activist employee name Christian Smalls. When Mr. Smalls went to the media, Amazon began a PR counteroffensive secretly strategizing to smear Mr. Smalls, an African American, as "not smart, not articulate."

These Amazon elections indicate that large companies, even when they are raising wages, seek to use such pay hikes to stave off greater worker power. That is one of the reasons that employers generally try to offer raises to workers during union drives. Like the proverbial "fist inside the velvet glove," the employer still maintains the power to reduce wages by claiming that business necessitates such a move. By contrast, the minimum wage law remains a floor which cannot be changed.

Starbucks is doing the same thing as Amazon. For years, the coffee giant has kept wages and benefits above the minimum wage to prevent unions from forming. As long as the minimum wage law is kept low, employers will aim to set their wages slightly above the minimum to deter workers from seeking a union. In many cases, this strategy works. In some cases, as on the Las Vegas Strip, the Culinary Union keeps wages high even for its nonunion workers. Thus, a low minimum wage keeps "threat effect" wages low.

THE POLITICAL ECONOMY OF THE FAIR LABOR STANDARDS ACT

The existing minimum wage and overtime laws are the product of intense lobbying by corporations to achieve regulatory arbitrage, to produce the most favorable business environment that can be legislated. As in many areas of legislation, protections are not distributed evenly; people of color have been specifically excluded within the legislative process. In the 1930s, in order to get federal protections

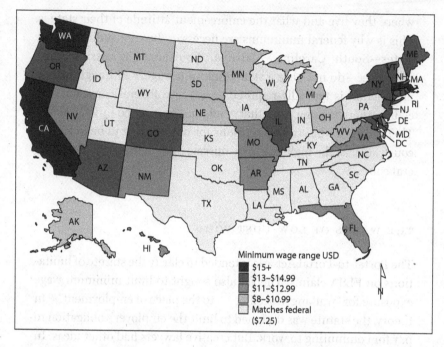

Map 1. Minimum wage by state. Source: U.S. Department of Labor data, 2023.

for collective bargaining and the votes of Southern senators, the National Labor Relations Act of 1935 exempted agricultural workers and domestic workers, many of whom were Black and Mexican. The Fair Labor Standards Act operated similarly, making protections available only at the state level after years of struggle.

The FLSA is a patchwork of exemptions and attempts to shave minutes and hours from the day, in the service of profit. Like many statutes when they are first enacted, the FLSA nonetheless was largely expansive in its initial coverage. Industry responded before the statute was ten years old, however, successfully lobbying Congress to enact the Portal-to-Portal Act of 1947.

The states are a patchwork of different minimum wage ranges, as Map 1 shows. This makes the experience of workers dependent on where they live and what the enforcement attitude of their state is. This is why federal minimums are necessary but not sufficient. Five states—South Carolina, Alabama, Louisiana, Mississippi, and Tennessee—do not have a state minimum wage.[28] Although federal jurisdiction is typically required to get into federal court on such claims, there is some work that would not be covered by federal law. There may also be strategic reasons for not wanting to be in federal court, such as the high rate of dismissals that plaintiffs suffer in federal court.[29]

THE WAGES OF LOW-COST FOOD

The Portal-to-Portal Act was intended to clarify the statute of limitations on FLSA claims. The act also sought to limit minimum wage exposure for "walking, traveling . . . to the place of employment."[30] In theory, the statute was designed to limit the employer's obligation to pay for commuting to work. But creative lawyers had other ideas. In *IBP v. Alvarez*, the International Beef Processors Company went to the U.S. Supreme Court to try to limit their liability to pay workers for the time spent walking from the time clock to the place where they put on their safety equipment. Although the Court ultimately rebuffed this theory, the case showed the lengths to which companies will go to shave time from "hours worked."

The processing of meat has always been unpleasant, dirty work. Waves of immigrants, first from Eastern Europe and the American South, then from Asia and Latin America, found their first jobs in the stockyards and the kill floors of the Midwest. A wave of African Americans went north to Chicago and other cities beginning in the 1880s and encountered discrimination, wage inequity, and unions that excluded them based on their race. Still, they struggled and organized to join unions and to get higher wages and, eventually, they began to find protection under the law of the workplace.

As earlier waves of immigrants moved into other parts of the economy, Mexican and other Latino immigrants took the places of this first wave of workers. These newer immigrants have become the permanent labor force at chicken and beef processing plants throughout the Midwest. Currently, from the minute they step onto company property, their movements are tracked through several surveillance technologies. These workers are the backbone of the fast-food industry.

Because they are in high demand, the workers often make more than the minimum wage in the state where they are working. Many are undocumented and only about 18 percent are unionized.[31] But as the experience of workers at a meat processing plant in Pasco, Washington, illustrates, companies are always looking for ways to reduce the wages of these vulnerable workers.

THE TIME-SHAVERS GO TO THE SUPREME COURT

Like many of her colleagues, Cecilia Alvarez worked a typical day shift for International Beef Processors. She arrived at the plant shortly before dawn, entered through the plant doors, and walked to the locker room. Here, she began donning the gear required to do her job—masks, gloves, lead aprons, boots. She, like many of her coworkers, was an active member of the union, and they all were concerned about safety. There was no question that the time she spent in the changing room putting on gear was "integral and indispensable" to her job.

In litigation, the focus was on walking—walking from the place where workers punched in to the place where they put on their gear. No one disputed that the time spent punching in and doffing the safety gear met the legal criteria and was covered. It was the walking to and from that was the issue. For most workers, this would not be a matter for contention, because they are not subject to a surveillance structure as many factory workers are.

WAREHOUSE WORKERS

Control was also key in *Integrity Staffing Solutions v. Busk*.[32] This case provides another example of the indignities faced by Amazon workers: these were workers at a fulfillment warehouse run by a firm called Integrity Staffing Solutions. The workers were required to go through a detector to minimize the threat of theft. These warehouse employees sued for compensation for the time they spent going through security checks at a Reno, Nevada, warehouse that contracted with Amazon and other retailers. The whole process of waiting to pass through the security checkpoint could take up to 25 minutes because the workers had to remove their keys, wallets, and belts and pass through a metal detector and also possibly be searched. Up to ten minutes of their lunchtime break also was used for this process. Plaintiffs alleged that the practices were violations of the FLSA and Nevada wage laws.

The employees wanted to receive compensation for waiting in line for the security checks, which the employer required to prevent the theft of merchandise. The Portal-to-Portal Act of 1947, which prevents the employee from receiving the compensation for time spent "preliminary" and "postliminary" to the worker's principal activities, did not answer the question of whether standing in line at a security check should be considered compensable "hours worked."

Justice Clarence Thomas wrote the opinion for the Court, holding that the time spent by warehouse workers undergoing security checks is not compensable under the FLSA. He declared that the screenings were not a principal activity nor integral to the employees' principal duties, and therefore were not compensable.[33] Justice Sonia Sotomayor, joined by Justice Elena Kagan, concurred in the judgment because the employer could have dispensed with the security screens without impairing job safety or effectiveness. In contrast to the Court's 2005 decision in *IBP v. Alvarez*, which held that the donning and doffing of safety gear for meatpackers was integral and indispensable as a safety matter, the Court here held that there was no safety reason for the time spent going through the detector.

LAW AND POLITICAL ECONOMY

Law and political economy (LPE) studies are becoming more common. LPE seeks to show the interests that are served by the law, and the ultimate product of the law—whether it is through legislation or adjudication—tend to fortify the privilege and inequality that many laws were meant to disrupt. Nowhere is the LPE phenomenon more evident than in the way that the FLSA has been molded by powerful interests to exclude vulnerable groups. This chapter views the creation of minimum wage law through the lens of LPE, showing that many of the exemptions and features of the law are not designed with workers' interests at heart, but rather to serve the interests of employers.

That even children have had to fight for the minimum wage is a story repeated throughout the history of workplace law. Employers repeatedly seek exemptions from laws that are meant to be broadly protective. Various industries go to legislators seeking carve-outs from the law. The Fair Labor Standards Act alone has 39 exemptions—everything from amusement and recreational establishments to shellfish haulers in Maine.

When legislators initially write laws, there do not need to be good reasons for exemptions. But there comes a point when the reason offered to a court for an exemption can be so irrational that it is rejected, even though judges generally apply a very deferential standard to exemptions.

CHALLENGING RACIAL CAPITALISM

Low minimum wages and a lack of enforcement are ultimately a feature of racial capitalism. Racial capitalism identifies the theory that the racial stratification inherent in society will inscribe itself in the economy. The important insight of racial capitalism about the current state of the economy is that economy has a dual nature—an instrumental one that seeks to fulfill the needs of capital through the labor of Black and brown workers and also a signifying feature that instantiates the racial hierarchy that already exists in society. Thus, as Professors Carmen Gonzalez and Athena Mutua write, it is "mutually constitutive," or, put another way, it is self-reinforcing.[34]

The remaining question is what should be done about the vicious cycle if race and class continue to affect the prospects of workers. The main takeaway of this book is that race and work are inextricably intertwined, and that once that is recognized by employers and policymakers, a higher minimum wage will continue to lift the lives of people of color and all workers.

As is discussed in Chapter 5, if the exemptions are racialized or based on animus to a particular group, the exemptions may be challenged on equal protection and due process grounds. While there is a high bar to challenging statutes on federal grounds, workers have had more luck suing under state constitutions. In 2018, for instance, the Washington State Supreme Court held that the exemption for farmworkers lacked a rational basis.[35] Two workers in the DeRuyter Brothers Dairy, Jose Martinez-Cuevas and Patricia Aguilar, who worked with their 300 coworkers on three eight-hour shifts— and usually many hours over 40 in a week—were denied minimum wage, overtime pay, and rest and meal breaks. Besides simply seeking what was legally owed to them, the class action led by Martinez-Cuevas and Aguilar sought to have the exemption from overtime pay for farmworkers declared unconstitutional.

This last claim was a bold move. The U.S. Constitution does not generally require legislatures to pass laws as long as there is just as rational reason for *not* legislating as there is for legislating. Many state constitutions are interpreted similarly. But the plaintiffs here used article II, section 35 of the Washington State constitution to argue that the legislature "shall" (i.e., must) pass necessary laws, the word *shall* operating as a "duty, rather than to confer discretion."[36] The court paid particular attention to the health and safety dangers and toil faced by the workers.[37] This was highly significant to the court, as was the fact that the workers involved here were immigrants. The court devoted significant attention to the underlying principles of fundamental constitutional rights and citizenship, even while basing its decision on a narrow, state-constitutional ground. In this way the decision was insulated from U.S. Supreme Court review, where most of the justices would likely be much more skeptical.

Other state courts have followed suit.[38] As is discussed in Chapter 5, there might be challenges to the exemptions for agriculture under the federal constitution. But other exemptions may and should be vulnerable to challenge. In my book *Marginal Workers*, I argue that workers of color and immigrants most frequently fall through the margins created even by workplace laws that are supposed to protect them.[39] In this chapter, I further develop the point that the exemptions and exclusions from protective labor laws are visited most heavily on workers of color and immigrants.

RACIAL POLITICAL ECONOMY

At its core, law and political economy studies emphasize that legal, political, and economic systems are symbiotic and interdependent. In the case of the United States, the capitalist system drives much of the politics as well as the legal system. In a racially stratified society such as ours, race tends to determine many outcomes in the economy. The idea that the proper functioning of capitalism depends on many workers laboring at or below the line might be called racial political economy.

What the struggles for a higher minimum tells us is that race and politics work in tandem to keep the minimum wage low. But even when the minimum wage is increased or expanded, various aspects of the American legal system conspire to prevent workers from getting the wages that they are owed. Workers of color and immigrants are especially likely to be denied their legal wages.

WORKERS WIN VICTORIES AGAINST
A STACKED DECK

Despite the structural barriers that have kept the minimum wage stagnant at the federal level, workers have won victories within the system to get a higher minimum wage in many states and cities. In the Introduction and also Chapter 8, I discuss the movement for a living wage and the Fight for $15, two examples of national movements that have changed the conversation about the need for livable wages.

Multiple states, including some of the reddest states in the nation, have raised their state minimum wage above the federal level. Some have included indexing formulas to ensure that their minimum wage keeps pace with the cost of living. And some states, including Nevada, have put the minimum wage into their constitution. Many of these victories have relied on the assistance of organized labor, such as the Culinary Union in Las Vegas.

THE LABOR MOVEMENT'S STAKE IN
THE MINIMUM WAGE

In media stories about the Culinary Workers Union in Las Vegas, the name of the union is almost always qualified as "politically powerful." This is because the union's ability to get out the vote has made or defeated many candidates in Nevada and several other states. The Culinary Workers Union was able to get an initiative on the Nevada ballot in the early 2000s to tie the minimum wage to the federal level and put it in the state constitution. At the time, Nevada was a reliably red state in presidential elections, and Republicans controlled both houses of the legislature and the governor's mansion. The union thereby insulated the minimum wage from interference by the legislature by enshrining it in the Nevada constitution.

This initiative passed handily in the 2004 and 2006 elections, as required by the Nevada constitution, even when Republicans won statewide elections. Nevada has also changed politically in the last 20 years. It morphed into a hard-fought purple political battleground with a Democratic governor and legislature. Still, increases in the minimum wage have not risen as quickly as in some neighboring states. And enshrining the minimum wage in the state constitution has not eliminated many of the ambiguities in the law. Nevertheless, Nevada continues to have its share of battles over the minimum wage.

NEVADA'S CONSTITUTIONALIZING OF THE MINIMUM WAGE

As in many cities, taxi drivers in Las Vegas are often immigrants and people of color. In many cities, taxi drivers have organized in traditional unions and nonbargaining associations. Although some are considered independent contractors, many are employees who seek the minimum wage. Even with the Nevada constitutional provision, that has been a struggle.

Taxi companies fought paying the minimum wage to the drivers all the way to the Nevada Supreme Court, which found in favor of the drivers in 2019. The political economy of Las Vegas, because the city is a global tourist destination, means that the taxi companies are very powerful, even though their power has been reduced somewhat by the rise of ride-hail companies such as Uber and Lyft. Still, there remains a longstanding symbiosis between the taxi companies and the casino resorts.

In Las Vegas, then, taxi workers have a bit more bargaining power than elsewhere. In many cities, such as San Diego, there is a long-standing belief that taxi workers do not want to be in unions. The work of Professor Veena Dubal demonstrates that there is in fact widespread interest among cab drivers in collective action, and there has often even been effective collective action in the gig economy. She has also discussed the racial dynamics of the gig industry.[40]

EVEN IN SIN CITY, WAGES ARE NOT OPTIONAL

Topless dancers in Las Vegas run the gamut from high-profile dancers to those working at one of the many clubs which cater to tourists, residents, or bachelor parties. One of the clubs about a half mile from the Las Vegas Strip is Sapphire Gentleman's Club. As is described in Chapter 3, the club's scheme is to require the dancers to pay a stage rental fee as well as to evade all responsibility for paying the minimum wage. The dancers at Sapphire sued for the minimum wage, alleging that they were under the control of the club.

As with previous cases, the club maintained a set of "house rules" enforced against the dancers, who could be fined or fired for violations. The dancers also were subject to a system of demerits that could affect their status at the club. The only thing that gave the dancers any freedom was the ability to dance when they wanted to do so. The case went to the Nevada Supreme Court, which in another victory for dancers in wage cases, found the dancers should be classified as employees.

Attorney Leon Greenberg brought this case, and he confirmed that many of the dancers in the class he represented were people of color and immigrants who had experienced extensive discrimination. Greenberg was also among the attorneys who brought a successful tip-sharing case in the Ninth Circuit Court of Appeals.[41] Greenberg says he specializes in minimum wage lawsuits because proving wage and hour cases is more straightforward than race or gender discrimination cases.

SUBMERGING RACE CLAIMS FOR WAGE CLAIMS

Attorney Greenberg's strategy to avoid race discrimination claims in wage and hour cases makes sense in several ways. First, adding intersectional claims can harm the chances of success for all claims. Second, as many civil rights attorneys can attest, the hostility of the courts to Title VII claims has made FLSA claims more lucrative. This is in large part related to Supreme Court precedents that have severely narrowed the path for success in civil rights cases. This means that many overlapping and intersecting wage and race discrimination claims remain unaddressed. We can see this in the litigation trends over the last few decades. It has long been the case that race claims have been submerged to wage claims because of the increasing skepticism of federal judges to race and national origin claims.

THE WEAK PROMISE OF DISPARATE IMPACT

Although direct evidence of race discrimination in the setting of wages is hard to obtain, there is another theory that might provide redress for workers of color who are denied the minimum wage. Title VII prohibits discrimination on the bases of race, color, and creed. Discrimination can be either direct or based on "practices . . . [and] devices that have the effect of discrimination."[42]

In theory, groups that are the victims of wage theft could bring disparate impact claims alleging that they are paid disproportionately. Then they could force a company to justify those disparities. There are several immediate problems, however. First, pay is unlikely to be considered a "device, test, or qualification" that the employer is required to justify. Second, even if the employer could be required to justify a pay practice, there are so many nondiscriminatory reasons they could invoke to avoid liability.

Therefore, there have been very few attempts to fashion a challenge to discriminatory pay practices using disparate impact theory. The few examples when these claims were tried show the strategic and structural limitations of tying these claims together.[43]

PARTICULAR ISSUES FOR WOMEN OF COLOR

As the first work on intersectionality showed, women of color face issues that men of color or white women do not face. In her foundational article on intersectionality, Professor Kimberlé Williams Crenshaw showed how antidiscrimination protections on the grounds of race and gender leave Black women less protected than white women and Black men.[44]

Similarly, the Equal Pay Act and Title VII operate together in ways that disadvantage women of color. How? That is because of the Bennett Amendment. The Lilly Ledbetter Fair Pay Act was intended to overturn the Supreme Court decision in *Ledbetter v. Goodyear Tire*. This would allow women such as Lilly Ledbetter herself the opportunity to file a Title VII action based on gender discrimination.[45]

But Ledbetter could also have filed an Equal Pay Act claim. The reasons that she did not are probably complex. As in Title VII claims, however, there are defenses similar to the Bennett Amendment which make a claim very difficult to win. The employer can show that there is disparity in wages for the same job for "any other factor besides sex" of the employee.[46] This allows employers a great deal of latitude to set wages in potentially discriminatory ways. In order to find out where workers suffer from pay discrimination, many employees have to seek out information on the pay practices of their employer. Because the Lilly Ledbetter law did not mandate open access to information about employer pay practices, many instances of pay discrimination are still unaddressed.

CONCLUSION

There are many ways in which the law can be reformed to be more responsive to the needs of people of color and immigrants. Some litigation victories have been rolled back by powerful interests through counter-campaigns framed as ways to help people of color and immigrants, such as the campaign by gig companies to pass Proposition 22 in California. These counter-campaigns have thwarted the struggles of many workers who, through litigation and activism, are advocating for greater wage justice. In most cases, workers are seeking minimal protections that should be available to all workers, such as a minimum wage or workers' compensation. But the political economy is stacked against them. In the next chapter, I discuss reforms that might be possible even within the current political situation.

7 Improving the Minimum Wage as a Tool for Racial Justice

Workers of color and immigrants in the workforce today are survivors—survivors of centuries of subjugation and, more recently, of three social hurricanes that tore through the United States in 2020. The first hurricane was the global COVID-19 pandemic, which has claimed more than a million lives in the United States.[1] Then, the death of George Floyd in Minneapolis on May 25, 2020, created another hurricane involving racial justice and injustice.[2] And third, the presidential election of 2020 that culminated in the violent attack by supporters of losing candidate Donald Trump on the U.S. Capitol building on January 6, 2021, has led many Americans to ponder the very survival of American democracy.[3]

In this environment, the fight for raising the minimum wage has become less prominent than several other crises—the war in Ukraine, the conflagration in Israel and Palestine, inflation, and the recovery from or possible resurgence of the pandemic. These issues may overshadow the task of improving the minimum wage and the lot of low-wage workers. As I have argued in this book, though, raising the minimum wage will help all workers to weather each of these storms. The stagnant wages for low-wage workers are at the heart of so much that is wrong in America right now. It is workers of color and immigrants who suffer most when minimum wage laws are not enforced or their thresholds increased. And raising up the workers at the bottom has historically been shown to have the greatest impact throughout the economy. In this book, I have outlined the needs and challenges now faced by workers and discuss strategies to improve the conditions of their work. Some of these strategies are being actively employed by social movements and some involve innovations still to be explored.

In this chapter, I catalog the reforms that need to happen to make the minimum wage more just and inclusive. Removing many of the exemptions for domestic workers and agricultural workers would ensure that many more people of color and immigrants get the minimum wage. Finally, I lay out a new vision for a minimum salary to sustain a living wage and also to provide stability, without being dependent on the vicissitudes of employer scheduling practices.

Critical wage theory is needed in these times because it recognizes the racial aspects of the material conditions that keep workers of color at the lower levels of the economic scale. In this chapter I use critical wage theory as a lens to describe and promote reforms designed to improve the lives of all workers.

This chapter assesses the current likelihood of a political scenario that might lead to increases in the minimum wage nationwide. I also describe some of the problems of enforcing the minimum wage and how they might be remedied. The pandemic made reforms to how the minimum wage is implemented and enforced even more urgent, and possibly more palatable. In the wake of the pandemic and the Black Lives Matter movement, raising the minimum wage is also essential for racial justice.

THE PANDEMIC HURRICANE

On March 13, 2020, the world stopped. By that time, the National Basketball Association had shut down. Actors Tom Hanks and Rita Wilson announced that they had tested positive for the coronavirus in Australia. On that day, the global COVID-19 pandemic was first seen as a serious issue in the United States, after already raging in several other countries. From that point on, the pandemic changed every aspect of American life, especially in the workplace.

The most immediate change was that millions stopped going in to work. Millions in the service sector lost their jobs within days and unemployment rolls swelled throughout the entire country. Millions more transitioned to working from home or to new occupations that could be done remotely to avoid human contact and potential exposure to the disease at a time when there was no vaccine.

But not everyone could work from home. "Essential workers" were required to stay on the job despite dangerous conditions. At the beginning of the pandemic, this category included jobs where workers faced the public, such as in grocery stores, hospitals, and public transportation. These workers were lionized as heroes by many Americans. And yet, Congress did not raise the minimum wage or legislate any sort of risk premium to compensate these workers. Essential workers were at a higher risk than nonessential workers, yet they were not being paid essential wages.[4] As COVID-19 cases rose and hospitals were overwhelmed in the spring and summer of 2020, the workers in meatpacking and other industries with large populations of immigrant workers and workers of color suffered some of the highest rates of infection and death.[5]

At the beginning of the pandemic, some grocery chains offered hazard pay, but as the pandemic wore on, companies like Rite Aid and Kroger retracted their offers of hazard pay even though the worst of the pandemic had not ended. Congress extended hazard pay reimbursement through the Coronavirus Relief Act, but that ended in the middle of 2021.

Raising the minimum wage has been shown to lead to increases for all workers. The Economic Policy Institute has estimated that raising the wage would directly or indirectly lead to 29.6 to 35.5 million workers getting a raise.[6] The ripple effects of a rise in the minimum wage would be the most effective way to partially compensate millions of workers for the extra risks they bore during the pandemic. These benefits will help to ease racial inequities, but the inequities remain.

THE HURRICANE OF RACIAL JUSTICE AND INJUSTICE

While the first wave of the pandemic was raging through the country in the first half of 2020, the world again stopped after the killing of George Floyd by a police officer in Minneapolis. After video of the event went viral throughout the world, protests proliferated in cities internationally. As described in a recent book about the life of George Floyd, the path the 46-year-old took to the street where he ultimately lost his life was through a series of low-wage jobs. While his economic circumstances ultimately were not the reason he was the victim of police murder, he had worked in low-wage jobs most of his life.[7] He also labored in prison for the private entity then called Corrections Corporation of America (CCA), and like others in confinement, he worked for only cents a day.[8]

The protests in cities large and small shined new light on the issues of racial injustice and police misconduct that had been brewing for years. Companies and professional sports teams rushed to take up the Black Lives Matter mantle and to adopt diversity plans. Unfortunately, these same companies have failed to support, and indeed they even actively oppose, increases to the minimum wage.

THE TRUMPUBLICAN HURRICANE

The upheaval following the George Floyd murder careened the country toward the 2020 election and ultimately the attack on the Capitol on January 6, 2021. In the meantime, the labor market slowly returned to more normal functioning, though unemployment remained higher than average through June 2022, at 8.4 percent (it improved by December 2023, to a rate of 3.7 percent). Extended economic uncertainty continues to make economic security unattainable for large segments of the population.

The presidency of Donald Trump, starting from his Inauguration speech decrying "American carnage" to encouraging the insurrection at the Capitol that did result in actual carnage that day, also included a sustained assault on American workers of color and immigrants. Every action coming from government agencies charged with the enforcement of federal law seemed to reverse the intent of the laws to protect workers. This is not surprising given those who served during the Trump administration, including former Carl's Jr. executive Patrick Pizella and employer defense lawyers Alexander Acosta and Eugene Scalia. Other agencies retrenched, cancelling worker protections including the limiting of claims for graduate students and gig workers. Even after the election of President Joe Biden, considered by many to be the most pro-union president in history, there has continued to be much retrenchment which needs to be reversed. And the political winds in the country now shift quickly. This means that meaningful increases to the minimum wage are not likely.

However, in the post-George Floyd/post-COVID-19/post-Jan. 6 context, several reforms to the way employees are paid are needed to compensate workers of color and immigrants more fully for the work they do. Below I discuss different strategies to improve the economic lives of marginalized workers.

PAY TRANSPARENCY

Such extraordinary pay inequity exists in part because many workers are not aware of the arbitrary disparities that are hard to explain on grounds other than gender and race. And yet, Equal Pay Act and Title VII claims are relatively rare. The fact is that many workers do not know that they are victims of pay discrimination because they do not have access to information about what other workers are paid. Pay transparency laws aim to change that, with the City of Philadelphia becoming one of the first with a local transparency requirement.

But an older federal law, dating back to the New Deal, has long allowed a modicum of pay transparency. The National Labor Relations Act (NLRA) allows workers to discuss pay and benefits with each other without fear of retaliation. And, if one or more workers join together to demand pay records from the employer, they are legally entitled to information about the wages the employer pays employees. If an employee faces retaliation, rules that prohibit discussions of pay are illegal under the NLRA's protection of "concerted activities" for employees' "mutual aid or protection."[9]

Even with concerted activity or collective bargaining, which is inaccessible to a large portion of the workforce, however, many workers will not be able to obtain reliable information on pay practices. A federal law that would require such information on request would serve well to provide minimum wage workers with the information they need to determine whether there is pay discrimination. After all, in the low-wage hourly market, there is less justification for discretion, unless the employer has a regular schedule of wage increases based on seniority.

RISK PREMIUMS

In a properly functioning labor market, classical economics theory predicts that workers will get higher wages without government intervention when there is a heightened need for workers and a lack of workers willing to fill those needs. Large companies regularly attract attention to their wage increases. Amazon touted its $15 an hour wage during the spring of 2020 with ads on National Public Radio and the *New York Times* website at the same time the company was vigorously opposing the unionization of its employees at its warehouse in Bessemer, Alabama. That vote was later overturned, in part because the wage increases and other benefits the company was offering to try to fend off unionization were illegal. Other companies like Target and Walmart also followed suit and raised wages.

Even before the pandemic, the most dangerous jobs in the country have been filled by people of color and immigrants, particularly in the meatpacking and food service industries. In 2005, Human Rights Watch reported higher rates of injuries and death for Latinos and immigrants.[10] Yet, these jobs are still paid at lower rates than less dangerous jobs.

During COVID-19, instead of receiving a bonus as an incentive to return to work, workers at meatpacking plants throughout the country were compelled to stay on the job by the Defense Production Act. The wages paid to the workers did not reflect the risk involved in working literally shoulder to shoulder with fellow workers during the pandemic. Many became infected and a number died. Their wages at the time of their death will determine future economic prospects for the family members left behind. Once again, there is an iron triangle of sorts between low wages, occupational risk, and race and immigration status.

MARKET FAILURES

Incredibly, the pandemic also caused some to ask whether a minimum wage would be necessary in the post-COVID world because the labor shortages that many employers were facing led some to raise wages. Yet even employers who feel compelled to offer higher wages are not required to provide any set number of hours. Thus the market cannot be counted upon to ensure that workers earn a livable wage.

While Apple recently received attention when it raised its starting salary to $22 an hour, not every worker is going to be employed by Apple, and many are now being laid off. Conditions at an Apple store in Maryland led employees in June 2022 to be the first to vote for union representation. The reality was that this was not just a response to the supply and demand curves of the labor market, but also a reaction to growing interest in unionization at Apple stores and across the country, including in well-publicized efforts at Starbucks stores. But despite Amazon warehouses and Apple stores raising wages in response to the threat of unionization, many workers still work at the baseline minimum wage for these huge corporations. A large percentage of these workers are immigrants and workers of color.

Despite a few well-publicized examples, most wages stayed flat during the pandemic.[11] At the same time that the federal government was transferring $200 billion in unemployment funds to the states, the federal minimum wage remained at its 2009 level. Many workers saw receiving unemployment benefits as preferable to continuing to work at minimum wage jobs. And that has contributed to the worker shortage many businesses now are facing. This is another reason that the minimum wage should be raised.

FIRST, RAISE THE WAGE

As of now, the federal minimum wage sits at the same place it did in 2009—$7.25 an hour. Through two recessions, a global pandemic, and historic inflation, Congress apparently still disregards the economic plight of low-wage workers. In fact, exacerbated by the pandemic, economic inequality has increased dramatically, while the number of billionaires in the country has exploded.

During the pandemic, the minimum wage dropped to 21 percent less than it was worth in 2009, when adjusted for inflation.[12] This means that the wage is now worth less than $5.73 per hour, especially with the burden of inflation during the economic hurricane of the pandemic.

Even though the federal minimum wage has remained stagnant, many states have moved to fill the gap. Many states have reached or will soon exceed the $15 mark. In June 2022, the State of Hawai'i enacted an $18 an hour minimum wage, with an increased tip credit.[13] But these increases are contingent on the politics of particular states, and it is far from clear that the tipped minimum wage will change at the federal level without a major change in the political winds.

INDEXING AND AUTOMATIC INCREASES

I have described the hegemony of economics in stopping or blunting the minimum wage. But, as I have argued, the principles of racial justice must take precedence over economic reasons for a low minimum wage. Indeed, the facts have pointed to a higher minimum wage for some time, particularly in the COVID-19 era. But policymakers rarely rely on economic data to try to determine what is a *livable* wage. Rather, they often propose a rate that make sense for the industries that are regulated. This is a missed opportunity for legislators to ensure that the minimum wage is a living wage.

And there are pitfalls here too. Some minimum wage statutes, such as in Alaska, Colorado, and South Dakota, have tied the minimum wage to the inflation rate for several years.[14] Several others, such as California, New York, and Oregon in the last few years, have included automatic increases to the minimum wage tied to the inflation rate. Thus, when the inflation rate is low, wage increases are also low or nonexistent. This policy has some benefits. But when inflation suddenly goes up to 7 or 8 percent, wages do not catch up quickly enough.

It would be better if legislators set a standard increase at a certain percentage so that when inflation rapidly increases, low-wage workers have more of a cushion. This also would help even out some of the shocks to the economy. The automatic nature of the increases alone would aid low-wage earners significantly in their ability to plan their economic future. If the federal minimum wage enacted in 2009 of $7.25 per hour had been raised to take inflation into account annually, it would currently be over $10 per hour.[15]

WAGE BOARDS

Wage boards in certain cities for certain industries have been able to tailor minimum wages to working conditions. There is long historical precedent for this. In fact, the first attempts to pass the minimum wage involved wage boards, mostly led by women reformers seeking the right to vote and a minimum wage for women in the garment industry in the 1910s and the 1920s. These early reforms were the precursor to the industry standards set in many industries, including wage standards in the poultry industry, successfully challenged in *A.L.A. Schechter Poultry v. United States*. In that case from the pre–New Deal period when the Court regularly struck down protective labor laws, the Court in *Schechter* found that Congress had delegated too much authority to the administration to determine what fair "economic conditions" were.

The Court has not struck down a law under the excessive delegation principle since *Schechter*. This has allowed administrative agencies such as the Department of Labor to regulate broadly since for over 80 years. However, with the addition of new Justices Gorsuch, Kavanaugh and Barrett, the current Supreme Court has become more skeptical of agency regulation in several cases, with more pending. This means that it will be extremely difficult at the federal level to have wage boards that are targeted at particular industries or workers. This does not mean that such regulation at the state level is not possible in industries such as food production and fast-food service. As is discussed in Chapter 4, the political economy in each state will lead to incomplete protection for workers, but especially will leave workers of color and immigrants in the fast food and gig economy with incomplete protection.

THE FAILURE OF POLITICS

The minimum wage has enjoyed support from a broad section of the public. As with many policies that enjoy popular support, such as abortion rights, gun control, or union organizing, the political system has failed to generate the outcomes that most voters want. Some of this is attributable to various structural obstacles that stand in the way of popular will—the filibuster, the electoral college, and the composition of the U.S. Senate in which each state gets two senators, no matter what the size of the state's population.

But there are other reasons why the minimum wage is an example of a "sticky" policy once it is passed. Some of the public react negatively, judging that such policies benefit only "those people." Minimum wage increases are castigated in the same way as welfare benefits. Many Americans assume that welfare benefits are largely utilized by people of color and undocumented immigrants when, in fact, the largest share of welfare recipients are white. If politicians see an increase in the minimum wage as benefiting people other than their constituents, there will not be significant change.

INCREASE AND ENFORCE

One of the surest ways to improve the lot of the working poor is to increase their wages. The Fight for $15 has made a minimum wage of $15 an hour a reality in many states and cities. But in the ten years since this social movement began, the cost of living has increased.

Thus, the Fight for $15 should now be more like the Fight for $20 or $25 (as well as a union). But politics being what they are now, $15 per hour probably remains the best-case, practical scenario.

In each of the last three presidential elections, the minimum wage has been one of the main litmus tests, largely in the Democratic Party primary. In 2008, Senators Hillary Clinton and Barack Obama were asked what they thought the ideal minimum wage should be. Neither candidate committed to $15 per hour, but both suggested that a higher amount should be "studied." As we know, Senator Obama went on to win the presidential nomination and to serve two terms in the White House.

Soon after taking office, President Obama had the opportunity to sign legislation raising the minimum wage to $7.25 per hour—where it still stands now. This was done in part because of Obama's honeymoon period, and in part because Democrats held 60 seats in the Senate and a majority in the House of Representatives. Two years later, the political tide turned against the incumbent party and Obama faced a Republican majority in both houses of Congress. The minimum wage was not going anywhere then and that is where it has stayed since.

In 2012, Obama was the incumbent president, facing a very wealthy plutocrat. In the last weeks of the campaign, Governor George Romney was caught on tape claiming that the "47 percent of the country pay no taxes" but were being supported by the rest of the country while doing no work. His campaign never recovered from that hot-mic moment.

In 2016, Senator Bernie Sanders and Secretary of State Hillary Clinton sought the Democratic nomination. In the primary battle, Senator Sanders quickly called for a $15 an hour minimum wage, while Secretary Clinton and other primary candidates were more circumspect. When the race came down to the two top candidates, the minimum wage was a clear difference between Clinton and Sanders, but Secretary Clinton nonetheless won the nomination.

Clinton's subsequent loss to Donald Trump and the Republican takeover of Congress meant that there would be no minimum wage increase for the next four years. But it was hardly only the stagnation of the minimum wage during that time that negatively affected people of color and immigrants. The administration severely restricted the standards for joint employment, for example, in agencies like the Department of Labor and the National Labor Relations Board. The joint employer rule would allow for greater responsibility of contracting parties throughout the supply chain for minimum wage violations or the duty to bargain. The rule is intended to deal with the fissured workplace that Professor David Weil identified. And yet, the rule has been a site of intense battles between business interests and worker advocates and will undoubtedly remain in stasis regardless of which party occupies the White House.

During the 2020 general election campaign and the transition period, hopes were high for a quick increase to the minimum wage. President Biden has made several very important appointments to key economic positions on his cabinet, as well as within the Department of Labor and the offices of federal contract compliance. Realistically, nonlegislative means must also be explored to raise wages and the livelihood for workers.

WHAT HAPPENS WHEN THE POLITICAL SYSTEM WON'T WORK?

After the election of a Democratic president and Congress in 2020, many thought that the stars were aligned finally to enact the $15 per hour minimum wage bill. More than a few years later, however, a wage increase does not seem possible legislatively. The question that remains therefore is, what can be done administratively? Executive orders have been used more often in recent years in several areas, for everything from immigration to travel bans. The COVID-19 pandemic showed us that in times of crisis, the president has extraordinary powers that can be used to blunt the effects of economic catastrophe. These powers should be applied to the current economic crises, including what high inflation is causing. The president can work with his economic team and the Federal Reserve to ensure that wage increases are targeted. In most cases, the most pressing need to have a higher minimum wage would be in cities and coastal areas where higher inflation is more of an issue.

Some states and communities may choose to keep minimum wages low, deciding that is best for them. This stance raises the issue of universal standards versus relativism. The failure of Congress to raise the minimum wage is a failure of the political route to ensure decent standards across the board. As is described in Chapter 5, there may be a point when the failure of individual states to protect workers becomes a constitutional problem under the Thirteenth and Fourteenth Amendments. Until these theories are accepted by the Supreme Court (if they ever are), politics will continue to fail marginal workers.

END THE EXCLUSIONS

As is described in Chapters 3, 4, and 5, our labor laws are full of gaps and holes that workers fall through. The priority would be to end the exclusions of agricultural and domestic workers to federal minimum wage and overtime laws. That would mean that the protections of the Fair Labor Standards Act would finally not be susceptible to manipulation based on where the worker lives. But that of course would only be the beginning. The exclusions to federal law protecting the right to organize also need to be changed.

As is described in Chapter 6, the political economy of the minimum wage will not likely yield to expanding the eligibility of workers as employees instead of independent contractors. Further, there is currently no active legislation to change the exclusions.

Yet, exclusions of farm workers have been challenged successfully in state courts in Washington and Oregon by invoking the Fourteenth Amendment's equal protection language in their respective state constitutions. The same strategy could be used under the federal constitution, which applies to both the state and federal governments. The problem is that the current Supreme Court has hardly been hospitable to equal protection claims, even when there is a racial history to the distinction. See for example the 2022 case, *United States v. Valleo-Madero*. At first glance, and most importantly for defendant Jose Luis Valleo-Madero, the case was about federal social security claims for residents of Puerto Rico. The federal government sued Valleo-Madero, a U.S. citizen and a resident of Puerto Rico, for social security benefits he allegedly was paid improperly.

Unfortunately, the Court held that denial of Valleo-Madero's social security benefits was not a denial under the federal Equal Protection Clause, even though similarly situated residents of the U.S. territory of the Consolidated States of the Northern Mariana Islands do receive the same social security disability benefits that Valleo-Madero sought. Given this and many other restrictive decisions by the current Supreme Court and other federal judges, the kind of equal protection claims that were previously successful in state courts would most likely now receive a chilly reception at the federal level. The equal protection guarantees of other state constitutions, however, should be invoked by challenging statutes with irrational and unreasonable exemptions for some workers.

MAKE WORK MORE BENEFICIAL THAN UNEMPLOYMENT

One of the things that happened in the pandemic is that workers who did not earn enough wages often were not eligible for unemployment benefits. Data have shown that the unemployment rates for African Americans and other minorities remain disproportionately high. Thus, raising the minimum wage will have a beneficial impact on many workers.

This has not stopped some politicians from arguing that the minimum wage should be reduced or even eliminated. One of the main planks of 2021 California gubernatorial recall candidate Larry Elder was a "0.00" minimum wage. "Why an employer and employee can't negotiate on their own a proper wage is beyond me." Elder's *reductio ad absurdum* position is not surprising coming from the libertarian fringe, but the sentiment of doing away with the minimum wage is common among many conservatives. Many such conservatives have now become federal judges. But even judges who do not like the minimum wage are obligated to follow the law, and there is little ambiguity about $7.25 per hour. Ambiguity does lurk within the law's coverage, however. The broad construction of exemptions has the same effect as a "0.00" minimum wage.

MAKE UNPAID INTERNSHIPS HARDER TO HOST

Unpaid internships are often touted as a great way for young people to get experience and allow the employer to "take a risk" on a young person without the obligation of payment. Sometimes, there is an educational component. But many internships resemble the abusive relationship depicted in the 2006 movie *The Devil Wears Prada*— minus the uplifting ending of that film. Most of the time, there is little educational content in internships, but with proper oversight, they may provide academic credits. The goal of the Department of Labor has been to determine when an internship is a bona fide trainee situation and when the employer is simply trying to exploit labor.

Each year, an estimated two million people work as interns in the United States. Of that number, only 6 to 8 percent of Black and Latino students have paid internships, compared to 74 percent of their white counterparts. Like the other unpaid gigs discussed in this book, internships are not cost-free to the intern. Each internship costs the intern an average of $6,000 in housing, food, and transportation. These costs tend to prove more challenging to students and young people of color.

The best way to deal with the situation would be for Congress to confirm that all hours at an internship must at least be compensated with the minimum wage. But the inequalities of who can do internships will persist. So, will ending the internship rule be enough for decent work? Perhaps not. But requiring a minimum wage would be a step toward dignity. It would also mean that more young people who do not come from positions of privilege would be able to compete for internships in the business world.

END THE TIPPED WAGE, AND
DISCOURAGE TIPPING ITSELF

As is discussed in Chapter 4, activists have targeted the tipped wage for repeal and have argued instead for starting everyone at $7.25 per hour. This is the law in six of 50 states already—California, Nevada, Minnesota, Montana, Washington, and Oregon. This policy would go a long way toward dealing with the inequities of the tipping system that has led to the racial and gender disparities.

But even with the elimination of the tipped wage, the institution of tipping will retain many of the legacies of slavery and racism. A fairer option would be to replace tipping with a regulated service charge. Many restaurants, including some high-end locations in New York City, have gone to this model. Danny Meyer, the owner of Union Square Hospitality Group, which includes the upscale New York Gramercy Tavern, also owns the Shake Shack, a fast-casual burger chain. At all of his establishments, Meyer has replaced tipping with a 21 percent service charge.

As one might expect, the change took many of Meyer's employees aback. But the resulting distribution of income has had an impact on racial justice within the restaurants.[16] Meyer's estimate was that back-of-the-house staff income went up 20 percent and front-of-the-house staff saw a decrease of 20 percent, leading many of the FOH staff to leave the restaurant. The tip pooling model has been litigated in the Ninth Circuit Court of Appeals, the federal region which covers nine Western states. The Department of Labor rule preventing tip pooling for those outside the "chain of service," such as supervisors, was upheld by the court in the Ninth Circuit, which means that the issue could be different in any of the other circuits, leading once again to an unevenness in the protection of workers of color and immigrants who are tipped workers.

Even at restaurants that have survived the pandemic, tipping will not come back entirely. At some restaurants that levy a service charge, any gratuities left by patrons are donated to charity. This is a principled position, but as I discuss below, there are preferable alternatives to the model of paying an hourly wage plus tips.[17]

During the COVID-19 pandemic, uncertainty and the lack of customers led many restaurants to close, and the ones that remain in operation are contemplating the uncertain labor costs that come with shifting public health mandates. But restaurant workers have faced this uncertainty for years and will be unlikely to come back to restaurant work unless they are promised better conditions. Many restaurant workers have left the industry entirely.

At the same time, the federal government has increased payments to individuals during the pandemic and extended certain unemployment benefits. This has raised concerns that the infusion of funds into the economy would create inflationary pressures. Like concerns about the minimum wage, these critiques forget the cliff that the economy fell over when the pandemic hit. In Nevada, for example, the unemployment rate a month into the pandemic was 28.5 percent, with the famous Las Vegas Strip shut down for 78 days.[18] Thus, with the choice between historically high levels of inflation and economic devastation for the bottom of the labor market, the decision to send payments directly to individuals was the correct one. But the inability to get more stimulus money in the present-day political climate makes an increase to the federal minimum wage very unlikely.

As the One Fair Wage (OFW) movement has argued, tipping is a vestige of an era when African Americans were expected to be subservient to the needs of white patrons for whatever tips they deemed worthy of the service. OFW has argued that the lower minimum wage should be abolished and the uncertainties of tips should be replaced by set service charges that are divided equally among the staff. This approach has its difficulties related to the taxability of the new service charge, but it represents a major improvement to the unpredictability of tipping and the reality that workers of color receive less in tips than white workers. This is a race-conscious reform that will lead to better living standards for workers of color.

MANDATED RISK PREMIUMS

If the COVID-19 pandemic showed one thing, it is that the free market for wages does not adequately compensate for the risk involved in certain professions. The theory is that in construction or dock work and other hazardous occupations the risk premium is built into the higher wages offered. But this is not the case. One solution would be to legislate certain risk premiums into certain jobs. This is already done in some respect in the prevailing wage schedule but is not always enforced. The types of jobs that we think of as hazardous—construction, mining—are dominated by white men who generally command a higher wage. The pandemic has showed us that there are other jobs not usually thought of as dangerous but which can be very dangerous and yet many of them pay at or near the minimum wage.

AMENDING THE AMENDMENTS

As I argue in Chapter 5, our existing Constitution does provide a strong basis for enacting minimum labor standards. Nonetheless, there are movements to amend the Constitution, adding provisions that would explicitly enshrine labor rights as fundamental rights. For example, the Thirteenth Amendment contains a broad prohibition against slavery and involuntary servitude. It also contains a gaping exception that has contributed to policies that continue many aspects of racial subjugation, including the lack of adequate compensation for prison labor. So, should the Thirteenth Amendment be amended? The short answer is that if the Amendment were properly interpreted there would not need to be a change to the language, because the use of unpaid prison labor is not justified by the exception clause.

The impression that the Thirteenth Amendment allows unpaid prison labor has certainly found a place in the public imagination thanks to brilliant movies like *13TH*. Despite the "correct" interpretation of the law, the fact is that the exception clause has led to several movements to amend the Amendment, as well as prison strikes and litigation.

In Nevada, there has been litigation over the minimum wage statute for prisoners. Nevada has one of the broadest minimum wage statutes, with the Supreme Court recently finding taxi drivers and topless dancers to be employees. The question will be whether the law says what it means and enforces what it says.

USE BASIC INCOME TO SUPPLEMENT, NOT TO SUPPLANT, THE MINIMUM WAGE

There is much discussion about the possibility of instituting a policy of basic income as an alternative to the minimum wage. Some tech moguls such as Elon Musk and Mark Zuckerberg tout this policy as an alternative to the minimum wage for all workers. The idea has continued to gain traction with policymakers, such as the mayor of Stockton, California, Michael Tubbs, who spearheaded a basic income payment to all the city's residents. All indications are that this was well received by the city's residents and was certainly welcome during the darkest days of the pandemic.

The federal government also distributed subsidies during the pandemic. The Coronavirus Relief Act of 2020 passed Congress overwhelmingly and included $600 for each American. This meant that for some workers, the compensation for staying home could outstrip the hourly rate of compensation many workers would earn in the labor market. This led many to criticize the payment as a disincentive from working. "We are paying people not to work," some lamented. Some argued this would lead to a labor shortage after the pandemic because people could make more by staying home. Of course, this explanation ignored the fact that it was unsafe for many workers to return to work, or that some workers simply decided their minimum wage jobs did not warrant their return.

Of course, the same critics of the COVID relief checks did not line up behind an increase in the minimum wage to readjust the incentives to work. Instead, the debate continues. Eventually, any other COVID relief was bound up in the politics of President Biden's proposed legislation, Build Back Better.

The COVID relief debate did not resolve the question of instituting a minimum basic income, and at this point, there seems little chance that any minimum basic income program will pass. Even if it were politically possible, though, basic income would not an alternative to the minimum wage for several reasons. First, some proposed minimum basic income programs exclude the undocumented. Second, the level of support would be unlikely to completely replace wage work.

FROM THE MINIMUM WAGE TO A MINIMUM SALARY

Even if a minimum income is not implemented in most of the United States, there is one reform that would add more certainty to the lives of many low-wage earners—ending the hourly wage. The issue for many low-wage workers is stability, the kind of stability that high-wage, salaried workers have. Thus, the law should incentivize and facilitate employers to pay their workers a regular salary. Here are some ideas of how this might be implemented.

Currently, an employer must pay all wages at regular intervals for all hours worked, or face waiting-time penalties under their respective state laws. But what if, as in the case of workers exempt from overtime laws, workers received a minimum salary regardless of how many hours they worked during a particular pay period. With the salary set at a minimal level, the worker could "bank" hours with the employer for use later.

Some regulation of the employer's scheduling practices is needed to deal with both the failure to guarantee a certain number of working hours and the possible uncertainty for businesses of meeting a higher hourly minimum wage. The federal Fair Labor Standards Act (FLSA) of 1938 allows states the ability to legislate in this area, provided the resulting reforms equal the federal minimum wage per hour. I propose converting the hourly minimum wage into a livable weekly wage (LWW) that would give the employer a certain amount of flexibility in terms of scheduling and the employees some degree of certainty in terms of a regular income. This would be used in tandem with fair scheduling laws and practices to allow employees the ability to plan their family and home lives and to increase their skills through job training and higher education.

The optimal level of the LWW, and how it might differ across years or geographic areas, would have to be studied further to ensure both an efficient level for the employer and a minimum standard of living for employees. The Department of Labor would be able to change the minimum salary level to be exempt from overtime premiums for hours worked more than 40 per week, and these changes would impact the LWW. Thus, this policy would be undertaken in a holistic manner that considers not just increases in the minimum wage, but also impacts on scheduling and overtime policies. Under this system, employers could still pay an hourly wage, but it would be at a higher level per hour than the minimum salary.

Employers might decide to pay their workers a minimum salary for a few reasons. First, they might choose the lower hourly wage to gain predictability in their labor costs. Second, the certainty of a minimum payment might avoid litigation and disputes that can arise with hourly paychecks. Of course, any new system may lead to questions of implementation and application. But wage laws can be designed with safe harbors to allow employers to provide more certainty.

THE THREAT OF THE SUPREME COURT

The minimum wage has been slowly increasing in many states. This book argues that federal change is still needed. But what should the federal minimum wage be? Every measure shows that it has not kept pace with inflation. The first step would be to legislate an automatic inflationary adjustment. But there seems little appetite for that. Can it be done administratively? Two years ago, I would have said yes—if the Federal Reserve can raise interest rates, another part of the government should be able to raise wages. But with the Supreme Court the way it is now, I am no longer confident such a move would pass constitutional scrutiny, especially with the Court's radical conservative majority.

The U.S. Supreme Court, with its six Republican justices, has overturned *Roe v. Wade*, the 1973 precedent declaring a constitutional right to abortion. It has hobbled the administrative agencies to which Congress entrusted authority for dealing with a range of issues, from securities regulation to food safety to the workplace and to protecting the environment. And the current Supreme Court has recently invented doctrines that make it impossible for agencies to regulate on "major questions." Thus, most of what the Supreme Court decides a major question is, is based on their own values.

After recent Court decisions inscribing substantive values onto constitutional jurisprudence, many believe that economic regulation will be the next domino to fall. The 1905 decision in *Lochner v. New*

York has been discredited, but never overruled.[19] The Supreme Court has been packed with justices who have an inordinately narrow view of the powers of government.

In 2012, five justices agreed that the Affordable Care Act, aka Obamacare, was an invalid exercise of power under the Commerce Clause of the Constitution. Although the ACA was ultimately upheld under Congress's taxing power, the holding that the ACA was not properly enacted under the Commerce Clause remains the law. On its face, the premise that the health care does not "substantially affect" interstate commerce is ludicrous to most, but the Court for years has tried to subvert federal legislation by saying the Commerce Clause prevents it.[20]

It is only a matter of time before there is a challenge to the FLSA as being not sufficiently tied to interstate commerce. Even though the FLSA has been upheld against constitutional challenge since 1941, the current Supreme Court showed in overturning *Roe v. Wade* in 2022 that the Court majority has little respect even for bedrock, decades-old precedents. And even in 2012, there was already a majority of the Court willing to strike down the Obama health care law as outside Congress's power under the Commerce Clause.

The rightward tilt of the Supreme Court is not a new phenomenon. The Court under Chief Justice John Roberts has been documented as the most business-friendly since 1946, and this is saying something compared to the Court under previous Chief Justices William Rehnquist and Warren Burger.[21] Still, the addition of three justices appointed by President Trump (in seniority order, Neil Gorsuch, Brett Kavanaugh, and Amy Barrett) has supercharged the right-wing of the Court into a 6–3 majority that does not even require the vote of Chief Justice Roberts.

All attempts to bring about democratic change at the state and local level are now under threat because the Supreme Court will have the last word on the functioning of the political process. As shown in Chapter 6, the courts have sometimes struck down even popular measures like the minimum wage.

IS A CONSTITUTIONAL CHANGE NEEDED?

With the Supreme Court captured by a regressive majority, new constitutional theories will only go so far. Some states, such as Nevada, have chosen to put a minimum wage law into their state constitution. This is a prudent strategy in case the Supreme Court responds as it did in the 1930s, acting under the principles of *Lochner v. New York*.[22] Few states, however, have this extra layer of protection from a rogue Supreme Court.

The more difficult question is whether progressives should seek a constitutional amendment enshrining a living wage in the U.S. Constitution. As I explained in Chapter 6, there is a movement to amend the Thirteenth Amendment and remove the punishment exception. That would deal with some of the confusion around prison labor, but would still leave the economic impact of the amendment subject to interpretation by an increasingly reactionary federal court system.

The process of amending the Constitution is known to be onerous. Article 5 requires two-thirds of both houses of Congress to successfully propose an amendment, and then two-thirds of state legislatures must agree to enact the amendment. Although the minimum wage is popular, many state legislatures are unlikely to want to approve something dealing with specific economics. In states where the legislature is more hostile to labor regulation, it would be unlikely to pass in any event. But as was the case in Nevada, voters in many states could establish minimum wage laws in their constitutions through the initiative process. Despite the investment of time and money needed to mount successful initiative campaigns, it is clear that such activity will and must continue to keep the need for a higher federal minimum wage in front of the public.

The U.S. Supreme Court has shown itself to be completely unpredictable on such bedrock principles as the right to an abortion and congressional power over the economy. The basis for the Fair Labor Standards Act is Congress's power over interstate commerce. But as in 1937 when the Supreme Court overturned decisions of the early twentieth century, a resurgent conservative Court majority could decide that the Constitution's Commerce Clause does not provide the authority to pass minimum wage legislation. Just as the right to an abortion now depends on the state in which a pregnant person lives, the right to a minimum wage could also be thrown to the states and six states do not even have a minimum wage law. Thus, federal regulation of the minimum wage is essential.

WHAT A LOW MINIMUM WAGE SAYS ABOUT US

Law has instrumental and communicative functions. As Robert Cover wrote, "No set of legal institutions or prescriptions exists apart from the narratives that locate it and give it meaning."[23] A low and stagnant minimum wage communicates that society places little value on all workers, not just on those who happen to earn at that low level. Because so many immigrants and people of color work at or near the minimum wage, the message of exclusion for those Americans is even more clear—their work is not valued or valuable to the dominant society. Raising the wage would be an important step toward valuing those who do the work that all of us rely upon.

The idea of even having minimum wage law says something about how we value work. It is a normative commitment that we the people make to set a floor for minimally decent work. It is not unlike the decision made to end slavery—as an expression of the conditions that *no one should be allowed* to agree to work under. That is why there is no such thing as "voluntary servitude," despite the words of the Thirteenth Amendment, and there should never be anyone "agreeing" to work for less than the minimum wage. We as a country decided almost one hundred years ago to take these decisions out of the market to deal with the lack of bargaining power that afflicts so many workers in the country. Because of the lack of bargaining power still facing so many workers of color and immigrants today, a minimum wage—one that provides a decent standard of living—is crucial.

While this chapter outlines several reforms that could help in the enforcement of the minimum wage, the first step toward a racially just minimum wage is to increase the minimum wage to a livable level. There have been several attempts to define what a livable wage is, which I explore in the next chapter on a global scale.

Just as the Equal Pay Act failed to close the gender pay gap, so too has Title VII of the Civil Rights Act failed to close the pay gaps between workers of color and white workers. The Lilly Ledbetter Fair Pay Act was a major reversal of a bad Supreme Court decision, but the act did little for the racial pay gap. As a critical wage theory (CWT) approach recognizes, legal remedies are not sufficient and can also be counterproductive. The goal of CWT is to change the dialogue on the importance of establishing higher labor standards for people of color and immigrants.

8 The Future of the Minimum Wage in the Global Economy

The COVID-19 pandemic exposed many of the fault lines in worker protection that had existed for decades before the coronavirus stopped most business and the global economy in March 2020. In the aftermath of the pandemic, labor shortages and remote work have caused some to question whether a higher minimum wage is needed after all. Like unions, pensions, and other positive innovations of the New Deal, the minimum wage is often seen as a relic of an earlier era.

Yet, like the minimum wage, many of these good ideas are more elusive for workers than ever. Today, only one in ten workers is represented by a union. Few employees work an eight-hour day, as work responsibilities creep into family and personal time for millions of workers. The federal minimum wage has been stagnant at $7.25 per hour for more than a decade, and the longer it is stagnant, the more it is seen as irrelevant. Yet, as this book shows, more and more workers, particularly workers of color, are demanding enforceable labor standards and higher wages. This final chapter looks toward the future of the minimum wage and wage equity both in the United States and at the global level.[1]

Far from being a relic of the past, a higher minimum wage is needed even more in the age of automation and artificial intelligence. This chapter also looks at different methods of setting the minimum wage globally. It suggests how to envision the minimum wage as a living wage, and how to support a higher minimum wage in an era of increasing automation and globalization. Finally, I put the racial inequities that we see in the United States into a global context.

TRADE AND MINIMUM WAGES

With the increasing pressure to establish a fair distribution of advantages in the global economy, the relationship between trade and the minimum wage has remained important. Recent changes in trade policy in the United States have led to the opportunity to assess the trade-wage dichotomy. In terms of regulation, the two phenomena generally are viewed as unrelated. The new global reality provides an opportunity to reassess the dichotomy that considers social movements for a minimum wage as entirely separate from efforts to protect trade across national borders.[2]

The United States has for decades been aggressively free-trade oriented but at the same time has had fewer protections for workers than many of its trading partners. Some commentators have started asking whether there should be a global minimum wage to protect high-wage countries and also to lessen global inequality. These questions will become more important as regional trade agreements such as the Trans-Pacific Partnership (TTP) become less common, apparently in favor of bilateral trade agreements, while the issue of migration has become more salient for many countries.

With its increasing amount of manufacturing and stagnant minimum wage, the United States has become even more out of step with the standards in the rest of the developed world. One need only look at the results from the databases of the International Labour Organization (ILOLEX and NATLEX) on labor protections for workers and the World Bank's Global Preferential Trade Agreement database to determine whether countries that adopt free trade agreements also provide labor minimum wage protections. If and how the United States resolves both issues will largely determine whether linkages between trade and wages can be accomplished in the coming years.

In 1994, the North American Free Trade Agreement (NAFTA) contained 11 protective labor principles that each of the NAFTA countries (Canada, Mexico, and the United States) agreed to promote. Subsequent free trade agreements have also contained minimum wage protections. With each trade agreement since NAFTA, including the Jordan Free Trade Agreement (JOFTA), Central American-Dominican Republic Free Trade Agreement (CAFTA-DR), and Free Trade Area of the Americas Agreement, labor protections have become stronger. The new NAFTA, called the United States-Mexico-Canada Agreement (USMCA), has minimum wages built into it.

Why then has there been great skepticism about a global minimum wage? One reason is that free trade agreements have done little if anything to stem the trends of global inequality identified by many economists, such as Thomas Piketty in his book, *Capital in the Twenty-First Century* (2014). Until these inequality trends are slowed or reversed, there will continue to be resistance to free trade agreements, unless these agreements can meaningfully apply substantive labor standards.

The new NAFTA evinces greater interest in labor standards, though it omits any negotiations about migration. This will exacerbate both the inequality between nations and wage inequality within nations. It will continue to make it more likely that migration to higher wage countries will continue to inflame politics, which are already becoming increasingly poisonous. With the closing of legal migration routes becoming more prevalent, illegal immigration is certain to increase. The trade-migration dichotomy can only be ameliorated through minimum wage standards prevalent throughout multinational trade areas. There have been proposals that wages might be increased to $16 per hour in auto industries across borders, for example, but even these proposals are not the kind of wage standards that will solve the trade-migration dichotomy. Instead, low-wage countries will continue to push immigrants across borders if wages in these developing countries are low. But how should the proper wage be set? That is the key, and difficult, question in current and future trade negotiations.

The role of the International Labour Organization (ILO) will become increasingly important. In 2010, the ILO issued a rights-based approach for the treatment of workers but did not include a trade-based approach.[3] Further, in the United States, the ongoing issue of the "dreamers," or DACA recipients, further complicates the situation. These are undocumented migrants who were brought to the United States as children. Though their fate and that of migrants more generally remains a political conundrum, there must be discussion of the regularization of migrants, with particular attention in the United States to the flood of migrants across the southern border. Finally, there also may be ways to increase the flow of much-needed professionals that would benefit all countries.

Yet for all the issues with NAFTA, the issue of migration has never been addressed and NAFTA does not provide robust protection for international labor rights. Nevertheless, cases brought under the North American Agreement on Labor Cooperation (NAALC) have opened an opportunity for social movement organizing. Even in this context, however, the AFL-CIO position, for example, on immigration reform with regards to guest workers or any number of features of an immigration reform package that is affected by NAFTA legal advocacy and the solidarity of the cross-border coalitions that were formed thru NAFTA will have an impact on subsequent immigration reform. As technology makes labor on demand as quick as workers delivering Uber Eats, there will be increasing pressure to grant just-in-time workers temporary visas.

The recent passage of the USMCA once again highlights the battle for labor standards in trade agreements. More than 20 years after the passage of NAFTA, lingering issues remain about human rights, labor rights, and international trade. Whether trade agreements can have enforceable labor standards has been a perennial issue in the debate around trade agreements. The long march of free trade policies continues to lack legitimacy in the eyes of many observers, and yet the approval of more free trade agreements seems likely, no matter what the outcome of the 2024 elections.

Simultaneously, in many countries there is an ongoing, often passionate debate about migration, both authorized and unauthorized, and about refugees. The Fight for $15 movement has ignited drives for racial and economic justice around the world. The question remains whether the fervor of these social movements can translate into enforceable labor standards. Social movements to raise the minimum wage are increasingly successful in states and cities in the United States, and there have been regular demonstrations in cities around the world.

How trade agreements translate their goals into law and policy is of continuing interest among legal scholars and social scientists. With trade agreements on the front burner politically, now is the time to ask whether the push for higher wages can also go global. For many years, the focus of the ILO and other international labor bodies has been shoring up procedural labor rights rather than instituting substantive standards. But a return to substantive standards would do more to level the global economic playing field. Under the right conditions, the Fight for $15 social movement might be an entry point for standardization of minimum wages, or even a minimum income.

In countries such as Bangladesh, where the 2013 Rana Plaza disaster took place, workers still make only cents per hour. Clearly, companies continue to go to countries outside the United States, to pay lower wages.

In 1999, the Battle in Seattle put fair trade in the spotlight, and trade agreements thereafter continued to be tied to the ILO's conventions. However, those standards are difficult to enforce, and even in countries that follow the standards, there are variations in the setting of the minimum wage. And minimum wage standards are notoriously difficult to set on a global basis. With growing concern about inequality in the global economy, however, the time might be right for a new approach to regulating wages through trade agreements.

The key question is whether social movements can be mobilized on a global scale to push for the enforcement of these minimum wage protections in trade agreements. Then the follow-up question is whether these protections are enforceable and can be squared with somewhat better protections in individual countries. There have also been arguments that the minimum wage protections of various countries would be put at risk by TPP, because of the investor state arbitration system that can strike down laws that are deemed anticompetitive.[4] Clearly, one of the issues that must be clarified is whether the agreement can be used to strike down some of the labor standards that it aims to put in place.

Although most countries have minimum wage provisions, there is considerable diversity in their approaches. It remains an open question as to what is best for workers and for the general protection of labor standards. Further, would global minimum wage standards make trade agreements like the TPP more palatable to unions and activists who believe these agreements bring down work standards throughout the world?

Of course, the ILO's instruments that promote freedom of association (Convention No. 87) and collective bargaining (Convention No. 98) are intended to promote higher standards, but they do not prescribe the level at which wages must be set. The ILO has proposed a Decent Work initiative, and this is one place where standard setting of minimum wages may be available, to ensure that these wages are indeed living wages. But the great diversity of economies and working conditions, as well as the many countries (the United States among them) which have not ratified many of the ILO's conventions, make the ILO a difficult place to set wage standards. Therefore, trade agreements should have stronger and more enforceable minimum wage provisions. Indeed, this is the fear of think tanks such as the Cato Institute. Nevertheless, there is little public evidence that current trade agreements are being used or will be used for this purpose.

Social movements to raise the minimum wage have been highly visible in recent years in states and cities where fast-food workers and others fight for "$15 and a union." These workers are seeking to raise and enforce labor statutes at the federal, state, and local levels.[5]

As Margaret Keck and Kathryn Sikkink argue in their 1998 book *Activists Beyond Borders*, there are many examples where transnational advocacy work has made progress, even before the 1999 World Trade Organization (WTO) process.[6] There is a significant justice movement that is global—we have seen this in the days of action in cities such as Paris, Amsterdam, and Mexico City.

THE ROLE OF TRANSNATIONAL ADVOCACY NETWORKS FOR BETTER MINIMUM WAGE POLICY

The TPP debate has roiled the political world, and trade already had been at the center of presidential races. In 2020, both major political party candidates distanced themselves from the TPP debate. While several candidates have argued for better trade agreements, there is not likely to be a moratorium on trade agreements after the next election. At the same time, there is growing unease about the effects of trade on jobs. This has dovetailed with workplace disasters such as Rana Plaza in Bangladesh, where more than 1,100 people died and over 2,500 were injured in the collapse of a garment factory.

After the 2016 election, the Trump administration announced its intent to withdraw the United States from TPP negotiations. But much of the political upset that led to that withdrawal came from wage inequality in several key battleground states. Thus, wage inequality will continue to be an issue whether or not there is an expansion of trade agreements.

Can enforceable minimum wage standards be incorporated into trade agreements? What is needed is a wage-setting authority. To many, this proposal would seem to be the antithesis of free trade. It is also probable that governments would resist these efforts if they thought it would reduce their comparative advantages. In some ways this goes back to the trade-labor linkage of the WTO. Things have changed since the late 1990s. Besides growing skepticism about trade, the Fight for $15 movement has transcended borders and raised questions about the wages that multinational companies pay overseas.

The trade-migration nexus will be more important in the future as more bilateral trade agreements are negotiated. In addition, legal advocacy on both the domestic and the international level will change organizations and will help create a broader story that includes the role that lawyers can have in changing organizations. There is and will continue to be a correlation between openness to trade and openness to migration. Nonetheless, several different factors go into the specific migration policies of different countries, including legacies of race and class.

For many unions their members have long been mostly, and in some unions entirely, white and nonimmigrant. More recently there has been an influx of immigrant workers into a variety of industries such as meatpacking, textile work, and other big industries, reflecting both global and economic changes.

Basically, the question of what, if any, labor rights immigrant workers had in unions and/or in the workplace was mostly litigated in the 1980s and 1990s. The 1986 Immigration Reform and Control Act (IRCA) imposed employer sanctions on people who hire undocumented workers, and to an extent provided for legalization.

On the federal level, there has been historical change, beginning with the 1986 reform, during which the AFL-CIO changed its position from supporting employer sanctions, followed by a rift with other immigrant rights groups, leading to the 1990s and 2000s approach that was more about legalizing and trying to do away with sanctions because of the way they had been used to deter organizing activities and basically deny the right of association for all workers. Unions, including the SEIU and the ILGWU, had seen a large influx of immigrant workers into their ranks, especially the AFL-CIO, which was the umbrella group for 13 million union members in the country. The historical movement during this 14- to 16-year period was from a more punitive approach to immigrant workers in 1986 to the more accommodating statement of 2000, in which the AFL-CIO, for a number of different reasons, called for legalization and also the end of employer sanctions. Various successful immigrant worker organizing campaigns took place. The drywaller strike in Los Angeles and SEIU's Justice for Janitors movement are examples of labor becoming very active and more successful during this time period, which contradicts the idea that immigrant workers are unorganizable.[7]

In recent decades, the labor movement has begun to work much more with immigrant rights coalitions; two examples are organizing for day laborers and promoting immigrant freedom rights. The incorporation of immigrants into the U.S. labor movement is interesting largely because of the demographics but also because of how the presumed conflict between African American workers and Latino/immigrant workers is perceived. In this period, there has been not only an increase in Latino/Latina workers in the workforce (from 4.4 to 13.1 percent) but also a steady increase of Black workers joining unions. Given these demographics, the labor movement is now more open to incorporating immigrants. This attitude is a welcome change, considering the history of discrimination against immigrants in the U.S. labor movement. I briefly review this legal context, without distinguishing between documented versus undocumented workers, which distinction did not impact anything until the 1986 immigration law.

In the 1986 immigration law, the competition between immigrants and citizens/residents was a major impetus for the AFL-CIO to try to get sanctions passed, to keep immigrants out of the labor market, and to be able to tell their members that it was doing something about the perception that immigrants were a threat to union members' jobs. Then, there were several Supreme Court and circuit court decisions about whether undocumented immigrant workers were protected by the National Labor Relations Act, including the 1984 *Sure-Tan vs. NLRB* case, which was the first time the U.S. Supreme Court had really addressed this question. The broad language of "employee" in the act seemed to mean that undocumented workers were covered by the act; thus the only remaining question was what sort of remedies were available to them. This was answered harshly in *Hoffman Plastic Compounds vs. NLRB* in 2002. However, *Sure-Tan* led to several decisions holding that undocumented workers are also employees for purposes of a broad number of other labor and employment law statutes—including the Fair Labor Standards Act, in terms of its minimum wage and overtime provisions, and Title VII of the Civil Rights Act. The legal theory that undocumented workers had to be considered employees for the purposes of the law helped to sustain on-the-ground organizing. Yet the AFL-CIO in February 2000 proposed legislative package that excluded immigrant workers. Hence, it is our preliminary argument that the AFL-CIO's position in this litigation was ahead of the organization in terms of labor rights for immigrants and that its support of the immigrant worker as an employee ultimately had an effect in *Sure-Tan* and subsequent litigation. In addition, people with legal background could see tension between the push for full status as employees and an exclusionary attitude towards immigrants, who were then moving into position of power in the labor movement. This dissonance is something that must be explored in the future as well. The labor movement must continue to see the fortunes of the workers it represents at home to be tied to the fortunes of workers abroad. The raising and enforcing of living wage standards through trade agreements may serve that goal. Cooperation with international organizations and other countries is essential to make sure that wages are not set so high as to price some countries out of the global marketplace for labor.

GLOBAL MINIMUM WAGES: DO THEY RAISE STANDARDS FOR ALL?

The pattern of trade agreements typically has been an "enforce your own laws" model. Most people believe that universal minimum wages are not feasible given the differences in living standards around the world,. though there have been attempts to legislate an international minimum wage. U.S. Congressman Richard Gephardt proposed this approach during his unsuccessful presidential campaign in 2000.[8]

Nonetheless, going all the way back to NAFTA, the standards in several trade agreements have required the treaty parties to commit to "minimum standards" for wages, health and safety, and compensation. Because these are among the 11 principles that the NAFTA countries are committed to "promote," it is unclear what substantive obligations these standards place on governments, but possibly these could include a duty to establish their own minimum wage provision.

Obviously, there is not a requirement that all countries have specific minimum wage requirements, nor was there any argument—or at least not any USMCA complaint filed—that there should be a federal minimum wage or that the treaty parties should comply with the USMCA's principle on minimum standards. Nonetheless, it would seem that some kind of minimum wage protections, state or federal, are necessary, and that each country would need to enforce them.

This raises the question of whether all workers should be covered by some minimum wage law. In the United States, five states do not have a minimum wage law· Alabama, Louisiana, Mississippi, Tennessee, and South Carolina. Thus, there could be a complaint against the United States for failure to protect workers in those states where they are not subject to a state-imposed minimum wage for jobs not covered by the FLSA. The U.S. government should be implored to take all possible steps to ensure that state governments implement minimum wage standards for all workers. But the federal-state structure makes any positive response difficult to enforce.

A possible USMCA complaint might also address the failure to promote minimal living standards. This might be about many issues, including the tipped minimum wage of $2.13 an hour in effect in many states. Also, there is the subminimum wage, which allows for people with developmental disabilities to be paid less than the federal minimum wage. All these practices weigh down labor standards in the United States. A complaint against the United States could bring attention to these practices, putting pressure on the federal government to change its laws to abolish the tipped wage and the subminimum wage.

We know that the United States has been famously resistant to external pressure from international organizations and bodies, particularly regarding its labor practices. As Tamara Kay argues in *NAFTA and the Politics of Transnationalism*, such complaints nonetheless can have catalytic effects.[9] Although there have been fewer NAFTA-based complaints in recent years, many possibilities remain to address longstanding problems, particularly the need to provide a livable minimum wage.

THE ROLE OF THE INTERNATIONAL LABOUR ORGANIZATION

There are five ILO conventions that address wages: (1) Convention 94, addressing minimum standards in public contracts; (2) Convention

95, requiring ILO members to set up systems for the protection of wages at regular intervals and in case of employer insolvency; (3) Convention 131, requiring a state system to set wages and to *periodically review* them; (4) Convention 173, providing for protection of wages in cases of business insolvency and bankruptcy; and (5) Convention 100, on equal remuneration based on gender.

Convention 94 addresses minimum standards in public contracts, and Convention 95 requires ILO members to have a system to set standards. These first two conventions certainly present issues for those states that do not have minimum wage standards. Convention 131 requires ILO members to have a system to review those standards periodically. The final two conventions (173 and 100) also impact the setting of minimum wages.

The primary difficulty is that the ILO has not promulgated any standard for setting wages. The other problem is that there has never been a good definition of what a living wage is, whether in the United States or abroad. In cities with "living wage ordinances" or minimum wage laws, these local standards apply only to companies with local government contracts. In cities such as Los Angeles, Pasadena, and Santa Monica, the mandated wage levels generally are set above the poverty level. Thus, for example, in Los Angeles, their living wage ordinance rate in July 2023 went up to $16.78 per hour for city contractors who provide health benefits and a $18.03 for companies that do not pay for health benefits. These standards have been indexed with the Consumer Price Index (CPI). Because of the relatively small number of contracts held by any particular city, the impact of the living wage ordinance is not as great as it might be if these ordinances applied to all businesses. Fortunately, that will be changing soon in Los Angeles now that the statewide minimum wage is $16 per hour. Nonetheless, many people still find it difficult to live in Los Angeles on $16 per hour. Unlike what occurred in Alabama (discussed in Chapter 2), the state law does not prevent cities from legislating a higher minimum wage, as the City of West Hollywood recently did in setting the minimum in that city at $19.08

per hour. According to MIT's living wage calculator, however, workers require between $21 and $22.50 to earn a "living wage" in Los Angeles County[10]

A NEW APPROACH TO THE LIVING WAGE

Despite the success of the Fight for $15 social movement, how to translate minimum wage standards to the global arena remains perplexing. If there is an obligation for governments to have minimum wage laws on the books, what should the standard be? The ILO's Decent Work initiative aimed to bring up the standards for all workers. But this initiative stopped short of setting substantive standards.

Part of the problem with a global minimum wage is that we tend to set minimum wages by the hour. This does not account for scheduling requirements and other practices that easily can keep workers below a living wage. With universal basic income policies attracting more interest, minimum annual salary levels for both full time and part time work are targets the ILO might seek in each country. It is clear that trade linkages to minimum wage policies will continue to be debated as long as there is skepticism that trade agreements benefit workers, governments, and companies equally. While minimum wage setting on an international level continues to be difficult, greater attention to this aspect of labor standards by trade negotiators, governments, and international bodies would increase the legitimacy of the free trade regime. In the end, as is typical, companies will have the ultimate responsibility for guaranteeing fair wages and acceptable working conditions. This is why the guidance and cooperation of international bodies will be very important in encouraging all countries to assess their wage policies for racial gaps, as well as those that they monitor for gender pay gaps.

CONCLUSION

This chapter, and indeed most of the book, has focused on minimum wage setting for a reason—millions of workers in industries globally now struggle to get a minimum standard of living. The reason for the focus on the minimum wage is because in some industries even that remains subject to negotiation. Countering that resistance has also been the primary goal of many of the movements discussed in this book. Certainly, when it comes to the living wage movements of the past 30 years, those that were successful set minimum wages with specific attention to the high cost of living in certain cities. As I argue in this book, the next step is to ensure not just the setting of livable minimum wages, but also minimum standards to ensure low-wage workers receive a regular salary, just as millions of workers throughout the economy are used to receiving.

What a living wage should be is extremely contextual based on different, local factors. What is important is that the setting of these wages is arrived at through a democratic process that considers the racially exploitative nature of certain industries. And these minimum standards must then be enforced with particular attention to the immigrants and people of color who are so often the victims of wage theft. It is only then that minimum wage laws will be truly fair. While the decision about whether to raise and enforce labor standards is ultimately a political one to be decided at the local level, this book has argued that the ramifications of low wages and lack of enforcement ultimately fall disproportionately on people of color and immigrants, not only in the United States but also throughout the world. Policymakers should take these effects into account to ensure that there are not racial and migration gaps which would ensnare marginalized populations. It is only when the law is made and enforced with an eye towards these workers that we have an economy that truly works for all of us.

Notes

ACKNOWLEDGMENTS

1. Ruben J. Garcia, "The Thirteenth Amendment and Minimum Wage Laws," *Nevada Law Journal* 19 (2018): 479–507.

INTRODUCTION

1. David Rolf, *The Fight for $15: The Right Wage for a Working America* (New York: The New Press, 2016).

2. Jonathan Rosenblum, *Beyond $15: Immigrant Workers, Faith Activists, and the Revival of the Labor Movement* (Boston: Beacon Press, 2017).

3. Oren M. Levin-Waldman, *Restoring the Middle Class through Wage Policy: Arguments for a Minimum Wage* (New York: Palgrave Macmillan, 2018).

4. Guy Davidov and Brian Langille, *The Idea of Labour Law* (Oxford: Oxford University Press, 2011).

5. Michelle Wilde Anderson, *The Fight to Save the Town: Reimagining Discarded America* (New York: Avid Reader Press/Simon & Schuster, 2022).

6. François Bonnet, *The Upper Limit: How Low-Wage Work Defines Punishment and Welfare* (Oakland: University of California Press, 2019).

7. Paul Butler, "Poor People Lose: *Gideon* and the Critique of Rights," *Yale Law Journal*, 122 (2013).

8. See Gerald Rosenberg, *The Hollow Hope: Can the Courts Bring About Social Change?* (Chicago: University of Chicago Press, 1991), 338 ("U.S. courts can almost never be effective producers of significant social reform").

9. See Arindrajit Dube, "Minimum Wages and the Distribution of Family Incomes," *American Economic Journal: Applied Economics* 11, no. 4 (2019): 268–304, https://doi.org/10.1257/app.20170085 (showing that an increase of $4.75 an hour would have lifted 6.2 million workers from poverty, including many Black and Hispanic families); Ellora Derenoncourt and Claire Montialoux, "Minimum Wages and Racial Inequality," *Quarterly Journal of Economics* (2021): 169–228, https://doi.org/10.1093/qje/qjaa031.

10. Ben Zipperer, Testimony Before the U.S. House of Representatives Committee on Education and Labor, February 7, 2019 (finding that by 2024, according to the Family Budget Calculator of the Economic Policy Institute, even a $15 per hour minimum wage for full time work would be inadequate for basic necessities in all areas of the country), https://www.epi.org/publication/minimum-wage-testimony-feb-2019/.

11. Kirstin Downey, *The Woman Behind the New Deal: The Life of Frances Perkins, FDR's Secretary of Labor and His Moral Conscience* (New York: Anchor, 2009), 265.

12. Ibid., 268.

13. McKenna Ross, "Station Casinos Begins Demolition of 2 Local Properties," *Las Vegas Review-Journal*, September 12, 2022, https://www.reviewjournal.com/business/casinos-gaming/station-casinos-begins-demolition-of-2-local-properties-2638712/.

CHAPTER 1. A CRITICAL RACE THEORY OF WAGE JUSTICE

1. Ruben J. Garcia, "Critical Race Theory and Proposition 187: The Racial Politics of Immigration Law," *Chicano-Latino Law Review* 17 (1995): 118.

2. Ruben J. Garcia, "New Voices at Work: Race and Gender Identity Caucuses within the U.S. Labor Movement," *Hastings Law Journal* 54 (2002): 79.

3. Kimberlé Williams Crenshaw, "Race, Reform and Retrenchment: Transformation and Legitimation in Antidiscrimination Law," *Harvard Law Review* 101, no. 7 (May 1988): 1331.

4. David E. Bernstein, *Only One Place of Redress: African Americans, Labor Regulations, and the Courts from Reconstruction to the New Deal* (Durham: Duke University Press, 2000); Harry Hutchinson, "Waging War on the 'Unemployables'? Race, Low-Wage Work and Minimum Wages: The New Evidence," *Hofstra Labor and Employment Law Journal* 29 (2011): 25–47.

5. Bernstein, *Only One Place of Redress*.

6. Deborah A. Ballam, "Exploding the Original Myth Regarding Employment-At-Will: The True Origins of the Doctrine," *Berkeley Journal of Employment and Labor Law*, 17, no. 1 (1996), available at http://www.jstor.org/stable/24050714.

7. Mari Matsuda, "Looking to the Bottom: Critical Legal Studies and Reparations," *Harvard Civil Rights–Civil Liberties Law Review* 22 (1987): 323.

8. See Kimberlé Williams Crenshaw, "Unmasking Colorblindness in the Law: Lessons from the Formation of Critical Race Theory," in *Seeing Race Again: Countering Colorblindness in the Law,* ed. Kimberlé Williams Crenshaw et al., pp. 52–84 (Oakland: University of California Press, 2019).

9. Ruben J. Garcia, "New Voices at Work: Race and Gender Identity Caucuses within the U.S. Labor Movement," *Hastings Law Journal* 54 (2002): 79.

10. Ruben J. Garcia, "The Human Right to Workplace Safety in a Pandemic," *Washington University Journal of Law* 64 (2021): 113.

11. Jeanna Smialek, "The Nobel in Economics Goes to Three Who Find Experiments in Real Life," *New York Times*, October 11, 2021, https://www.nytimes.com/2021/10/11/business/nobel-economics-prize-david-card-joshua-angrist-guido-imbens.html.

12. Derrick Bell, "Racial Realism," *Connecticut Law Review* 24, no. 2 (Winter 1992): 363–379.

13. Matsuda, "Looking to the Bottom," 325.

14. Kimberlé Williams Crenshaw, "Mapping the Margins: Intersectionality, Identity Politics, and Violence against Women of Color," *Stanford Law Review* 43, no. 6 (July 1991).

15. Ian Haney López, *Merge Left: Fusing Race and Class, Winning Elections, and Saving America* (New York: The New Press, 2019).

16. Francisco Valdes, "Legal Reform and Social Justice: An Introduction to LatCrit Theory, Praxis and Community," *University of Miami Law Review* 14, no. 2 (2005): 148.

17. Bell, "Racial Realism," 363.

CHAPTER 2. MOVEMENTS FRAMING THE MINIMUM
WAGE AS A MATTER OF RACIAL JUSTICE

1. Stephanie Luce, *Fighting for a Living Wage* (Ithaca: Cornell University Press, 2004).

2. Stuart Silverstein, "Santa Monica Makes a Notably Aggressive Living Wage Proposal," *Los Angeles Times*, September 28, 1999, https://www.latimes.com/archives/la-xpm-1999-sep-28-fi-14929-story.html.

3. Judy Marblestone and Kathleen S. Erskine, "The Movement Takes the Lead," in *Cause Lawyers and Social Movements*, ed. Austin Sarat and Stuart Scheingold (Stanford: Stanford University Press, 2006).

4. Robert Pollin et al., "How Santa Monica Workers Would Have Benefitted from a $10.75 Living Wage," in *A Measure of Fairness*, ed. Robert Pollin (Ithaca: Cornell University Press, 2018).

5. City of Santa Monica, Living Wage Ordinance, Santa Monica Municipal Code § 4.65 (2023).

6. Scott Cummings, *An Equal Place: Lawyers in the Struggle for Los Angeles* (New York: Oxford University Press, 2021), 27.

7. "Food Labor Research Network," UC Berkeley, http://onefairwage.site/research.

8. Vivien Hart, *Bound by Our Constitution: Women, Workers, and the Minimum Wage* (Princeton: Princeton University Press, 1994), 68–69.

9. Ruth Milkman and Kent Wong, *Voices from the Front Lines: Organizing Immigrant Workers in Los Angeles* (Los Angeles: UCLA Center for Labor Research and Education: 2000).

10. Paul Frymer, *Black and Blue: African Americans, the Labor Movement, and the Decline of the Democratic Party* (Princeton: Princeton University Press, 2007).

11. Philip Dray, *There Is Power in a Union: The Epic Story of Labor in America* (New York: Anchor, 2011).

12. Employee Retirement Income Security Act, 93rd U.S. Congress, 94-406 (1974).

13. Cummings, *An Equal Place*, 9.

14. Ruth Milkman and Kent Wong, *Voices from the Front Lines: Organizing Immigrant Workers in Los Angeles* (Los Angeles: UCLA Center for Labor Research and Education, 2000), 11.

15. Karesha Manns, "I'm a McDonald's Worker Going on Strike Today. Here's Why We Deserve a $15 Minimum Wage," January 15, 2021, https://www.businessinsider.com/mcdonalds-employee-worker-mlk-15-minimum-wage-covid-19-essential-2021-1.

16. Nevada Revised Statutes 608.250(1)(d).

17. Barbara Brents, et al., *The State of Sex: Tourism, Sex and Sin in the New American Heartland* (New York: Routledge, 2009).

18. Dynamex Operations West, Inc. v. Superior Court, 4 Cal. 5th 903 (Cal. 2018).

19. California Labor Code § 2750.3 (2019).

20. Martin Luther King, Jr., speech, "I Have a Dream," August 28, 1963, Washington, D.C.

21. Noah Zatz, "The Minimum Wage as a Civil Rights Protection: An Alternative to Antipoverty Arguments?" *University of Chicago Legal Forum* 3 (2009): 1, 5.

22. Brishen Rogers, "Justice at Work: Minimum Wage Laws and Social Equality," *Texas Law Review* (2014): 1543, 1582–1586.

23. Moshe Maravit, *Why Labor Organizing Should Be a Civil Right* (New York: The Century Foundation Press, 2012).

24. Rachel Kahn Best et al., "Multiple Disadvantages: An Empirical Test of Intersectionality in EEO Litigation," *Law and Society Review*, 45 (2011): 991.

CHAPTER 3. IMMIGRANTS, DAY LABORERS, AND EXOTIC DANCERS

1. Margot Rutman, "Exotic Dancers' Employment Law Regulations," *Temple Political and Civil Rights Law Review* 8 (1999): 515.

2. McFeeley v. Jackson St. Entertainment, LLC, 825 F.3d 235, 247 (4th Cir. 2016).

3. Hart v. Rick's Cabaret International, Inc., 967 F. Supp. 2d 901 (S.D.N.Y. 2013) (holding dancers had been misclassified under the Federal Labor Standards Act as well as New York state minimum wage laws and were entitled to back pay because the club had significant control over their work life and earning potential).

4. McFeeley v. Jackson St. Entertainment, LLC, 825 F.3d 235 (4th Cir. 2016) (holding dancers were employees under the economic realities test and entitled to wages under the FLSA and Maryland state law); Pizzarelli v. Cadillac Lounge, LLC, No. 15–254 WES, 2018 U.S. Dist. LEXIS 117338 (D.R.I. 2018) (holding that despite a dancer's only having worked at the Cadillac Lounge over the course of a year, with her work possibly interrupted by performing at other clubs, she was still considered an employee under both the FLSA and Rhode Island state law).

5. Barbara Brents et al., *The State of Sex: Tourism, Sex and Sin in the New American Heartland* (New York: Routledge, 2009), 62.

6. Ibid.

7. Sheerine Alemzadeh, "Baring Inequality: Revisiting the Legalization Debate through the Lens of Strippers' Rights," *Michigan Journal of Gender and Law* 19 (2013).

8. Pamela Paul, "What It Means to Call Prostitution Sex Work," *New York Times*, August 17, 2023, https://www.nytimes.com/2023/08/17/opinion/prostitution-sex-work.html.

9. Berta Esperanza Hernández-Truyol and Jane E. Larson, "Sexual Labor and Human Rights," *Columbia Human Rights Law Review* 37 (2006): 391–445.

10. Caity Gwin, "Goals on the Pole: Strippers' Fight for Workplace Rights: Legal Tools at Our Disposal," in *Sex Work Now*, ed. Bernadette Barton, Barb Brents, and Angela Jones (New York: New York University Press, forthcoming) (describing the strike and campaign for unionization by Star Garden workers and other dancers nationally).

11. Russell Weaver and Anne Marie Brady, "Building Responsible Projects in New York City: Assessing the Impact of Prevailing Wage Benefits on Workers, Contractors, and the New York City Economy," Cornell Industrial and Labor Relations School, The Worker Institute, https://ecommons.cornell.edu/server/api/core/bitstreams/2615d93d-fc5e-4b1f-90c0-c28702110688/content.

12. U.S. Department of Labor, Instructions for Completing Payroll Form, WH-347.

13. Aurelia Glass, "Prevailing Wages Can Build Good Jobs into America's Electric Vehicle Industry," *CAP*, July 6, 2022, https://www.americanprogress.org/article/prevailing-wages-can-build-good-jobs-into-americas-electric-vehicle-industry/.

14. Michael's Painting and Painting L.A., Inc., 337 N.L.R.B. 860 (2002), enforced, 85 Fed. Apps. 614 (9th Cir. 2004).

15. Ibid.

16. These facts are reported in the National Labor Relations Board decision, Michael's Painting and Painting L.A., Inc., 337 N.L.R.B. 860 (2002), enforced, 85 Fed. Apps. 614 (9th Cir. 2004).

17. David Bernstein, *Only One Place of Redress: African Americans, Labor Regulations, and the Courts from Reconstruction to the New Deal* (Durham: Duke University Press, 2000), 102–104.

18. Ibid., 104.

19. Davis Bacon Act, 71st U.S. Congress, 71-798 (1931).

20. Michael's Painting and Painting L.A., Inc., 337 N.L.R.B. 860 (2002), enforced, 85 Fed. Apps. 614 (9th Cir. 2004).

21. Ayesha Bell Hardaway, "The Paradox of the Right to Contract: Non-compete Agreements as Thirteenth Amendment Violations," *Seattle University Law Review* 39 (2016) (arguing that noncompete agreements between employers and workers earning low wages while performing unskilled labor are a violation of the Thirteenth Amendment).

22. Mark A. Graber, "The Second Freedmen's Bureau Bill's Constitution," *Texas Law Review* 94 (2016): 1361, 1366 (showing how the Second Freedmen's Bureau bill's constitution was better structured to place economic inequality and dependency at the core of American constitutionalism than the judicially driven constitutionalism of the present).

23. Michael's Painting and Painting L.A., Inc., 337 N.L.R.B. 860 (2002), enforced, 85 Fed. Apps. 614 (9th Cir. 2004).

24. Ruben J. Garcia, "Across the Borders: Immigrant Status and Identity in Law and LatCrit Theory," *Florida Law Review* 55 (2003): 511.

25. "U.S. Department of Labor Sues Chain of RI Nails Salons for Retaliating against Employees," August 27, 2022, https://www.golocalprov.com/business/u.s.-department-of-labor-sues-chain-of-ri-nails-salons-for-retaliating-agai.

26. See, e.g., Michael A. Olivas, *No Undocumented Child Left Behind: Plyler v. Doe and the Education of Undocumented Schoolchildren* (New York: New York University Press, 2012); Kevin Johnson, *The Huddled Masses Myth: Immigration and Civil Rights* (Philadelphia: Temple University Press, 2008).

27. Hoffman Plastic Compounds, 525 U.S. 135 (2002).

28. Patel v. Quality Inn South, 846 F.2d 700 (11th Cir. 1988).

29. Jennifer Gordon, *Suburban Sweatshops: The Fight for Immigrant Rights* (Cambridge, MA: Harvard University Press, 2005).

30. McNamara-O'Hara Service Contracts Act, 89th Congress Public Law Number (1965).

31. See Ruben J. Garcia, "Labor and Property: Guestworkers, International Trade, and the Democracy Deficit," *Journal of Gender, Race and Justice* (2006): 27, 51.

32. David Weil, *The Fissured Workplace: Why Work Became So Bad for So Many and What Can Be Done to Improve It* (Cambridge, MA: Harvard University Press, 2014).

33. Becerra v. Expert Janitorial, 332 P.3d 415 (2014).

34. Ibid.

35. "Day Labor in Las Vegas: Employer Indiscretions in Sin City," Arriba Las Vegas Workers Center, January 2018, https://arribalasvegas.org/wp-content/uploads/2019/04/Day-Labor-in-Las-Vegas-compressed.pdf.

36. Weil, *The Fissured Workplace*, 236.

37. Ibid., 215 (Fig. 9.1).

38. "Wage and Hour Division Needs Improved Investigative Processes and Ability to Suspend Statute of Limitations to Better Protect Workers against Wage Theft," Government Accountability Office, U.S. Department of Labor (2009).

39. "Department of Labor: Wage and Hour Division's Complaint Intake and Investigative Processes Leave Low Wage Workers Vulnerable to Wage Theft," Government Accountability Office (2009), https://www.gao.gov/products/gao-09-458t.

40. "Department of Labor: Case Studies from Ongoing Work Show Examples in which Wage and Hour Division Did Not Adequately Pursue Labor Violations," Government Accountability Office (2008), https://www.gao.gov/products/gao-08-973t.

41. "Fair Labor Standards Act: Better Use of Available Resources and Consistent Reporting Could Improve Compliance," Government Accountability Office (2008), https://www.gao.gov/products/gao-08-962t.

CHAPTER 4. LEGALLY SANCTIONED SUBMINIMUM WAGES

1. Sylvia Allegretto and David Cooper, *Twenty-Three Years and Still Waiting for Change: Why It's Time to Give Tipped Workers the Regular Minimum Wage* (Washington D.C.: Economic Policy Institute, 2014), accessed March 20, 2023, https://files.epi.org/2014/EPI-CWED-BP379

.pdf; Ian Ayres et al., "To Insure Prejudice: Racial Disparities in Taxicab Tipping," *Yale Law Journal* 114 (2005): 1613–1674.

2. Fair Labor Standards Act of 1938, 75th U.S. Congress, 75–718 (1938).

3. "How Biden's COVID Relief Plan Cures the Racist Subminimum Wage," One Fair Wage, Food Labor Research Center, UC Berkeley, National Black Workers' Center Project (February 2021), https://onefairwage.site /wp-content/uploads/2021/02/OFW_EndingLegacyOfSlavery-2.pdf.

4. Ofer Azar, "The Effect of the Minimum Wage for Tipped Workers on Firm Strategy, Employees and Social Welfare," *Labour Economics* 19 (2012).

5. Jonathan Grossman, "The Fair Labor Standards Act of 1938: Maximum Struggle for A Minimum Wage," https://www.dol.gov/general/aboutdol /history/flsa1938.

6. Michael Lynn, "Tipping in Restaurants around the Globe: An Interdisciplinary Review," in *Handbook of Contemporary Behavioral Economics*, ed. Morris Altman (New York: M. E. Sharpe, 2006), 629.

7. Oregon Restaurant and Lodging Association v. Perez, 816 F.3d 1080 (9th Cir. 2018).

8. Wynn Las Vegas, LLC, v. Baldonado, 311 P.3d 1179 (Nev. 2013).

9. Al Mancini, "In Las Vegas, Server Is a Serious, Well-Paying Career," *Las Vegas Review Journal*, September 1, 2018, https://www .reviewjournal.com/entertainment/food/in-las-vegas-restaurant-server-is -serious-well-paying-career/.

10. Wynn Las Vegas, LLC, v. Baldonado, 311 P.3d 1179 (Nev. 2013).

11. William Whitaker, "The Tip Credit Provisions of the Fair Labor Standards Act," *Congressional Research Service Report*, March 24, 2006, https://www.everycrsreport.com/files/20060324_RL33348_ ad85f13a3a41cd5fafd56b16338e820ac7136692.pdf (noting that industry saw the 1961 amendment as a loss, given that its previous exposure up to that point was zero dollars per hour for tipped workers).

12. Wynn Las Vegas, LLC, v. Baldonado, 311 P.3d 1179 (Nev. 2013).

13. Kerry Segrave, *Tipping: An American Social History of Gratuities* (Jefferson, NC: McFarland, 1998).

14. Fair Labor Standards Act of 1938, as amended 99th U.S. Congress, 75–718 (1986).

15. "The Glass Floor: Sexual Harassment in the Restaurant Industry, Report of the Restaurant Opportunities Center," last modified October 7, 2014, https://nature.berkeley.edu/agroecologylab/wp-content/uploads/2020 /06/The-Glass-Floor-Sexual-Harassment-in-the-Restaurant-Industry.pdf.

16. Rajesh Nayak and Paul Sonn, *Restoring the Minimum Wage for America's Tipped Workers*, National Employment Law Project Report (August 2009). 1–22.

17. Ruben J. Garcia, "Politically Engaged Unionism: The Culinary Workers Union in Las Vegas," in *The Cambridge Handbook of U.S. Labor Law for the Twenty-First Century*, ed. Richard Bales and Charlotte Garden (Cambridge: Cambridge University Press, 2019).

18. Meshna v. Scrivanos, 27 N.Ed.3d 1253 (Mass. 2015) (finding that employer has clearly communicated no-tipping policy, employer does not violate the law by retaining money left by customers for tips).

19. "Subminimum Wage," U.S. Department of Labor, accessed March 30, 2023, https://www.dol.gov/general/topic/wages/subminimumwage; "Minimum Wage for Tipped Employees," U.S. Department of Labor, January 1, 2024, https://www.dol.gov/whd/state/tipped.htm.

20. Ibid.

21. Ibid.

22. Employment Under Special Certificates, 29 U.S.C. § 214(c) (1989).

23. Lydia DePillis, "Disabled People Are Allowed to Work for Pennies per Hour—But Maybe Not for Much Longer," *Washington Post*, February 12, 2016, https://www.washingtonpost.com/news/wonk/wp/2016/02/12/disabled-people-are-allowed-to-work-for-pennies-per-hour-but-maybe-not-for-much-longer/?utm_term=.cb1c75c2996e.

24. Samuel R. Bagenstos, "The Case against the Section 14(c) Subminimum Wage Program," *Report for the Georgia Advocacy Office* (2011), available at http://thegao.org/wp-content/uploads/2012/09/14c_report_sam_bagenstos-1.pdf; Samuel R. Bagenstos, "Disability Rights and Labor: Is This Conflict Really Necessary?" *University of Michigan Law Journal* 97 (2017); Americans with Disabilities Act of 1990, 101st U.S. Congress, 101–336 (1990).

25. James Gray Pope, "Labor's Constitution of Freedom," *Yale Law Journal* 106 (1997): 941, 945–946.

26. Hawai'i Rev. Stat. s 481 B-14; Mass. Gen. Laws Ch. 149 s 152A.

CHAPTER 5. LEGACIES OF RACE AND SLAVERY

1. Scott Cummings, *An Equal Place: Lawyers in the Struggle for Los Angeles* (New York: Oxford University Press, 2021), 47–48 (noting the work on the case by Della Bahan and Janet Herold of Rothner, Segall, Bahan, and Greenstone; Julie Su of the Asian Pacific Legal Center; Dan Stormer

of Hasdell and Stormer; Lora Jo Foo of the Asian Law Caucus; Lucas Guttentag and Leti Volpp from the ACLU Immigrants' Rights Project; and Mark Rosenbaum, Daniel Tokaji, and David Schwartz of the ACLU of Southern California).

2. Annie Correal, "Hindu Sect Is Accused of Using Forced Labor to Build N.J. Temple," *New York Times*, May 11, 2021, https://www.nytimes.com/2021/05/11/nyregion/nj-hindu-temple-india-baps.html.

3. Joseph Fishkin and William E. Forbath, *The Anti-oligarchy Constitution: Reconstructing the Economic Foundations of American Democracy* (Cambridge, MA: Harvard University Press, 2022), 419 (stating how basic principles of the democracy of opportunity remain affirmative of constitutional obligations of government); Rebecca E. Zietlow, "A Positive Right to Free Labor," *Seattle University Law Review* 39 (2016): 859–899 (explaining how Thirteenth Amendment contains a positive guarantee of rights).

4. James Gray Pope, "Labor's Constitution of Freedom," *Yale Law Journal* 106 (1997): 941; Lea VanderVelde, "The Labor Vision of the Thirteenth Amendment," *University of Pennsylvania Law Review* 138 (1989) (arguing the Thirteenth Amendment addresses fair and just labor relations).

5. VanderVelde, "The Labor Vision of the Thirteenth Amendment," 437, 495.

6. Rebecca Zietlow, "James Ashley's Thirteenth Amendment," *Columbia Law Review* (2012): 1697–1731 (describing Representative James Ashley's theories of racial and class-based oppression concerning the Thirteenth Amendment).

7. Rebecca Zietlow, "The Rights of Citizenship: Two Framers, Two Amendments," *Pennsylvania Journal of Constitutional Law* 11 (2009): 1269–1288 (discussing views of citizenship held by Representatives Ashley and Bingham).

8. Esther S. McDonald, "Patenting Human Life and the Rebirth of the Thirteenth Amendment," *Notre Dame Law Review* 78 (2003): 1359–1387 (discussing the claim that the Thirteenth Amendment's prohibition against slavery prohibits the patenting of human embryos).

9. Jamal Greene, "Thirteenth Amendment Optimism," *Columbia Law Review* 112 (2012): 1733–1768 (explaining some pessimism about Thirteenth Amendment optimism).

10. West Coast Hotel Co. v. Parrish, 300 U.S. 379 (1937).

11. The Matthew Shepard and James Byrd Jr. Hate Crimes Prevention Act, 111th U.S. Congress, 18 U.S.C. § 245(b)(2) (2009) (the 2009 Hate

Crimes Prevention Act was enacted pursuant to the Thirteenth Amendment).

12. Michael Vorenberg, *Final Freedom: The Civil War, the Abolition of Slavery, and the Thirteenth Amendment* (Cambridge: Cambridge University Press, 2004), 28.

13. Risa L. Goluboff, *The Lost Promise of Civil Rights* (Cambridge, MA: Harvard University Press, 2010), 151–152.

14. Jacobus tenBroek, "Thirteenth Amendment to the Constitution of the United States: Consummation to Abolition and Key to the Fourteenth Amendment," *California Law Review* 39, no. 2 (1951): 171.

15. State v. J.P., 2004 Fla. LEXIS 2101, 30 Fla. L. Weekly S 331 (Fla. Nov. 18, 2004).

16. U.S. Constitution Amendment 14.

17. On fundamental rights and incorporation, see McDonald v. City of Chicago, 561 U.S. 742 (2010).

18. Substantive due process in the labor context has so far been applied to cases like Coppage v. Kansas, 236 U.S. 1 (1915) (upholding yellow dog contracts).

19. See Lochner v. New York, 198 U.S. 45, 52, 25 S. Ct. 539 (1905) (striking down maximum hours law for bakers in New York).

20. Zietlow, "A Positive Right to Free Labor," 884.

21. Michael C. Duff, "The Thirteenth Amendment: Meaning, Enforcement, and Contemporary Implications: Panel III: The Limits of Authority: Thirteenth Amendment Optimism," *Columbia Law Review* 112 (2013).

22. James Gray Pope, "Contract, Race, and Freedom of Labor in the Law of Involuntary Servitude," *Yale Law Journal* 119 (2010).

23. Ayesha Bell Hardaway, "The Paradox of the Right to Contract: Noncompete Agreements as Thirteenth Amendment Violations," *Seattle University Law Review* 39 (2016): 957–981.

24. Ibid.

25. Ibid.

26. Philip Dray, *There Is Power in a Union: The Epic Story of Labor in America* (New York: Anchor, 2011), 17.

27. Douglas A. Blackmon, *Slavery by Another Name: The Re-enslavement of Black People in America from the Civil War to World War II* (New York: Anchor, 2008), 263.

28. Clifford F. Thies, "The First Minimum Wage Laws," *Cato Journal* 10 (1991): 716.

29. Duff, *The Thirteenth Amendment*.

30. Akhil Reed Amar and Daniel Widawsky, "Child Abuse as Slavery: A Thirteenth Amendment Response to Deshaney," *Harvard Law Review* 105 (1992): 1359, 1364; Baher Azmy, "Unshackling the Thirteenth Amendment: Modern Slavery and a Reconstructed Civil Rights Agenda," *Fordham Law Review* 71 (2002): 984–987.

31. Cox v. Cosentino, 876 F. 2d 1 (1989).

32. Matthew A. Kelly, "Early Federal Regulation of Hours of Labor in the United States," *Industrial and Labor Relations Review* 3, no. 3 (1950): 362–374.

33. Lochner v. New York, 198 U.S. 45, 52, 25 S. Ct. 539 (1905).

34. William E. Forbath, "The New Deal Constitution in Exile," *Duke Law Journal* 51 (2001): 165, 201.

35. Ibid.

36. U.S. Constitution Amendment 13, Section 2.

37. Clayton Antitrust Act of 1914, 63rd U.S. Congress, 63-212 (1914) (stating "The labor of a human being is not a commodity or article of commerce").

38. Clifford F. Thies, "The First Minimum Wage Laws," *Cato Journal* 10 (1991): 715.

39. Robert Asher, "The 1911 Wisconsin Workmen's Compensation Law: A Study in Conservative Labor Reform," *Wisconsin Magazine of History* 57 (Winter 1973–1974): 123, 140.

40. David R. Roediger and Phillip Sheldon Foner, *Our Own Time: A History of American Labor and the Working Day* (New York: Verso, 1989), 123, 139–140.

41. "Labor Law Highlights, 1915–2015," *Monthly Labor Review*, https://www.bls.gov/opub/mlr/2015/article/pdf/labor-law-highlights-1915-2015.pdf.

42. William E. Forbath, *Law and the Shaping of the American Labor Movement* (Cambridge, MA: Harvard University Press, 1989).

43. Deshaney v. Winnebago County Department of Social Services, 489 U.S. 189 (1989).

44. Zietlow, "A Positive Right to Free Labor," 879–880.

45. Jordon G. Weissman, "What Would Happen if We Got Rid of the Minimum Wage?" *Slate*, May 24, 2015, http://www.slate.com/articles/business/moneybox/2014/05/ending_the_minimum_wage_what_happens_if_we_got_rid_of_the_mimimum_wage.html.

46. Gillian B. White, "Should Cities Have a Different Minimum Wage Than Their State?" *The Atlantic*, January 15, 2015, https://www.theatlantic.com/business/archive/2015/01/should-cities-have-a-different-minimum-wage-than-their-state/384516/.

47. Jennifer Grady, "What Is the Living Wage Movement?" *Library Worklife*,2004,http://ala-apa.org/newsletter/2004/06/16/what-is-the-living-wage-movement/.

48. Pope, "Contract, Race, and Freedom of Labor in the Law of Involuntary Servitude," 943.

49. Aviam Soifer, "Federal Protection, Paternalism, and the Virtually Forgotten Prohibition of Voluntary Peonage," *Columbia Law Review* 112, no. 7 (November 2012).

50. Ibid.

51. Annalyn Kurtz and Tal Yellin, "Minimum Wage Since 1938," *CNN*, April 9, 2019, https://money.cnn.com/interactive/economy/minimum-wage-since-1938/.

52. "State Minimum Wage Laws," U.S. Department of Labor, January 1, 2023, https://www.dol.gov/whd/minwage/america.htm.

53. Judiciary and Judicial Procedure 28 U.S.C. § 1331 (1980).

54. "Fact Sheet 14: Coverage Under the Fair Labor Standards Act (FLSA)," U.S. Department of Labor, July 2009, https://www.dol.gov/whd/regs/compliance/whdfs14.htm.

55. Daniel V. Dorris, "Comment: Fair Labor Standards Act Preemption of State Wage-and-Hour Law Claims," *University of Chicago Law Review* 76 (2009): 1251.

56. Wal-Mart Stores, Inc. v. Dukes, 564 U.S. 338 (2011) (coverage under the Fair Labor Standards Act is found where the enterprise generates a gross annual volume of more than $500,000).

57. U.S. Constitution Amendment 13, Section 1.

58. "Fact Sheet 14, Coverage Under the Fair Labor Standards Act (FLSA)."

59. Ruben J. Garcia, "Prison Strike Is Reminder How Commonplace Prison Labor Is, and That It May Run Afoul of the Law," *The Conversation*, August 30, 2018, https://theconversation.com/us-prisoners-strike-is-reminder-how-commonplace-inmate-labor-is-and-that-it-may-run-afoul-of-the-law-101948.

60. Alexander v. Sara, Inc., 559 F. Supp. 42 (1983) (no jurisdiction for federal wage claims; no state minimum wage claims under Louisiana law).

61. For example, litigation involving the GEO Group, a private contractor managing immigration detention centers in Colorado, went to the U.S. Court of Appeals for the Tenth Circuit. Menocal v. GEO Group, 882 F.3d 905 (10th Cir. 2018).

62. Ibid.

63. National Guestworker Alliance litigation against Allied Signal, http://www.guestworkeralliance.org/category/litigation/.

64. Ibid.

65. Moodie et al. v. Kiawah Island Inn Co., LLC, 124 F. Supp. 3d 711, 715 (D. S.C. 2015).

66. Deshaney v. Winnebago County Department of Social Services, 489 U.S. 189 (1989).

67. Deepa Das Acevedo, "Unbundling Freedom in the Sharing Economy," *Alabama Law* 91 (2017): 793, 812.

68. Ibid.

69. "Car Rentals for Gig Workers as Low as $260/week," Uber, https://www.uber.com/drive/vehicle-solutions/.

70. Pollock v. Williams, 332 U.S. 4 (1944); Bailey v. Alabama, 219 U.S. 219 (1911).

71. See United States v. Kozminski, 487 U.S. 938 (1988).

72. Conspiracy against Rights, 18 U.S.C. § 241 (1996); Sale into Involuntary Servitude, 18 U.S.C. § 1584 (2008).

73. Ibid.

74. "Shield from Justice: Police Brutality and Accountability in the United States," Federal Passivity, Human Rights Watch, accessed March 25, 2023, https://www.hrw.org/legacy/reports98/police/uspo33.htm.

75. Rhonda Brownstein, "Are There Limits to Prosecutorial Discretion," *Southern Poverty Law Center*, January 1, 2003, https://www.splcenter.org/fighting-hate/intelligence-report/2003/are-there-limits-prosecutorial-discretion.

76. For state responsibility for labor violations, see Livadas v. Bradshaw, 512 U.S.C. § 104 (1994).

77. Tobias Barrington Wolff, "The Thirteenth Amendment and Global Slavery," *Columbia Law Review* 102 (2002).

78. "State Minimum Wage Laws," U.S. Department of Labor, January 1, 2023, https://www.dol.gov/whd/minwage/america.htm.

79. Ibid.

80. Ibid.

81. "Fact Sheet 14: Coverage Under the Fair Labor Standards Act (FLSA).

82. Human Rights First, Blog, "Domestic Servitude: An Especially Hidden Form of Labor Trafficking," August 2, 2016, https://humanrightsfirst.org/library/domestic-servitude-an-especially-hidden-form-of-labor-trafficking/.

83. If there is a lack of minimum wage remedies under federal law, the state law would fill gaps. But if there is no minimum wage, the worker would be without a remedy. See David Jamieson, "Student Guestworkers at Hershey's Plant Allege Exploitative Conditions," *HuffPost*, updated December 6, 2017, https://www.huffingtonpost.com/2011/08/17/student-guestworkers-at-hershey-plant_n_930014.html; Anthony Man, "South Florida a 'Hotspot' for Human Trafficking," *Orlando Sun Sentinel*, January 13, 2018, https://www.sun-sentinel.com/news/nationworld /fl-reg-human-trafficking-visas-deutch-frankel-20180111-story.html.

84. Griselda Nevarez, "Latino Workers Helped Rebuild New Orleans, but Many Weren't Paid," *NBC News*, August 28, 2015, https://www .nbcnews.com/storyline/hurricane-katrina-anniversary/ latino-workers-helped-rebuild-new-orleans-many-werent-paid-n417571.

85. Michelle Chen, "These Workers Came From Overseas to Help Rebuild After Hurricane Katrina and Were Treated Like Prisoners," February 20, 2015, https://www.thenation.com/article/archive/these-workers-came-overseas-help-rebuild-after-hurricane-katrina-and-were -treated-prison/.

86. "Fair Labor Standards Act: Better Use of Available Resources and Consistent Reporting Could Improve Compliance," Government Accountability Office (2008), https://www.gao.gov/products/gao-08-962t.

87. "Subminimum Wage," U.S. Department of Labor, accessed March 30, 2023, https://www.dol.gov/general/topic/wages/subminimumwage; "Minimum Wages for Tipped Employees." U.S. Department of Labor, accessed March 30, 2023, https://www.dol.gov/whd/state/tipped.htm.

88. Ibid.

89. Michelle Alexander, "Tipping Is a Legacy of Slavery," *New York Times*, February 5, 2021, https://www.nytimes.com/2021/02/05/opinion /minimum-wage-racism.html.

90. Employment Under Special Certificates, 29 U.S.C. § 214(c) (1989).

91. Lydia DePillis, "Disabled People Are Allowed to Work for Pennies per Hour—But Maybe Not for Much Longer," *Washington Post*, February 12, 2016, https://www.washingtonpost.com/news/wonk/wp/2016/02/12 /disabled-people-are-allowed-to-work-for-pennies-per-hour-but-maybe-not-for-much-longer/?utm_term=.cb1c75c2996e.

92. See Samuel R. Bagenstos, "The Case against the Section 14(c) Subminimum Wage Program," *Report for the Georgia Advocacy Office* (2011), available at http://thegao.org/wp-content/uploads/2012/09/14c_report_

sam_bagenstos-1.pdf; Samuel R. Bagenstos, "Disability Rights and Labor: Is This Conflict Really Necessary?" *Indiana Law Journal* 97 (2017): 277–298. See also Americans with Disabilities Act of 1990, 1990 Enacted S. 933, 104 Stat. 327, 101 P.L. 336, 101st U.S. Congress, 101-336 (1990).

93. "Department of Developmental Services," Connecticut's Official State Website, accessed March 25, 2023, http://www.ct.gov/dds/lib/dds /employment/the_case_against_14c_sub_minumum_wage_program.pdf.

94. Pope, "Labor's Constitution of Freedom."

95. U.S. Department of Labor, Fair Labor Standards Act Advisor, https://webapps.dol.gov/elaws/faq/esa/flsa/002.htm; Dana Liebelson, "The Minimum Wage Loophole That's Screwing Over Waiters and Waitresses," *Mother Jones*, May 12, 2014, http://www.motherjones.com /politics/2014/05/minimum-wage-tip-map-waiters-waitresses-servers/.

96. Ibid.

97. Kathryn Casteel, "The Minimum Wage Movement Is Leaving Tipped Workers Behind," *FiveThirtyEight*, February 7, 2017, https://fivethirtyeight .com/features/the-minimum-wage-movement-is-leaving-tipped-workers- behind/.

98. Noah Zatz, "Working beyond the Reach or Grasp of Employment Law," in *The Gloves-Off Economy: Problems and Possibilities at the Bottom of America's Labor Market*, ed. Annette Bernhardt, Heather Boushey, Laura Dresser, and Chris Tilly (Champaign: Labor and Employment Relations Association, University of Illinois at Urbana-Champaign, 2008), 31–64.

99. Alexander Tsesis, "Into the Light of Day: Relevance of the Thirteenth Amendment to Contemporary Law," *Columbia Law Review* 1447 (2012): 1447 (addressing the Thirteenth Amendment in relation to other constitutional provisions, the significance of the Amendment in restructuring federalism, the limits of the Amendment's grant of congressional and judicial authority, and the implications to current affairs and contemporary constitutional theory).

100. Kerry Segrave, *Tipping: An American Social History of Gratuities* (Jefferson, NC: McFarland, 1998).

101. "End Legacy of Slavery, One Fair Wage for All," One Fair Wage Food Labor Research Center, UC Berkeley National Black Workers' Center Project, Restaurant Opportunities Centers Report, February 1, 2021, https://onefairwage.site/wp-content/uploads/2021/02/OFW_EndingLe- gacyOfSlavery-2.pdf.

102. Saru Jayaraman, *Forked: A New Standard for American Dining* (New York: Oxford University Press, 2016).

103. "Editorial: In Hiking the Minimum Wage, Don't Leave Tipped Workers Behind," *Los Angeles Times*, May 3, 2015, http://www.latimes.com/opinion/editorials/la-ed-tipped-minimum-wage-20150503-story.html.

104. "Minimum Wages for Tipped Employees," U.S. Department of Labor, accessed March 21, 2023, https://www.dol.gov/whd/state/tipped.htm.

105. Ibid.

106. Saru Jayaraman, *Behind the Kitchen Door* (Ithaca: Cornell University, 2013), 103–156; Segrave, *Tipping*, 51–52.

107. Village of Arlington Heights v. Metro Development Corporation, 429 U.S. 252 (1977); Hunter v. Erickson, 393 U.S. 569 (1969).

108. Schutte v. Coalition to Defend Affirmative Action, 572 U.S. 291 (2014).

109. Ibid.

110. Maria L. Ontiveros, "Noncitizen Immigrant Labor and the Thirteenth Amendment: Challenging Guest Worker Programs," *University of Toledo Law Review* 923, no. 3 (2006) (analyzing "guest worker programs" through the Thirteenth Amendment).

111. tenBroek, "Thirteenth Amendment to the Constitution of the United States."

112. Bailey v. Alabama, 211 US 452 (1908).

113. Bailey v. Alabama, 219 US 219 (1911).

114. West Coast Hotel Co. v. Parrish, 300 U.S. 379, 387, 57 S. Ct. 578, 580, 81 L. Ed. 703 (1937).

115. Alexander v. Sara, Inc., 559 F. Supp. 42 (1983).

116. Deshaney v. Winnebago County Department of Social Services, 489 U.S. 189 (1989).

117. Rebecca E. Zietlow, "Free at Last! Anti-subordination and the Thirteenth Amendment," *Boston University Law Review* 255 (2010) (discussing how Section 2 of the Thirteenth Amendment is a source of rights for individuals to belong and participate in our society).

118. Adam Winkler, *Gunfight: The Battle over the Right to Bear Arms in America* (New York: W. W. Norton, 2011). See District of Columbia v. Heller, 554 U.S. 570 (2008).

119. Kate Andrias, "The New Labor Law," *Yale Law Journal* 126 (2016): 2, 9 (identifying a new labor law that has the potential to help achieve greater equality, both economic and political).

120. Lynn Thompson and Andy Martinez, "Seattle City Council Approves Historic $15 Minimum Wage," *Seattle Times*, June 2, 2014, updated January 25, 2016, https://www.seattletimes.com/seattle-news/seattle-city-council-approves-historic-15-minimum-wage/.

121. Chamber of Commerce v. City of Seattle (9th Cir. 2017) (challenge to the Seattle Minimum Wage).

122. "State Minimum Wage Laws," U.S. Department of Labor, January 1, 2023, https://www.dol.gov/whd/minwage/america.htm.

123. Ibid. (paying attention to California).

124. Karl Russell, "A Higher Minimum Wage in 2017," *New York Times*, January 5, 2017, https://www.nytimes.com/interactive/2017/01/05/business/economy/state-minimum-wages.html.

125. See U.S. Constitution Amendment 10.

126. David Rolf, *The Fight for $15: The Right Wage for a Working America* (New York: The New Press, 2016).

127. Chamber of Commerce and ERISA challenge, Seattle 9th Cir. 2016; The ERISA Industry Committee v. City of Seattle, No. 20-35472 (9th Cir. 2020).

128. Ibid.

129. "Poverty Thresholds," U.S. Census Bureau, accessed March 21, 2023, https://www.census.gov/data/tables/time-series/demo/income-poverty/historical-poverty-thresholds.html.

130. These states are South Carolina, Louisiana, Alabama, Mississippi, and Tennessee. "State Minimum Wages," National Conference of State Legislatures, August 30, 2022, http://www.ncsl.org/research/labor-and-employment/state-minimum-wage-chart.aspx.

131. Ahiza Garcia, "$10.10 Minimum Wage Stuck Down in Birmingham, Alabama," *CNN Business*, February 27, 2016, https://money.cnn.com/2016/02/27/news/economy/minimum-wage-birmingham-alabama/index.html.

132. Melanie Trottman, "Workers Sue Over Alabama Wage Law, Citing Civil Rights," *Wall Street Journal*, April 28, 2016, https://www.wsj.com/articles/workers-sue-over-alabama-wage-law-citing-civil-rights-1461853686.

133. U.S. Constitution Article I, Section 7, Clauses 2, 3.

134. See Jones v. Alfred Mayer Co., 392 U.S. 409 (1968).

135. Ibid.

CHAPTER 6. THE RACIAL POLITICAL ECONOMY

1. George Skelton, "It's No Wonder Hundreds of Millions Have Been Spent on Prop. 22. A Lot Is at Stake," *Los Angeles Times*, October 16, 2020, https://www.latimes.com/california/story/2020-10-16/skelton-proposition-22-uber-lyft-independent-contractors.

2. Dynamex Operations West, Inc. v. Superior Court, 4 Cal. 5th 903, 415 P.3d 1 (Cal. 2018).

3. Definitions, 29 U.S.C. § 152(3) (1978).

4. National Collegiate Athletic Association v. Alston, 594 U.S. ___ (2021).

5. Angela B. Cornell and Mark Barenberg, *The Cambridge Handbook of Labor and Democracy* (Cambridge: Cambridge University Press, 2022).

6. Veena Dubal, "Essentially Dispossessed," *South Atlantic Quarterly* 121 (2022): 285.

7. "Labor Force Characteristics by Race and Ethnicity," Bureau of Labor Statistics, January 2023, https://www.bls.gov/opub/reports/race-and-ethnicity/2021/home.

8. Sarah Maslin Nir, "Benefits, and Some Resistance, as New York Cracks Down on Nail Salon Abuses," *New York Times*, July 16, 2015, https://www.nytimes.com/2015/07/17/nyregion/benefits-and-some-resistance-as-new-york-cracks-down-on-nail-salon-abuses.html.

9. Noah Zatz, "Working beyond the Reach or Grasp of Employment Law," in *The Gloves-Off Economy: Problems and Possibilities at the Bottom of America's Labor Market*, ed. Annette Bernhardt, Heather Boushey, Laura Dresser, and Chris Tilly (Champaign: Labor and Employment Relations Association, University of Illinois at Urbana-Champaign, 2008), 31–64.

10. Ibid.

11. Dynamex Operations West, Inc. v. Superior Court, 4 Cal. 5th 903 (Cal. 2018).

12. Ibid.

13. Guy Davidov and Brian Langille, *The Idea of Labour Law* (Oxford: Oxford University Press, 2011).

14. Dynamex Operations West, Inc. v. Superior Court, 4 Cal. 5th 903 (Cal. 2018).

15. "The Contract of Employment," Cal. Lab. Code Section 2750.3 (2020).

16. "Local Taxpayer, Public Safety, and Transportation Protection Act of 2010" (text of Proposition 22).

17. Doruk Cengiz et al., "CEP Discussion Paper No. 1531," Centre for Economic Performance, February 2018, https://cep.lse.ac.uk/pubs /download/dp1531.pdf.

18. Michael Reich, "An $18 Wage for California," *Institute for Research on Labor and Employment*, https://irle.berkeley.edu/publications /irle-policy-brief/an-18-minimum-wage-for-california/.

19. Davidov and Langille, *The Idea of Labour Law*.

20. "Day Labor in Las Vegas: Employer Indiscretions in Sin City," Arriba Las Vegas Workers Center, January 2018, https://arribalasvegas .org/wp-content/uploads/2019/04/Day-Labor-in-Las-Vegas-compressed .pdf.

21. Shannon Walsh, director, *The Gig Is Up* (London: Dogwoof Pictures, 2021), https://tubitv.com/movies/654449/the-gig-is-up?start=true& tracking=google-feed&utm_source=google-feed.

22. Alana Semuels, "The Internet Is Enabling a New Kind of Poorly Paid Hell," *The Atlantic*, January 23, 2018, https://www.theatlantic .com/technology/archive/2018/08/fiverr-online-gig-economy/569083/.

23. National Collegiate Athletic Association v. Alston, 594 U.S. ___ (2021).

24. Paul Krugman, "Who's Radical Now? The Case of Minimum Wages," *New York Times*, January 19, 2021.

25. François Bonnet, *The Upper Limit: How Low-Wage Work Defines Punishment and Welfare* (Oakland: University of California Press, 2019).

26. Kirstin Downey, *The Woman Behind the New Deal: The Life of Frances Perkins, FDR's Secretary of Labor and His Moral Conscience* (New York: Anchor, 2009).

27. Andrea Hsu, "Do-Over Union Election at Amazon's Bessemer Warehouse Is Too Close to Call," *NPR*, March 31, 2022, https://www .npr.org/2022/03/31/1090123017/do-over-union-election-at-amazons -bessemer-warehouse-is-too-close-to-call. The union ultimately lost the election but is challenging the results in the National Labor Relations Board.

28. U.S. Department of Labor, www.dol.gov.

29. Alexander J. S. Colvin and Mark D. Gough, "Mandatory Employment Arbitration," *Annual Review of Law and Social Science*, 19 (2023): 131–144 at 133 (one study found that wage and hour plaintiffs prevail in just over half (56%) of cases).

30. Congressional Findings and Declaration of Policy, 29 U.S.C. § 251 (1947).

31. Current Population Survey via UnionStats.com as reported by Alvin Chang et al., "The Pandemic Exposed the Meatpacking Industry's Power," *The Guardian*, November 16, 2021, https://www.theguardian.com /environment/2021/nov/16/meatpacking-industry-covid-outbreaks-workers.

32. Integrity Staffing Solutions, Inc. v. Busk, 574 U.S. 27 (2014).

33. Ibid.

34. Carmen Gonzalez and Athena Mutua, "Mapping Racial Law Capitalism: Implications for Law," *Journal of Law and Political Economy* 2, no. 2 (2022): 127, https://ssrn.com/abstract=4180690.

35. Gene Johnson, "Washington Supreme Court: Farmworkers to Get Overtime Pay," Associated Press, November 5, 2020, https://apnews.com /article/washington-agriculture-d4d155379061da6798e1790342093ed4.

36. Martinez-Cuevas, et al. v. Deruyter Brothers Dairy Inc, et al. Wash. S. Ct. No 96267-7 (Nov. 5, 2020).

37. Ibid.

38. Jamie Goldberg, "Oregon Farmworkers File Petition Challenging Regulations That Exclude Agricultural Workers From Overtime Pay," *The Oregonian*, December 21, 2021.

39. Ruben J. Garcia, *Marginal Workers: How Legal Fault Lines Divide Workers and Leave Them without Protection* (New York: New York University Press, 2013). In this book, I focused on how federal collective bargaining and antidiscrimination law often work at odds with each other and how they can be reformed to provide a minimum floor.

40. Veena Dubal, "The New Racial Wage Code," *Harvard Law and Policy Review* 15 (2022): 511.

41. Cezarz v. Wynn, 2:13-cv-00109-RCJ-CWH (D. Nev. Jan. 10, 2014).

42. Civil Action for Deprivation of Rights, 42 U.S.C. § 1983 (1996).

43. Rachel Kahn Best et al., "Multiple Disadvantages: An Empirical Test of Intersectionality Theory in EEO Litigation," *Law and Society Review* 45 (2011): 991–1025, https://sites.lsa.umich.edu/rachelbest/wp-content/uploads/sites/208/2014/12/lasr463.pdf.

44. Kimberlé Williams Crenshaw, "Demarginalizing the Intersection of Race and Gender," *University of Chicago Legal Forum* 8 (1989) : 139–167, https://chicagounbound.uchicago.edu/cgi/viewcontent. cgi?article=1052&context=uclf.

45. Ledbetter v. Goodyear Tire and Rubber Co., 550 U.S.C. 618 (2007).

46. Findings and Declaration of Policy, 29 U.S.C. 151 (1947).

CHAPTER 7. IMPROVING THE MINIMUM WAGE
AS A TOOL FOR RACIAL JUSTICE

1. "Global Coronavirus Tracker," last modified June 18, 2022, https://covid.cdc.gov.

2. Robert Samuels and Toluse Olorunnipa, *His Name Is George Floyd: One Man's Life and the Struggle for Racial Justice* (New York: Viking, 2022).

3. "The Future of American Democracy: A Special Series," *The New Yorker*, last modified March 30, 2023, https://www.newyorker.com/news/the-future-of-democracy?verso=true.

4. Leah Douglas, "Coronavirus Infections at U.S. Meat Plants Far Higher Than Previous Estimates—House Subcommittee," Reuters, October 28, 2021, https://www.reuters.com/world/us/coronavirus-infections-us-meat-plants-far-higher-than-previous-estimates-house-2021-10-28/.

5. Tina L. Saitone et al., "COVID-19 Morbidity and Mortality in U.S. Meatpacking Counties," *Food Policy* 101 (2021).

6. David Cooper, "Raising the Minimum Wage to $15 by 2024 Would Lift Pay for Nearly 40 Million Workers," *Economic Policy Institute*, February 5, 2019, https://www.epi.org/publication/raising-the-federal-minimum-wage-to-15-by-2024-would-lift-pay-for-nearly-40-million-workers/.

7. Samuelson and Olorunnipa, *His Name Is George Floyd*, 166.

8. Ibid., 129–131. As is discussed in Chapter 5, the Corrections Corporation of America (CCA) is now called CoreCivic.

9. *Right of Employees as to Organization, Collective Bargaining, etc.*, U.S.C. 29 § 157 (1947).

10. "Blood, Sweat, and Fear: Workers Rights in U.S. Meat and Poultry Plants," Human Rights Watch, accessed March 22, 2023, https://www.hrw.org/report/2005/01/24/blood-sweat-and-fear/workers-rights-us-meat-and-poultry-plants.

11. United States Occupational Health and Safety Administration (OSHA) Coronavirus (COVID-19) resources page, https://www.osha.gov/coronavirus.

12. Ben Zipperer, "The Minimum Wage Has Lost 21 percent of Its Value Since Congress Last Raised the Wage," Economic Political Institute, July 22, 2021, https://www.epi.org/blog/the-minimum-wage-has-lost-21-of-its-value-since-congress-last-raised-the-wage/.

13. Chris Marr, "Hawaii Governor Signs $18 Minimum Wage Law, First of Its Kind," *Bloomberg Law*, June 22, 2022, https://news.bloomberglaw.com/daily-labor-report/hawaii-governor-signs-18-minimum-wage-law-first-of-its-kind.

14. Ibid.

15. Lorie Konish, "High Inflation Leads Federal Minimum Wage to Reach Lowest Value since 1956, Report Finds," *CNBC*, July 15, 2022, https://www.cnbc.com/2022/07/15/inflation-leads-federal-minimum-wage-to-reach-lowest-value-since-1956.html.

16. Serena Dai, "Danny Meyer Admits Large Portion of Staff Left Over No-Tipping Changes," *Eater New York*, February 6, 2018, https://ny.eater.com/2018/2/6/16978464/danny-meyer-tipping-staff-turnover.

17. "Letters: Rick Bayless: Chicago Restaurants Are Working to Become More Equitable, Sustainable," *Chicago Tribune*, June 9, 2021, https://www.chicagotribune.com/opinion/letters/ct-letters-vp-061021-20210609-s4stweqpw5dj5lvnn3z2ld3inq-story.html.

18. Blake Hounshell, "Is Nevada Turning Red?" *New York Times*, June 13, 2022, https://www.nytimes.com/live/2022/06/13/us/midterm-primary-elections.

19. Lochner v. New York, 198 U.S. 45 (1905).

20. National Federation of Independent Business v. Sebelius, 567 U.S. 519 (2012).

21. Lee Epstein et al., "How Business Fares in the Supreme Court," *Minnesota Law Review* 97 (2013): 1431–1472, https://www.minnesotalawreview.org/wp-content/uploads/2013/04/EpsteinLanderPosner_MLR.pdf.

22. Lochner v. New York, 198 U.S. 45 (1905).

23. Robert M. Cover, "The Supreme Court 1982 Term, Foreword: Nomos and Narrative," *Harvard Law Review* 97 (1982): 4.

CHAPTER 8. THE FUTURE OF THE MINIMUM
WAGE IN THE GLOBAL ECONOMY

1. Brishen Rogers, "The Law and Political Economy of Workplace Technological Change," *Harvard Civil Rights-Civil Liberties Law Review* 55 (2020).

2. "International Labour Migration: A Rights-Based Approach," International Labour Organization, April 29, 2010, https://www.ilo.org/global/publications/books/WCMS_125361/lang--en/index.htm.

3. Ibid.

4. Alan Morrison, "Is the Trans-Pacific Partnership Unconstitutional?" *The Atlantic*, June 23, 2015, https://www.theatlantic.com/politics /archive/2015/06/23/tpp-isds-constitution/396389/.

5. Margaret E. Keck and Kathryn Sikkink, *Activists Beyond Borders* (Ithaca: Cornell University Press, 1998).

6. Ellen Meiksins Wood, *Rising from the Ashes? Labor in The Age of "Global" Capitalism* (New York: Monthly Review Press, 1998).

7. Hector Delgado, *New Immigrants in Old Unions* (Philadelphia: Temple University Press, 1994). Delgado talks about why this idea of immigrant workers being un-organizable is false.

8. Ronald Brownstein, "Gephardt's Revolution Begins with a Global Minimum Wage," *Los Angeles Times*, January 12, 2004, https://www .latimes.com/archives/la-xpm-2004-jan-12-na-outlook12-story.html.

9. Tamara Kay, *NAFTA and the Politics of Transnationalism* (Cambridge: Cambridge University Press, 2011); Tamara Kay and R. L. Evans, *Trade Battles: Activism and the Politicization of the International Trade Policy* (New York: Oxford University Press, 2018).

10. Amy K. Glasmeier, Living Wage Calculator 2023, Massachusetts Institute of Technology, https://livingwage.mit.edu.

Bibliography

LEGAL CASES

A.L.A. Schechter Poultry Corp. v. United States, 295 U.S. 495, 55 S. Ct. 837, 79 L. Ed. 1570 (1935).

Alexander v. Sara, Inc., 559 F. Supp. 42 (1983).

Bailey v. Alabama, 211 U.S. 452 (1908).

Bailey v. Alabama, 219 U.S. 219 (1911).

Becerra v. Expert Janitorial, 332 P.3d 415 (2014).

Bureerong v. Uvawas, 922 F. Supp. 1450 (C.D. Cal. 1996).

Cezarz v. Wynn, 2:13-cv-00109-RCJ-CWH (D. Nev. Jan. 10, 2014).

Chamber of Commerce v. City of Seattle (9th Cir. 2017).

Coppage v. Kansas, 236 U.S. 1 (1915).

Cox v. Cosentino, 876 F.2d 1 (1989).

Depianti v. Jan-Pro Franchising Int'l, 39 F. Supp. 3d 112 (D. Mass. 2014), aff'd, 873 F.3d 21 (1st Cir. 2017).

Deshaney v. Winnebago County Department of Social Services, 489 U.S. 189 (1989).

District of Columbia v. Heller, 554 U.S. 570 (2008).

Dobbs v. Jackson Women's Health Organization, No. 19-1392, 597 U.S. 215 (2022).

Dynamex Operations West, Inc. v. Superior Court, 4 Cal. 5th 903 (Cal. 2018).

Emporium Capwell v. Western Addition Community Organization, 420 U.S. 50, 95 S. Ct. 977, 43 L. Ed. 2d 12 (1975).

The ERISA Industry Committee v. City of Seattle, No. 20–35472 (9th Cir. 2020).

Hart v. Rick's Cabaret International, Inc., 967 F. Supp.2d 901 (S.D.N.Y. 2013).

Hoffman Plastic Compounds, Inc. v. NLRB, 535 U.S. 137 (2002).

Hunter v. Erickson, 393 U.S. 569 (1969).

Integrity Staffing Solutions, Inc. v. Busk, 574 U.S. 27 (2014).

International Beef Processors Co. v. Alvarez, 546 U.S. 21 (2005).

Jones v. Alfred Mayor Co., 392 U.S. 409 (1968).

Ledbetter v. Goodyear Tire and Rubber Co., 550 U.S. 618 (2007).

Lewis v. the Governor of Alabama, 944 F.3d. 1287 (11th Cir. 2019) (en banc).

Livadas v. Bradshaw, 512 U.S. 104 (1994).

Lochner v. New York, 198 U.S 45, 52, 25 S.Ct. 539 (1905).

Martinez-Cuevas, et al. v. Deruyter Brothers Dairy Inc, et al. Wash. S. Ct. No 96267-7 (Nov. 5, 2020).

McDonald v. City of Chicago, 561 U.S. 742 (2010).

McFeeley v. Jackson St. Entertainment, LLC, 825 F.3d 325 (4th Cir. 2016).

Menocal v. Geo Group, 882 F.3d 905 (10th Cir. 2018).

Meshna v. Scrivanos, 27 N.Ed.3d 1253 (Mass. 2015).

Michael's Painting and Painting L.A., Inc., 337 N.L.R.B. 860 (2002), enforced, 85 Fed. Apps. 614 (9th Cir. 2004).

Moodie v. Kiawah Island Inn Co., LLC, 124 F. Supp. 3d 711, 715 (D. S.C. 2015).

Morillion v. Royal Packing Co., 22 Cal 4th 575 (2000).

National Collegiate Athletic Association v. Alston, 594 U.S. ___ (2021).

National Federation of Independent Business v. Sebelius, 567 U.S. 519 (2012).

Oregon Restaurant and Lodging Association v. Perez, 816 F.3d 1080 (9th Cir. 2018).

Patel v. Quality Inn South, 846 F.2d 700 (11th Cir. 1988).

Pizzarelli v. Cadillac Lounge, LLC, No. 15–254 WES, 2018 U.S. Dist. LEXIS 117338 (D.R.I. 2018).

Pollock v. Williams, 332 U.S. 4 (1994).

Schutte v. Coalition to Defend Affirmative Action, 572 U.S. 291 (2014).

State v. J. P., 2004 Fl. LEXIS 2101, 30 Fla. L. Weekly S 331 (Fla. Nov. 18, 2004).

Sure-Tan, Inc. v. NLRB, 467 U.S. 883 (1984).

United States v. Kozminski, 487 U.S. 938 (1988).

United States v. Valleo-Madero, 596 U.S. __ (2022)

Village of Arlington Heights v. Metro Development Corporation, 429 U.S. 252 (1977).

Wal-Mart Stores, Inc. v. Dukes, 564 U.S. 338 (2011).

West Coast Hotel Co. v. Parrish, 300 U.S. 379 387, 57 S. Ct. 578, 580, 81 L. Ed. 703 (1937).

Wynn Las Vegas, LLC, v. Baldonado, 311 P.3d 1179 (Nev. 2013).

OTHER SOURCES: BOOKS, ARTICLES, POLICY, AND LEGISLATION

Alemzadeh, Sheerine. "Baring Inequality: Revisiting the Legalization Debate through the Lens of Strippers' Rights." *Michigan Journal of Gender and Law* 19 (2013): 339–372. https://repository.law.umich.edu /cgi/viewcontent.cgi?article=1026&context=mjgl.

Alexander, Michelle. "Tipping Is a Legacy of Slavery." *New York Times*, February 5, 2021. https://www.nytimes.com/2021/02/05/opinion /minimum-wage-racism.html.

Allegreta, Sylvia, and David Cooper. *Twenty-Three Years and Still Waiting for Change: Why It's Time to Give Tipped Workers the Regular Minimum Wage*. Washington, D.C.: Economic Policy Institute, 2014. Accessed March 30, 2023. https://files.epi.org/2014/EPI-CWED-BP379.pdf.

Amar, Akhil Reed, and Daniel Widawsky. "Child Abuse as Slavery: A Thirteenth Amendment Response to Deshaney." *Harvard Law Review* 105 (1992): 1359–1385. https://doi.org/10.2307/1341734.

Americans with Disabilities Act of 1990, 101st U.S. Congress, 101-336 (1990).

Anderson, Michelle Wilde. *The Fight to Save the Town: Reimagining Discarded America*. New York: Avid Reader Press/Simon & Schuster, 2022.

Andrias, Kate. "The New Labor Law." *Yale Law Journal* 126 (2016): 2–126. https://www.yalelawjournal.org/pdf/a.2.Andrias.100_sa4cc96k.pdf.

Asher, Robert. "The 1911 Wisconsin Workmen's Compensation Law: A Study in Conservative Labor Reform." *Wisconsin Magazine of Story* 57 (Winter 1973–1974): 120–140. https://www.jstor.org/stable/4634868.

Autor, David H., et al. "The Contribution of the Minimum Wage to US Wage Inequality over Three Decades: A Reassessment." *American*

Economic Journal: Applied Economics 8, no.1 (January 2016): 58–99. https://doi.org/10.1257/app.20140073.

Ayres, Ian, et al. "To Insure Prejudice: Racial Disparities in Taxicab Tipping." *Yale Law Journal* 114 (2005): 1613–1674. https://www.yalelawjournal.org/pdf/207_wd54xsc1.pdf.

Azar, Ofer. "The Effect of the Minimum Wage for Tipped Workers on Firm Strategy, Employees and Social Welfare." *Labour Economics* 19 (2012): 748–755. https://doi.org/10.1016/j.labeco.2012.07.002.

Aziz, Sahar. *The Racial Muslim: When Racism Quashes Religious Freedom*. Oakland: University of California Press, 2022.

Azmy, Baher. "Unshackling the Thirteenth Amendment: Modern Slavery and a Reconstructed Civil Rights Agenda." *Fordham Law Review* 71 (2002): 981–1061. https://ir.lawnet.fordham.edu/cgi/viewcontent.cgi?article=3872&context=flr.

Bagenstos, Samuel R. "The Case against the Section 14(c) Subminimum Wage Program." *Report for the Georgia Advocacy Office* (2011). Available at http://thegao.org/wp-content/uploads/2012/09/14c_report_sam_bagenstos-1.pdf.

———. "Disability Rights and Labor: Is This Conflict Really Necessary?" *Indiana Law Journal* 97 (2017): 277–298. https://repository.law.umich.edu/cgi/viewcontent.cgi?article=2851&context=articles.

Bell, Derrick. "Racial Realism." *Connecticut Law Review* 24, no. 2 (Winter 1992): 363–380. https://www.law.nyu.edu/sites/default/files/Racial%20Realism.pdf.

Bernstein, David. E. *Only One Place of Redress: African Americans, Labor Regulations, and the Courts from Reconstruction to the New Deal*. Durham: Duke University Press, 2000.

Best, Rachel Kahn, et al. "Multiple Disadvantages: An Empirical Test of Intersectionality Theory in EEO Litigation." *Law and Society Review* 45 (2011): 991–1025. https://sites.lsa.umich.edu/rachelbest/wp-content/uploads/sites/208/2014/12/lasr463.pdf.

Blackmon, Douglas A. *Slavery by Another Name: The Re-enslavement of Black People in America from the Civil War to World War II*. New York: Anchor, 2008.

"Blood, Sweat, and Fear: Workers Rights in U.S. Meat and Poultry Plants." Human Rights Watch, accessed March 22, 2023. https://www.hrw.org/report/2005/01/24/blood-sweat-and-fear/workers-rights-us-meat-and-poultry-plants.

Bonnet, François. *The Upper Limit: How Low-Wage Work Defines Punishment and Welfare*. Oakland: University of California Press, 2019.

Brents, Barbara, et al. *The State of Sex: Tourism, Sex and Sin in the New American Heartland*. New York: Routledge, 2009.

Brooks, Siobhan. *Unequal Desire: Race and Erotic Capital in the Stripping Industry*. New York: State University of New York Press, 2010.

Brownstein, Rhonda. "Are There Limits to Prosecutorial Discretion?" *Southern Poverty Law Center*, January 1, 2003. https://www.splcenter.org/fighting-hate/intelligence-report/2003/are-there-limits-prosecutorial-discretion.

Brownstein, Ronald. "Gephardt's Revolution Begins with a Global Minimum Wage." *Los Angeles Times*, January 12, 2004. https://www.latimes.com/archives/la-xpm-2004-jan-12-na-outlook12-story.html.

Bureau of Labor Statistics. "Labor Force Characteristics by Race and Ethnicity." January 2023. https://www.bls.gov/opub/reports/race-and-ethnicity/2021/home.

Butler, Paul. "Poor People Lose: *Gideon* and the Critique of Rights." *Yale Law Journal*, 122 (2013): 2176–2204. https://scholarship.law.georgetown.edu/facpub/1249.

Card, David, and Alan B. Krueger. "Minimum Wages and Employment: A Case Study of the Fast-Food Industry in New Jersey and Pennsylvania." *American Economic Review*, American Economic Association, 84, no. 4 (1994): 772–793.

Casteel, Kathryn. "The Minimum Wage Movement Is Leaving Tipped Workers Behind." *FiveThirtyEight*, February 7, 2017. https://fivethirtyeight.com/features/the-minimum-wage-movement-is-leaving-tipped-workers-behind/.

Cengiz, Doruk, et al. "CEP Discussion Paper No. 1531." Centre for Economic Performance, February 2018. https://cep.lse.ac.uk/pubs/download/dp1531.pdf.

Cherry, Miriam A., "Virtual Work and Invisible Labor." In *Invisible Work: Hidden Work in the Contemporary World*. Oakland: University of California Press, 2016.

Clausing, Kimberly. *Open: The Progressive Case for Free Trade, Immigration, and Global Capital*. Cambridge, MA: Harvard University Press, 2019.

Cooper, David. "Raising the Minimum Wage to $15 by 2024 Would Lift Pay for Nearly 40 Million Workers, Economic Policy Institute."

Economic Policy Institute, February 5, 2019. https://www.epi.org
/publication/raising-the-federal-minimum-wage-to-15-by-2024-would
-lift-pay-for-nearly-40-million-workers/.

Cornell, Angela B., and Mark Barenberg. *The Cambridge Handbook of Labor and Democracy.* Cambridge: Cambridge University Press, 2022.

Correal, Annie. "Hindu Sect Is Accused of Using Forced Labor to Build N.J. Temple." *New York Times*, May 11, 2021. https://www.nytimes
.com/2021/05/11/nyregion/nj-hindu-temple-india-baps.html.

Cover, Robert M. "The Supreme Court 1982 Term, Foreword: Nomos and Narrative." *Harvard Law Review* 97 (1982): 4–68. https://openyls.law
.yale.edu/bitstream/handle/20.500.13051/2047/Nomos_and
_Narrative.pdf?sequence=2&isAllowed=y.

Crenshaw, Kimberlé Williams. "Demarginalizing the Intersection of Race and Gender." *University of Chicago Legal Forum* 8 (1989): 139–167.
https://chicagounbound.uchicago.edu/cgi/viewcontent.cgi?article=
1052&context=uclf.

———. "Mapping the Margins: Intersectionality, Identity Politics, and Violence against Women of Color." *Stanford Law Review* 43, no. 6 (July 1991): 1241–1299. https://www.berkeleycitycollege.edu/slo/files/2021
/05/Crenshaw-Mapping-the-Margins-Intersectionality-and-Vioence
-against-WOC.pdf.

———. "Race, Reform, and Retrenchment: Transformation and Legitimation in Antidiscrimination Law." *Harvard Law Review* 101, no. 7 (May 1988): 1331–1387. https://doi.org/10.2307/1341398.

———. "Unmasking Colorblindness in the Law: Lessons from the Formation of Critical Race Theory." In *Seeing Race Again: Countering Colorblindness Across the Disciplines,* ed. Kimberlé Williams Crenshaw, et al., 52–84. Oakland: University of California Press, 2019.

Cummings, Scott. *An Equal Place: Lawyers in the Struggle for Los Angeles.* New York: Oxford University Press, 2021.

Dai, Serena. "Danny Meyer Admits Large Portion of Staff Left Over No-Tipping Changes." *Eater New York*, February 6, 2018. https://ny
.eater.com/2018/2/6/16978464/danny-meyer-tipping-staff-turnover.

Das Acevedo, Deepa. "Unbundling Freedom in the Sharing Economy." *Alabama Law* 91 (2017): 793–837. https://scholarship.law.ua.edu/cgi
/viewcontent.cgi?article=1076&context=fac_articles.

"Day Labor in Las Vegas: Employer Indiscretions in Sin City." Arriba Las Vegas Workers Center, January 2018. https://arribalasvegas.org
/wp-content/uploads/2019/04/Day-Labor-in-Las-Vegas-compressed.pdf.

Davidov, Guy, and Brian Langille. *The Idea of Labour Law*. Oxford: Oxford University Press, 2011.

Delgado, Hector Delgado. *New Immigrants in Old Unions*. Philadelphia: Temple University Press, 1994.

"Department of Developmental Services." Connecticut's Official State Website, accessed March 25, 2023. http://www.ct.gov/dds/lib/dds /employment/the_case_against_14c_sub_minumum_wage_program .pdf.

"Department of Labor: Case Studies from Ongoing Work Show Examples in which Wage and Hour Division Did Not Adequately Pursue Labor Violations." Government Accountability Office (2008). https://www. gao.gov/products/gao-08-973t.

"Department of Labor: Wage and Hour Division's Complaint Intake and Investigative Processes Leave Low Wage Workers Vulnerable to Wage Theft." Government Accountability Office (2009). https://www.gao .gov/products/gao-09-458t.

DePillis, Lydia. "Disabled People Are Allowed to Work for Pennies per Hour—but Maybe Not for Much Longer." *Washington Post*, February 12, 2016. https://www.washingtonpost.com/news/wonk/wp/2016 /02/12/disabled-people-are-allowed-to-work-for-pennies-per-hour -but-maybe-not-for-much-longer/?utm_term=.cb1c75c2996e.

Derenoncourt, Ellora and Claire Montialoux, "Minimum Wages and Racial Inequality." *Quarterly Journal of Economics* (2021): 169–228. https://doi.org/10.1093/qje/qjaa031.

Digirolamo, Vincent. *Crying the News: A History of America's Newsboys*. New York: Oxford University Press, 2019.

Dorris, Daniel V. "Comment: Fair Labor Standards Act Preemption of State Wage-and-Hour Law Claims." *University of Chicago Law Review* 76 (2009): 1251–1286. https://www.jstor.org/stable/27793404.

Douglas, Leah. "Coronavirus Infections at U.S. Meat Plants Far Higher Than Previous Estimates—House Subcommittee." Reuters, October 28, 2021. https://www.reuters.com/world/us/coronavirus-infections -us-meat-plants-far-higher-than-previous-estimates-house-2021 -10-27/.

Downey, Kirstin. *The Woman Behind the New Deal: The Life of Frances Perkins, FDR's Secretary of Labor and His Moral Conscience*. New York: Anchor, 2009.

Dray, Philip. *There Is Power in a Union: The Epic Story of Labor in America*. New York: Anchor, 2011.

Dreier, Hannah. "As Migrant Children Were Put to Work, U.S. Ignored Warnings." *New York Times*, April 17, 2023. https://www.nytimes.com/2023/04/17/us/politics/migrant-child-labor-biden.html.

Dubal, Veena. "Essentially Dispossessed." *South Atlantic Quarterly* 121 (2022): 285–296. http://dx.doi.org/10.2139/ssrn.4090023.

———. "The New Racial Wage Code." *Harvard Law and Policy Review* 15 (2022): 511.

Dube, Arindrajit, "Minimum Wages and the Distribution of Family Incomes." *American Economic Journal: Applied Economics* 11, no. 4 (2019): 268–304. https://doi.org/10.1257/app.20170085.

"Editorial: In Hiking the Minimum Wage, Don't Leave Tipped Workers Behind." *Los Angeles Times*, May 3, 2015. http://www.latimes.com/opinion/editorials/la-ed-tipped-minimum-wage-20150503-story.html.

"End Legacy of Slavery, One Fair Wage for All." Restaurant Opportunities Council Report, February 1, 2021. https://onefairwage.site/wp-content/uploads/2021/02/OFW_EndingLegacyOfSlavery-2.pdf.

Epps, Garrett. *Democracy Reborn: The Fourteenth Amendment and the Fight for Equal Rights in Post–Civil War America*. New York: Henry Holt and Company, 2006.

Epstein, Lee, et al. "How Business Fares in the Supreme Court." *Minnesota Law Review* 97 (2013): 1431–1472. https://www.minnesotalawreview.org/wp-content/uploads/2013/04/EpsteinLanderPosner_MLR.pdf.

Equal Employment Opportunity Commission. "Maritime Autowash Will Pay $300,000 in EEOC Race and National Origin Discrimination Case." December 19, 2018. https://www.eeoc.gov/newsroom/maritime-autowash-will-pay-300000-eeoc-race-and-national-origin-discrimination-case.

Eskridge, William N. *A Republic of Statutes: The New American Constitution*. New Haven: Yale University Press, 2010.

"Fact Sheet 14: Coverage Under the Fair Labor Standards Act (FLSA)." U.S. Department of Labor, July 2009. https://www.dol.gov/whd/regs/compliance/whdfs14.htm.

"Fair Labor Standards Act: Better Use of Available Resources and Consistent Reporting Could Improve Compliance." Government Accountability Office (2008). https://www.gao.gov/products/gao-08-962t.

Fair Labor Standards Act of 1938, 75th U.S. Congress, 75-718 (1938).

Fishkin, Joseph, and William E. Forbath. *The Anti-oligarchy Constitution: Reconstructing the Economic Foundations of American Democracy*. Cambridge, MA: Harvard University Press, 2022.

"Food Labor Research Network." UC Berkeley. http://onefairwage.site
/research.

Forbath, William E. "The New Deal Constitution in Exile." *Duke Law Journal* 51 (2001): 165–222. https://doi.org/10.2307/1373232.

———. *Law and the Shaping of the American Labor Movement.* Cambridge, MA: Harvard University Press, 1989.

"The Future of American Democracy: A Special Series from *The New Yorker*." *The New Yorker*, last modified March 30, 2023. https://www
.newyorker.com/news/the-future-of-democracy?verso=true

Frymer, Paul. *Black and Blue: African Americans, the Labor Movement, and the Decline of the Democratic Party.* Princeton: Princeton University Press, 2007.

Galemba, Rebecca Berke. *Laboring for Justice: The Fight against Wage Theft in an American City.* Stanford: Stanford University Press, 2023.

Garcia, Ahiza. "$10.10 Minimum Wage Stuck Down in Birmingham, Alabama." *CNN Business*, February 27, 2016. https://money.cnn.com
/2016/02/27/news/economy/minimum-wage-birmingham-alabama
/index.html.

Garcia, Ruben J. "Across the Borders: Immigrant Status and Identity in Law and LatCrit Theory." *Florida Law Review* 55 (2003): 511–537.
https://scholars.law.unlv.edu/cgi/viewcontent.cgi?article=1676&contex
t=facpub.

———. "Critical Race Theory and Proposition 187: The Racial Politics of Immigration Law." *Chicano-Latino Law Review*, 17 (1995): 118–154.
https://scholars.law.unlv.edu/cgi/viewcontent.cgi?article=1675&contex
t=facpub.

———. "The Human Right to Workplace Safety in a Pandemic." *Washington University Journal of Law and Policy* 64 (2021): 113–149. https://
journals.library.wustl.edu/lawpolicy/article/1039/galley/17874/view/.

———. "Labor and Property: Guestworkers, International Trade, and the Democracy Deficit." *Journal of Gender, Race and Justice* (2006):
27–65.

———. *Marginal Workers: How Legal Fault Lines Divide Workers and Leave Them without Protection.* New York: New York University Press,
2012.

———. "New Voices at Work: Races and Gender Identity Caucuses within the U.S. Labor Movement." *Hastings Law Journal* 54 (2002): 79–165.
https://repository.uchastings.edu/cgi/viewcontent.cgi?article=3502&co
ntext=hastings_law_journal.

———."Politically Engaged Unionism: The Culinary Workers Union in Las Vegas." In *The Cambridge Handbook of U.S. Labor Law for the Twenty-First Century*, ed. Richard Bales and Charlotte Garden, 373–380. Cambridge: Cambridge University Press, 2019.

———. "Prison Strike Is Reminder How Commonplace Prison Labor Is, and That It May Run Afoul of the Law." *The Conversation*, August 30, 2018.https://theconversation.com/us-prisoners-strike-is-reminder-how-commonplace-inmate-labor-is-and-that-it-may-run-afoul-of-the-law-101948.

———. "The Thirteenth Amendment and Minimum Wage Laws." *Nevada Law Journal* 19 (2018): 479–508.

"The Glass Floor: Sexual Harassment in the Restaurant Industry, Report of the Restaurant Opportunities Center." Last modified October 7, 2014. https://nature.berkeley.edu/agroecologylab/wp-content/uploads/2020/06/The-Glass-Floor-Sexual-Harassment-in-the-Restaurant-Industry.pdf.

Gleeson, Shannon M. *Conflicting Commitments: The Politics of Enforcing Immigrant Worker Rights in San Jose and Houston*. Ithaca: Cornell University Press, 2012.

———. *Precarious Claims: The Promise and Failure of Workplace Protections in the United States*. Oakland: University of California Press, 2016.

Goluboff, Risa L. *The Lost Promise of Civil Rights*. Cambridge, MA: Harvard University Press, 2010.

Gonzalez, Carmen, and Athena Mutua. "Mapping Racial Law Capitalism: Implications for Law." *Journal of Law and Political Economy* 2, no. 2 (2022): 127–201.

Gordon, Jennifer. *Suburban Sweatshops: The Fight for Immigrant Rights*. Cambridge, MA: Harvard University Press, 2005.

Graber, Mark A. "The Second Freedmen's Bureau Bill's Constitution." *Texas Law Review* 94 (2016): 1361–1402. https://texaslawreview.org/wp-content/uploads/2016/09/Graber.pdf.

Grady, Jennifer. "What Is the Living Wage Movement?" *Library Worklife*, 2004. http://ala-apa.org/newsletter/2004/06/16/what-is-the-living-wage-movement/.

Grant, Melissa Gira. *Playing the Whore*. New York: Verso, 2014.

Greene, Jamal. "Thirteenth Amendment Optimism." *Columbia Law Review* 112 (2012): 1733–1768. https://scholarship.law.columbia.edu/cgi/viewcontent.cgi?article=1648&context=faculty_scholarship.

Gwin, Caity. "Goals on the Pole: Strippers' Fight for Workplace Rights: Legal Tools at Our Disposal." In *Sex Work Now*, ed. Bernadette Barton, Barb Brents, and Angela Jones. New York: New York University Press, forthcoming.

Hardaway, Ayesha Bell. "The Paradox of the Right to Contract: Noncompete Agreements as Thirteenth Amendment Violations." *Seattle University Law Review* 39 (2016): 957–981. https://digitalcommons.law.seattleu.edu/cgi/viewcontent.cgi?article=2334&context=sulr.

Hart, Vivien. *Bound by Our Constitution: Women, Workers, and the Minimum Wage*. Princeton: Princeton University Press, 1994.

Hatton, Erin. *Coerced: Work Under Threat of Punishment*. Oakland: University of California Press, 2020.

———. *Labor and Punishment: Work In and Out of Prison*. Oakland: University of California Press, 2021.

Hernández-Truyol, Berta Esperanza, and Jane E. Larson, "Sexual Labor and Human Rights." *Columbia Human Rights Law Review* 37 (2006): 391–445.

Hounshell, Blake. "Is Nevada Turning Red?" *New York Times*, June 15, 2022. https://www.nytimes.com/live/2022/06/13/us/midterm-primary-elections.

Hutchinson, Harry. "Waging War on the 'Unemployables'? Race, Low-Wage Work and Minimum Wages: The New Evidence," *Hofstra Labor and Employment Law Journal* 29 (2011): 25–47.

Hsu, Andrea. "Do-Over Union Election at Amazon's Bessemer Warehouse Is Too Close to Call." *NPR*, March 31, 2022. https://www.npr.org/2022/03/31/1090123017/do-over-union-election-at-amazons-bessemer-warehouse-is-too-close-to-call.

"International Labour Migration: A Rights-Based Approach." International Labour Organization, April 29, 2010. https://www.ilo.org/global/publications/books/WCMS_125361/lang--en/index.htm.

Jamieson, David. "Student Guestworkers at Hershey's Plant Allege Exploitative Conditions." *HuffPost*, updated December 6, 2017. https://www.huffingtonpost.com/2011/08/17/student-guestworkers-at-hershey-plant_n_930014.html.

Jayaraman, Saru. *Behind the Kitchen Door*. Ithaca: Cornell University Press, 2013.

———. *Forked: A New Standard of American Dining*. New York: Oxford University Press, 2016.

Johnson, Gene. "Washington Supreme Court: Farmworkers to Get Overtime Pay." Associated Press, November 5, 2020. https://apnews .com/article/washington-agriculture-d4d155379061da6798e179034209 3ed4.

Kahlenberg, Richard D. *Why Labor Organizing Should Be a Civil Right.* New York: The Century Foundation Press, 2012.

Karlamanga, Soumya. "California's Statewide Minimum Wage Is Now $16 an Hour." *New York Times,* January 2, 2024.

Kay, Tamara. *NAFTA and the Politics of Transnationalism.* Cambridge: Cambridge University Press, 2011.

Kay, Tamara, and R. L. Evans. *Trade Battles: Activism and the Politicization of the International Trade Policy.* New York: Oxford University Press, 201

Keck, Margaret E., and Kathryn Sikkink. *Activists Beyond Borders.* Ithaca: Cornell University Press, 1998.

Kens, Paul. *Judicial Power and Reform Politics: The Anatomy of* Lochner v. New York. Lawrence: University Press of Kansas, 1990.

King, Shaun. "How the 13th Amendment Didn't Really Abolish Slavery, but Let It Live On in U.S. Prisons." *Daily News,* September 21, 2016. http://www.nydailynews.com/news/national/king-13th-amendment -didn-abolish-slavery-article-1.2801218.

Kurtz, Annalyn, and Tal Yellin. "Minimum Wage Since 1938." *CNN,* April 9, 2019. https://money.cnn.com/interactive/economy/minimum-wage -since-1938/.

"Labor Law Highlights, 1915–2015." *Monthly Labor Review,* October 2015. https://www.bls.gov/opub/mlr/2015/article/pdf/labor-law -highlights-1915-2015.pdf.

Lamoreaux, Naomi R., and William J. Novak. *Corporations and American Democracy.* Cambridge, MA: Harvard University Press, 2017.

"Letters: Rick Bayless: Chicago Restaurants Are Working to Become More Equitable, Sustainable." *Chicago Tribune,* June 9, 2021.

Levin, Benjamin. "Criminal Employment Law." *University of Colorado Law School* 39 (2018): 2265–2325. https://scholar.law.colorado.edu/cgi /viewcontent.cgi?article=2292&context=faculty-articles.

———. "Criminal Labor Law." *Berkeley Journal of Employment and Labor Law* 37, no. 2 (2016): 43–100. https://www.jstor.org/stable/26356859.

———. "Wage Theft Criminalization." *UC Davis Law Review* (2021): 1429–1506. https://lawreview.law.ucdavis.edu/issues/54/3/articles /files/54-3_Levin.pdf.

Levin-Waldman, Oren M. *Restoring the Middle Class through Wage Policy: Arguments for a Minimum Wage*. New York: Palgrave Macmillan, 2018.

Linder, Marc. *Farewell to the Self-Employed: Deconstructing a Socioeconomic and Legal Solipsism*. New York: Greenwood Press, 1992.

———. *Wars of Attrition: Vietnam, the Business Roundtable, and the Decline of Construction Unions*. Iowa City: Fanpìhuà Press, 2000.

López, Ian Haney. *Merge Left: Fusing Race and Class, Winning Elections, and Saving America*. New York: The New Press, 2019.

Luce, Stephanie. *Fighting for a Living Wage*. Ithaca: Cornell University Press, 2004.

Lynn, Michael. "Tipping in Restaurants around the Globe: An Interdisciplinary Review." In *Handbook of Contemporary Behavioral Economics*, ed. Morris Altman, 626–645. New York: M. E. Sharpe Publishing, 2006.

Man, Anthony. "South Florida a 'Hotspot' for Human Trafficking." *Orlando Sun Sentinel*, January 13, 2018. https://www.sun-sentinel.com/news/nationworld/fl-reg-human-trafficking-visas-deutch-frankel-20180111-story.html.

Mancini, Al. "In Las Vegas, Server Is a Serious, Well-Paying Career." *Las Vegas Review Journal*, September 1, 2018. https://www.reviewjournal.com/entertainment/food/in-las-vegas-restaurant-server-is-serious-well-paying-career/.

Maravit, Moshe. *Why Labor Organizing Should Be a Civil Right*. New York: The Century Foundation Press, 2012.

Marbleston, Judy, and Kathleen S. Erskine. "The Movement Takes the Lead." In *Cause Lawyers and Social Movement*, ed. Austin Sarat and Stuart Scheingold, 249–277. Stanford: Stanford University Press, 2006.

Marr, Chris. "Hawaii Governor Signs $18 Minimum Wage Law, First of Its Kind." *Bloomberg Law*, June 22, 2022. https://news.bloomberglaw.com/daily-labor-report/hawaii-governor-signs-18-minimum-wage-law-first-of-its-kind.

Martinez, Jenny S. *The Slave Trade and the Origins of International Human Rights Law*. New York: Oxford University Press, 2012.

Maslin Nir, Sarah. "Benefits, and Some Resistance, as New York Cracks Down on Nail Salon Abuses. *New York Times*, July 16, 2015. https://www.nytimes.com/2015/07/17/nyregion/benefits-and-some-resistance-as-new-york-cracks-down-on-nail-salon-abuses.html.

Matsuda, Mari. "Looking to the Bottom: Critical Legal Studies and Reparations." *Harvard Civil Rights–Civil Liberties Law Review* 22 (1987): 323–399.

McDonald, Esther S. "Patenting Human Life and the Rebirth of the Thirteenth Amendment." *Notre Dame Law Review* 78 (2003): 1359–1387. https://scholarship.law.nd.edu/cgi/viewcontent.cgi?article=1482&context=ndlr.

McGhee, Heather. *The Sum of Us: What Racism Costs Everyone and How We Can Prosper Together.* New York: One World, 2021.

Milkman, Ruth, and Kent Wong. *Voices from the Front Lines: Organizing Immigrant Workers in Los Angeles.* Los Angeles: UCLA Center for Labor Research and Education, 2000.

"Minimum Wages for Tipped Employees." U.S. Department of Labor, accessed March 30, 2023. https://www.dol.gov/whd/state/tipped.htm.

Morrison, Alan. "Is the Trans-Pacific Partnership Unconstitutional?" *The Atlantic*, June 23, 2015. https://www.theatlantic.com/politics/archive/2015/06/tpp-isds-constitution/396389/.

Müller, Torsten. "Minimum Wage Developments in 2022—Fighting the Cost-of-Living Crisis." *European Economic, Employment and Social Policy* (February 2023): 1–10. https://www.etui.org/sites/default/files/2023-03/Minimum%20wage%20developments%20in%202022-fighting%20the%20cost-of-living%20crisis_2023.pdf.

National Conference of State Legislatures. "State Minimum Wages." August 30, 2022. http://www.ncsl.org/research/labor-and-employment/state-minimum-wage-chart.aspx

Nayak, Rajesh, and Paul Sonn. *Restoring the Minimum Wage for America's Tipped Workers.* National Employment Law Project Report, August 2009.

Ness, Immanuel. *Guest Workers and Resistance to U.S. Corporate Despotism.* Urbana: University of Illinois Press, 2011.

Nevarez, Griselda. "Latino Workers Helped Rebuild New Orleans, but Many Weren't Paid." *NBC News*, August 28, 2015. https://www.nbcnews.com/storyline/hurricane-katrina-anniversary/latino-workers-helped-rebuild-new-orleans-many-werent-paid-n417571.

Ontiveros, Maria L. "Noncitizen Immigrant Labor and the Thirteenth Amendment: Challenging Guest Worker Programs." *University of Toledo Law Review* 38 (2006–2007): 923–939. https://heinonline.org/HOL/LandingPage?handle=hein.journals/utol38&div=62&id=&page=.

Orleck, Annelise. *"We Are All Fast-Food Workers Now": The Global Uprising against Poverty Wages*. Boston: Beacon Press, 2018.

Perea, Juan F. "The Echoes of Slavery: Recognizing the Racist Origins of the Agricultural and Domestic Worker Exclusion from the National Labor Relations Act." *Ohio State Law Journal* 95 (2011): 95–138. https://kb.osu.edu/bitstream/handle/1811/71439/OSLJ_V72N1_0095 .pdf.

Pollin, Robert, et al. "How Santa Monica Workers Would Have Benefited from a $10.75 Living Wage." In *A Measure of Fairness*, ed. Robert Pollin, 118–134. Ithaca: Cornell University Press, 2018.

Poo, Ai-Jen. *The Age of Dignity: Preparing for the Elder Boom in a Changing America*. New York: The New Press, 2016.

Pope, James Gray. "Contract, Race, and Freedom of Labor in the Law of Involuntary Servitude." *Yale Law Journal* 119 (2010): 1474–1567. https:// www.yalelawjournal.org/pdf/880_8jeqgf27.pdf.

———. "Labor's Constitution of Freedom." *Yale Law Journal* 106 (1997): 941–1031. https://openyls.law.yale.edu/bitstream/handle/20.500.13051 /9001/38_106YaleLJ941_1996_1997_.pdf?sequence=2.

"Poverty Thresholds." U.S. Census Bureau, accessed March 25, 2023. https://www.census.gov/data/tables/time-series/demo/income-poverty /historical-poverty-thresholds.html.

Prassl, Jeremias. *The Concept of the Employer*. Oxford: Oxford University Press, 2015.

Rauch, Jonathan. *The Constitution of Knowledge*. Washington, D.C.: Brookings Institution Press, 2021.

Rahman, K. Sabeel. *Democracy against Domination*. New York: Oxford University Press, 2017.

Reddy, Diana S. "After the Law of Apolitical Economy: Reclaiming the Normative Stakes of Labor Unions." *Yale Law Journal* (2023): 1391–1461. https://www.yalelawjournal.org/pdf/132.5.Reddy_vu6m11dz.pdf

Reich, Michael et al. *When Mandates Work: Raising Labor Standards at the Local Level*. Berkeley: University of California Press, 2014.

Roediger, David R., and Phillip Sheldon Foner. *Our Own Time: A History of American Labor and the Working Day*. New York: Verso, 1989.

Rogers, Brishen. "Justice at Work: Minimum Wage Laws and Social Equality." *Texas Law Review* (2014): 1543, 1582–1586.

———. "The Law and Political Economy of Workplace Technological Change." *Harvard Civil Rights–Civil Liberties law Review* 55 (2020): 531–584.

Rolf, David. *The Fight for $15: The Right Wage for a Working America.* New York: The New Press, 2016.

Rosenberg, Gerald N. *The Hollow Hope: Can the Courts Bring About Social Change?* Chicago: University of Chicago Press, 1991.

Rosenblat, Alex. *Uberland: How Algorithms Are Rewriting the Rules of Work.* Oakland: University of California Press, 2018.

Rosenblum, Jonathan. *Beyond $15: Immigration Workers, Faith Activists, and the Revival of the Labor Movement.* Boston: Beacon Press, 2017.

Rosenfeld, Jake. *You're Paid What You're Worth: And Other Myths of the Modern Economy.* Cambridge, MA: Harvard University Press, 2021.

Ross, McKenna. "Station Casinos Begins Demolition of 2 Local Properties." *Las Vegas Review-Journal,* September 12, 2022. https://www.reviewjournal.com/business/casinos-gaming/station-casinos-begins-demolition-of-2-local-properties-2638712/.

Ross, Robert J. S. *Slaves to Fashion: Poverty and Abuse in the New Sweatshops.* Ann Arbor: University of Michigan Press, 2004.

Russell, Kari. "A Higher Minimum Wage in 2017." *New York Times,* January 5, 2017. https://www.nytimes.com/interactive/2017/01/05/business/economy/state-minimum-wages.html.

Ryssal, Kai, and Livi Burdette. "How Ride-Hail Companies Use Data to Pay Drivers Less." *Marketplace,* April 10, 2023. https://www.marketplace.org/2023/04/10/how-ride-hail-companies-use-data-to-pay-drivers-less/.

Saitone, Tina L., et al. "COVID-19 Morbidity and Mortality in U.S. Meatpacking Counties." *Food Policy* 101 (2021): 1–19. https://doi.org/10.1016/j.foodpol.2021.102072.

Samuels, Robert, and Toluse Olorunnipa. *His Name Is George Floyd: One Man's Life and the Struggle for Racial Justice.* New York: Viking, 2022.

Sarat, Austin, and Stuart A. Scheingold. *Cause Lawyers and Social Movements.* Stanford: Stanford University Press, 2006.

Saucedo, Leticia M. "The Employer Preference for the Subservient Worker and the Making of the Brown Collar Workplace." *Ohio State Law Journal* 67 (2006): 961–1021.

Segrave, Kerry. *Tipping: An American Social History of Gratuities.* Jefferson, NC: McFarland, 1998.

Semuels, Alana. "The Internet Is Enabling a New Kind of Poorly Paid Hell." *The Atlantic,* January 23, 2018. https://www.theatlantic.com/technology/archive/2018/08/fiverr-online-gig-economy/569083/.

Shane, Peter M. *Democracy's Chief Executive: Interpreting the Constitution and Defining the Future of the Presidency.* Oakland: University of California Press, 2022.

"Shield from Justice: Police Brutality and Accountability in the United States." Federal Passivity, Human Rights Watch, accessed March 25, 2023. https://www.hrw.org/legacy/reports98/police /uspo33.htm.

Skelton, George. "It's No Wonder Hundreds of Millions Have Been Spent on Prop. 22. A Lot Is at Stake." *Los Angeles Times*, October 16, 2020. https://www.latimes.com/california/story/2020-10-16/skelton -proposition-22-uber-lyft-independent-contractors.

Smialek, Jeanna. "The Nobel in Economics Goes to Three Who Find Experiments in Real Life." *New York Times*, October 11, 2021. https:// www.nytimes.com/2021/10/11/business/nobel-economics-prize-david -card-joshua-angrist-guido-imbens.html.

Soifer, Aviam. "Federal Protection, Paternalism, and the Virtually Forgotten Prohibition of Voluntary Peonage." *Columbia Law Review* 112, no. 7 (November 2012): 1607–1640. https://www.jstor.org/stable /41708160.

———. "The Floor and More." In *The Promises of Liberty: The History and Contemporary Relevance of the Thirteenth Amendment*, ed. Alexander Tsesis, 196–225. New York: Columbia University Press, 2010.

———. *Law and the Company We Keep.* Cambridge, MA: Harvard University Press, 1998.

———. "Old Lines in New Battles: An Overlooked Yet Useful Statute to Confront Exploitation of Undocumented Workers by Employers and by Ice." *Nevada Law Journal* 19, no. 2 (Winter 2018): 397–412. https:// scholars.law.unlv.edu/cgi/viewcontent.cgi?article=1782&context=nlj.

Soni, Saket. *The Great Escape: A True Story of Forced Labor and Immigrant Dreams in America.* Chapel Hill, NC: Algonquin Books of Chapel Hill, 2023.

Southworth, Ann. *Lawyers of the Right: Professionalizing the Conservative Coalition.* Chicago: University of Chicago Press, 2008.

"State Minimum Wage Laws." U.S. Department of Labor, January 1, 2023. https://www.dol.gov/whd/minwage/america.htm.

"Subminimum Wage." U.S. Department of Labor, accessed March 30, 2023. https://www.dol.gov/general/topic/wages/subminimumwage.

tenBroek, Jacob. "Thirteenth Amendment to the Constitution of the United States: Consummation to Abolition and Key to the Fourteenth

Amendment." *California Law Review* 39, no. 2 (1951): 171–203. https://doi.org/10.2307/3478033.

Theodore, Nik. "Day-Labor Worker Centers: Advancing New Models of Equity and Inclusion in the Informal Economy." *Economic Development Quarterly* (2023): 1–12. https://doi.org/10.1177/08912424231165004.

Thies, Clifford F. "The First Minimum Wage Laws." *Cato Journal* 10 (1991): 715–746. https://www.cato.org/sites/cato.org/files/serials/files/cato-journal/1991/1/cj10n3–7.pdf.

Thompson, Lynn, and Andy Martinez. "Seattle City Council Approves Historic $15 Minimum Wage." *Seattle Times*, June 2, 2014, updated January 25, 2016. https://www.seattletimes.com/seattle-news/seattle-city-council-approves-historic-15-minimum-wage/.

Trottman, Melanie. "Workers Sue Over Alabama Wage Law, Citing Civil Rights." *Wall Street Journal*, April 28, 2016. https://www.wsj.com/articles/workers-sue-over-alabama-wage-law-citing-civil-rights-1461853686.

Tsesis, Alexander. *Destructive Messages: How Hate Speech Paves the Way for Harmful Social Movements.* New York: New York University Press, 2002.

———. "Into the Light of Day: Relevance of the Thirteenth Amendment to Contemporary Law." *Columbia Law Review* 1447 (2012): 1447–1458. https://www.jstor.org/stable/41708155.

———. *The Thirteenth Amendment and American Freedom.* New York: New York University Press, 2004.

———. *We Shall Overcome: A History of Civil Rights and the Law.* New Haven: Yale University Press, 2008.

Valdes, Francisco. "Legal Reform and Social Justice: An Introduction to LatCrit Theory, Praxis and Community." *University of Miami Law Review* 14, no. 2 (2005): 148–173. https://repository.law.miami.edu/cgi/viewcontent.cgi?article=1512&context=fac_articles.

VanderVelde, Lea. "The Labor Vision of the Thirteenth Amendment." *University of Pennsylvania Law Review* 138 (1989): 437–504. https://scholarship.law.upenn.edu/cgi/viewcontent.cgi?article=3786&context=penn_law_review.

Vinel, Jean-Christian. *The Employee: A Political History.* Philadelphia: University of Pennsylvania Press, 2013.

Vorenberg, Michael. *Final Freedom: The Civil War, the Abolition of Slavery, and the Thirteenth Amendment.* Cambridge: Cambridge University Press, 2004.

Walsh, Shannon, director. *The Gig Is Up*. London: Dogwoof Pictures, 2021. https://tubitv.com/movies/654449/the-gig-is-up?start=true& tracking=google-feed&utm_source=google-feed.

Weil, David. *The Fissured Workplace: Why Work Became So Bad for So Many and What Can Be Done to Improve It*. Cambridge, MA: Harvard University Press, 2014.

Weinrib, Laura. *The Taming of Free Speech: America's Civil Liberties Compromise*. Cambridge, MA: Harvard University Press, 2016.

Weissman, Jordan G. "What Would Happen if We Tore Up the Minimum Wage?" *Slate*, May 24, 2015. http://www.slate.com/articles/business /moneybox/2014/05/ending_the_minimum_wage_what_happens_if _we_tear_up_the_pay_floor.html.

Whitaker, William. "The Tip Credit Provisions of the Fair Labor Standards Act." *Congressional Research Service Report*, March 24, 2006. https://www.everycrsreport.com/files/20060324_RL33348_ ad85f13a3a41cd5fafd56b16338e820ac7136692.pdf.

White, Gillian B. "Should Cities Have a Different Minimum Wage Than Their State?" *The Atlantic*, January 15, 2015. https://www.theatlantic .com/business/archive/2015/01/should-cities-have-a-different-minimum- wage-than-their-state/384516/.

Wilde Anderson, Michelle. *The Fight to Save the Town: Reimagining Discarded America*. New York: Avid Reader Press/Simon & Schuster, 2022.

Wilson, Eli Revelle Yano. *Front of the House, Back of the House: Race and Inequality in the Lives of Restaurant Workers*. New York: New York University Press, 2021.

Winkler, Adam. *Gunfight: The Battle over the Right to Bear Arms in America*. New York: W. W. Norton, 2011.

Witt, John Fabian. *The Accidental Republic: Crippled Workingmen, Destitute Widows, and the Remaking of American Law*. Cambridge, MA: Harvard University Press, 2004.

Wolff, Tobias Barrington. "The Thirteenth Amendment and Global Slavery." *Columbia Law Review* 102 (2002): 973–1050. ttps://doi.org/10 .2307/1123649.

Wood, Ellen Meiksins. *Rising from the Ashes? Labor in The Age of "Global" Capitalism*. New York: Monthly Review Press, 1998.

Zatz, Noah. "The Minimum Wage as a Civil Rights Protection: An Alternative to Antipoverty Arguments?" *University of Chicago Legal*

Forum 3 (2009): 1–47. https://chicagounbound.uchicago.edu/cgi /viewcontent.cgi?article=1439&context=uclf.

———. "Working beyond the Reach or Grasp of Employment Law." In *The Gloves-Off Economy: Problems and Possibilities at the Bottom of America's Labor Market*, ed. Annette Bernhardt, Heather Boushey, Laura Dresser, and Chris Tilly, 31–64. Champaign: Labor and Employment Relations Association, University of Illinois at Urbana -Champaign, 2008.

Zietlow, Rebecca E. "A Positive Right to Free Labor." *Seattle University Law Review* 39 (2016): 859–899. https://digitalcommons.law.seattleu .edu/cgi/viewcontent.cgi?article=2331&context=sulr.

———. "Free at Last! Anti-subordination and the Thirteenth Amendment." *Boston University Law Review* 255 (2010): 255–312. https:// www.bu.edu/law/journals-archive/bulr/documents/zietlow.pdf.

———. "James Ashley's Thirteenth Amendment." *Columbia Law Review* (2012): 1697–1731. https://www.jstor.org/stable/41708162.

———. "The Rights of Citizenship: Two Framers, Two Amendments." *Pennsylvania Journal of Constitutional Law* 11 (2009): 1269–1288. https://scholarship.law.upenn.edu/cgi/viewcontent.cgi?article= 1172&context=jcl.

Zipperer, Ben. "The Minimum Wage Has Lost 21 percent of Its Value Since Congress Last Raised the Wage." Economic Political Institute, July 22, 2021. https://www.epi.org/blog/the-minimum-wage-has-lost- 21-of-its-value-since-congress-last-raised-the-wage/.

Index

Allied Signal Shipyard (Signal International LLC). *See* guest workers

Amalgamated Clothing and Textile Workers Union (ACTWU): supported liberal labor legislation in the 1930s, 33–34

Amazon corporation: effort to unionize at Bessemer (Alabama) warehouse, 100–101, 122–23; successful drive to unionize Staten Island warehouse, 101–2; use of subcontractors in operation of warehouses, 106; use of U.S. workers for minimal, repetitive tasks, 100

American Federation of Labor–Congress of Industrial Organizations (AFL-CIO): merger (1955), 34; position on immigrants and impact on legal cases, 152; support for legalization and opposition to employer sanctions, 151

Americans with Disabilities Act of 1990 (ADA), 41, 70; as civil rights statute, 40–41; did not address subminimum wage for disabled persons, 70–71, 87

Apple Inc.: immigrants and workers of color make up significant proportion of workers at, 123; laid off workers, 123; raised starting salary to $22 an hour, 123; raising of wages aimed at staving off unionization, 123; store workers in Maryland voted for union representation, 123

Arriba Las Vegas Workers Center, 57; assist low-wage immigrant workers obtain wages due, 61–62

Bell, Derrick: and racial realism, 25

Bernstein, David: argues that prevailing wage laws should be repealed, 51; critical of prevailing wage statutes, 15; prevailing wage laws created to protect white union workers, 15; prevailing wages negatively impact African Americans, 51

Biden, Joseph R. (president): continued some of predecessor's reversal of

Biden, Joseph R *(continued)*
    federal enforcement, 120; most pro-
    union president, 120; proposed Build
    Back Better law, 136
Black Lives Matter (BLM): corporate sup-
    port for, 119; goals of, 6; and inequi-
    ties in workplace, education, and
    government, 25; struggle for higher
    wages and labor rights, 6
Brotherhood of Sleeping Car Porters:
    organized along racial and gender
    lines, 33

Card, David, 20
Century City police violence (1990), 35
chain of service: Department of Labor
    rule upheld in court, 133; described,
    66, 69; hierarchy in hospitality sector,
    66; incentives to discriminate, 69;
    racially organized, 66, 69
Civil Rights Act of 1866, 76
Civil Rights Act of 1964: integrated labor
    rights as civil rights, 41; limits of legal
    claims using Title VII, 27, 43; link to
    Fair Labor Standards Act of 1938, 24;
    supported by United Auto Workers
    (UAW), 34; supported by United
    Steelworkers (USW), 34; Title VII
    bans occupational segregations, 27;
    Title VII failed to close pay gap
    between white and non-white work-
    ers, 142
Civil Rights Act of 1991, 42
"civil rights law" vs. "labor law": long-
    standing split, 40
collective bargaining agreements: impor-
    tant avenue for greater domestic
    worker power, 22; covered workers
    below New Deal wage level, 1; histori-
    cal role of unions in enforcing, 61;
    important vehicle to raise wages, 6,
    70; International Labour Organiza-
    tion Convention No. 98 and, 148; law
    can disadvantage workers of color, 17;
    10 percent of workers represented by a
    union, 143; as vehicle to more equita-
    bly regulate tips, 69;
college athlete workers, 37
Contreras, Miguel, 35

Coronavirus Relief Act of 2020: distribu-
    tion of $600 for some U.S. residents,
    136; hazard pay reimbursement, 118–19
Cover, Robert: on legal institutions and
    actions having a local context, 141
COVID-19 pandemic: alleged shortage of
    workers, 19; altered the workplace,
    118; broad impacts of, 118–19; and
    constructs of "essential" jobs/workers,
    10; disproportionate impact on immi-
    grants and minorities, 10; and eco-
    nomic inequality, 9; employers able to
    operate with fewer workers, 19;
    exposed the weaknesses in worker
    protection, 143; and extraordinary
    presidential powers, 128; impact on
    restaurants, 133; more than a million
    deaths in the U.S. during, 116
Crenshaw, Kimberlé Williams: develop-
    ment of critical race theory (CRT), 14;
    differential treatment of legal claims,
    23, 114; and intersectionality, 6; mar-
    ginalization of women of color by Title
    VII, 27; paradox of intersectionality in
    legal claims, 6
critical race praxis: defined, 24
critical race theory (CRT): aims to identify
    potential remedies for racialized minori-
    ties, 17; Biden rescinded predecessor's
    executive order on, 13; and commodifi-
    cation of labor, 18; concern with sys-
    temic racism in labor market, 20;
    counterpoint to law and economic
    movement, 20; critics view of, 14–15;
    described, 14–15; emergence and chal-
    lenge to critical legal studies, 16–17;
    encompasses a normative concern, 20;
    higher minimum wage necessary for
    greater racial justice, 16, 18; limited
    application to labor and employment
    law, 15; linkage between race and class,
    22, 28; need to recognize articulation
    between race and wage discrimination,
    21; and paradox of employment laws,
    17–18; and Proposition 187, 14; and rec-
    ognition that law fails marginal workers,
    16, 17; role in linking social movements,
    24; seeks to explain law's subordination
    of people of color, 17; spread beyond law

schools, 13–14; and structural determinism, 17; Trump executive order on, 13
critical wage theory (CWT): benefit to workers of color, 3; explained, 2; as framework to examine economic subordination of workers, 117; importance of improving racial minorities and the use of, 16; and legal revolution in the 1930s, 3; normative arguments, 3–4; not limited to analysis of statistical data, 3; and raising and enforcing minimum wages, 3; related to racial justice, 4
Culinary Workers Union Local 226: and coalescence of groups of color, 34; covers over 60,000 workers on Las Vegas Strip, 69; effort to regularize tipping system, 69; less than 10 percent of hospitality workers covered by collective bargaining agreements, 69–70; as politically powerful, 110; success in linking state to federal minimum wage in Nevada constitution, 110–11
Cummings, Scott: analysis of garment workers campaign against Guess?, 32; importance of cross-racial organizing, 32; on broadening Los Angeles's worker retention ordinance, 36

Davis Bacon Act of 1931: established prevailing wages for government contracts, 51; positive impact on workers, 51–52
day laborers: assisted by Arriba Las Vegas Workers Center, 61–62; labor movement interest in organizing, 151; share misclassification with guest workers and sex workers, 12; victims of misclassification and wage theft, 12
Defense Production Act: meatpacking workers compelled to work under, 122
dignity deficit, 8
disabled workers in sheltered workshops: Americans with Disabilities Act of 1990 did not end disparate wages for, 70–71, 87; formal exploitation of, 70–71; legally sanctioned subminimum wage for, 2, 65, 70, 81, 86; and involuntary servitude, 71; may earn less than $1 an hour, 70, 87; Wage and Hour Division (WHD) administrator can issue partial exemptions to minimum wages for, 62. See also Thirteenth Amendment
Durazo, María Elena: Asian and Latino distribution in work tasks, 35–36; diversity in union membership, 35; president of Hotel Employees and Restaurant Employees (HERE) Union Local 11, 35; role in creation of worker retention ordinance (WRO), 36; supported creation of Los Angeles for a New Economy (LAANE), 35

Economic Policy Institute (EPI): on impact of raising minimum wage, 119
eight-hour workday, 9; enacted by Congress in 1868, 79; few people actually work an, 143; Haymarket protestors in 1887, 79; initially applied only to federal employees, 79; promoted by the Women's Trade Union League, 33
El Monte sweatshop case. See Uvawas
enforcement of labor laws: failure in, 10–11
Equal Pay Act of 1963: failed to close pay gap between white and non-white workers, 142; link to Fair Labor Standards Act of 1938, 42; protects against pay disparities based on sex, 42. See also Ledbetter, Lilly
essential workers: Congress provided hazard pay reimbursement to employers, 119; COVID-19 pandemic and the label, 10
exotic dancers: appellate court judge on application of Fair Labor Standards Act of 1938 to, 47; considered employees by courts, 46–47, 49; as contested term, 48; creation of a union of, 49; demands for overtime pay and minimum wages, 66; seeking minimum wages, 3; misclassification as "independent contractors," 46; successful wage case (Reich v. Circle C Investments), 48. See also sex workers

Fair Labor Standards Act of 1938 (FLSA): amendments in 1948 required employers to pay at least $2.13 an hour, 68; based on Congress's power to regulate interstate commerce, 140; created the minimum hourly wage, 68; enacted in response to activism and labor movement, 33; excluded agricultural workers and domestic workers, 15; excludes people of color and women, 16; exemptions to minimum wage, 70, 86; interstate commerce and, 139; limits of legal claims using Title VII and, 43; link to Equal Pay Act of 1963, 42; occupational exclusions impact on Black and Mexican laborers, 103; occupational exemptions in, 107; "paycheck rule" and, 42; racial origins of, 15; racial political economy of, 102–4; states allowed to legislate working hours, 137; tipped minimum wage and, 88; upheld against constitutional challenges, 139; Wilkinson, J. Harvie (judge), opinion on, 47; workers worked only for tips until 1948, 68

federal minimum wage: current level set in 2009, 1, 123, 125; disproportionate harm on people of color and immigrants, 2, 4, 5; enforcement of, 6; indexing to productivity and inflation, 8; low-wage work and, 3; as measure of how workers and work are valued, 7; millions of workers paid below or at, 4; minimal standard of living and, 4, 5; racial and sexual discrimination, 2, 19; reduction of race-based market failures, 10; set at $7.25 per hour, 1, 123, 125

federal subminimum wages: legacy of racism in, 8; sheltered workshops for disabled and, 2; social justice and elimination of, 7; tipped workers and, 64; wait staff at restaurants and, 2. See also legally sanctioned subminimum wages

Fight for $15: and actual cost of living, 16–27; broad success of, 126, 147, 150; and drive for racial and economic justice, 147; impact on overseas wages,

150, 156; organizing in Santa Monica (California), 31; potential for standardization of minimum wages, or a minimum income, 147; role of immigrants and people of color in, 24; role of Service Employees International Union (SEIU) in, 36; sought a $15 minimum wage and creation of union, 1, 53, 126–27, 149; and substantive standards, 156; success in fast-food sector, 1, 7–8

Floyd, George: killed by police officers, 6, 25, 116, 119; and low-wage jobs, 119; prison laborer, 119; proliferation of protests, 9, 119

Fourteenth Amendment (1868): developed jurisprudence, 74; and enforcement of federal labor laws, 84; limited governmental obligations under, 77–78; limited state obligations under, 80; and Oregon and Washington challenge to exclusion of agricultural workers from minimum wage, 129–30; and positive governmental obligations, 75; and rights against government interference, 75; Thirteenth Amendment and, 77, 78; Thirteenth Amendment and litigation, 74, 75–76, 84; weakness in, 77; and welfare rights movement, 89

ghost workers, 100

gig workers: ABC test, 38; California legislative enactment of Dynamex, 39; cases against Uber, Door Dash, and Instacart, 38; and "casualization" of employment, 38; drivers as de facto employees, 38; Gonzalez, Lorena, authored California Assembly Bill 5, 39; industry structured to avoid payment of minimum wage, overtime, and workers' compensation, 38; parallel to sex work industry, 38; potential legal actions against corporation related to "involuntary servitude," 85; pro-employee bias in the law (Dynamex v. Superior Court), 38; Uber and liens on privately-owned cars, 84–85. See also Thirteenth Amendment global minimum wage, 144, 147; and absence of universal minimum wage requirement, 153; difficult to set, 148; Gephardt, Richard (congressman), proposal for, 153; and problem with setting minimum wage by the hour, 156; skepticism about, 145

Gompers, Samuel: founder and president of American Federation of Labor (AFL), 34

governmental complicity in subminimum wages, 84; five states with no minimum wage for work not covered by Fair Labor Standards Act of 1938, 86, 91

Greenstone, Ellen: and case of exotic dancers regarding wages, 45; former attorney with United Farm Workers (UFW), 45; partner at Rothner, Segall, and Greenstone, 29

guest workers: Allied Signal Shipyard (Signal International LLC) did not pay minimum wage or overtime to, 58; Allied Signal Shipyard trafficked Indian, 58–59; assisted by Southern Poverty Law Center against abusive employers, 83; exploitation of J-1 visa, 86; held in slavery in Florida, 86; and increasing pressures to expand temporary worker visas, 147; litigation against Allied Signal Shipyard, 58; South Carolina golf resort exploitation of H-2B, 83; in states with no minimum wage, worst abuses suffered by, 83; victims of misclassification and wage theft, 12

Hoffman Plastic Compounds: court decision on immigrant workers' back pay claims (*Hoffman v. National Labor Relations Board*, 2002), 55; undocumented workers not entitled to remedies because of immigration status, 55, 152; and undocumented workers' right to receive minimum wages, 55–56

home health care workers: and classification as "partial public employees," 22; earn low wages, 22; misclassification as independent contractors, 22

hospitality industry: chain of service hierarchy in, 66; pooling of tips and floor persons in casinos, 67; problems defining who is a supervisor in, 66–67

Hutchinson, Harry: minimum wage laws and Black unemployment, 15; New Deal minimum wage law as action to benefit white workers, 15

immigrants exploit other immigrants, 53–54; Chinese nail salon, 54; employer retaliation against worker regarding minimum wage and overtime pay complaints, 54

instrumental and communicative functions of law, 141

International Labour Organization (ILO): and enforcement of conventions, 148; and labor protections for workers, 154–55; and procedural labor rights, 147; conventions on freedom of association (No. 87) and collective bargaining (No. 98) do not address wage levels, 148, 154–55; conventions not been ratified by nation-states, 149; Decent Work initiative, 148, 156; ILOLEX and NATLEX databases at, 145; rights-based and trade-based approaches, 146

International Ladies Garment Workers Union (ILGWU): organizes along racial and gender lines, 33; supported liberal labor legislation in the 1930s, 33–34

intersectional legal claims, 43, 113

involuntary servitude, 78; and voluntary arrangements, 78; debt bondage, peonage and, 78. *See also* Thirteenth Amendment

iron triangle: link between low wages, occupational risks, and race and immigration status, 122

janitorial workers: documented and undocumented workers employed as, 59–60; employer explanation for payment of low wages, 60–61; Expert Janitorial used different subcontractors, 60; Jan-Pro classification of workers as "independent businesses," 59;

janitorial workers *(continued)*
lawsuit against Expert Janitorial subcontractor *(Becerra v. Expert Janitorial)*, 60; multiple state lawsuits against Jan-Pro *(Depianti v. Jan-Pro)*, 59–60; presence of interlocking contracts, 61; victims in Jan-Pro business promotion, 59

King, Martin Luther, Jr. (Reverend): Fight for $15 and, 36; minimum wage and, 40; March on Washington (1963), 40
King, Rodney, 35

labor rights: as fundamental rights, 77; importance of labor movement linking national efforts with workers abroad, 152–53; increased role of immigrants in labor movement, 151
Latina and Latino critical legal theory (LatCrit): and critical race praxis, 24; and critical race theory (CRT), 24;
law and political economy (LPE): explained, 107, 109; and how the Fair Labor Standards Act of 1938 excludes vulnerable groups, 107;
Ledbetter, Lilly: limitations in Lilly Ledbetter Fair Pay Act of 2009, 42–43
legally sanctioned subminimum wages: for disabled workers, 65; principally affects women and people of color, 65; six states require minimum wage for tipped workers, 64; tip credit rule, 65
living wage, 7; definition, 11, 155, 157; as a human right, 11–12; important link to setting level of minimum wage, 80–81, 124, 144; labor movement support for, 33–34; Los Angeles ordinance (1997), 29; Massachusetts Institute of Technology (MIT) calculator of, 156; municipal ordinances (LWOs) limited to government contractors, 155; Pasadena ordinance (2016), 29; raising minimum wage and, 5; repeal of Santa Monica's LWO, 30–31; Santa Monica ordinance (2001), 29–31; trade agreements and enforcement of, 153
López, Ian Haney: class and race framework resonates broadly, 23, 32; on

narratives that can garner white support along class lines, 23; research on race and elections, 23
Los Angeles Alliance for a New Economy (LAANE): emerged among local individuals and workers, 35. *See also* Contreras, Miguel; Durazo, María Elena

market failure, 25; associated with racialization, 10; and employer valuation of the labor of people of color and immigrants, 15; as failure to adequately compensate workers and risks involved, 10; global minimum wage actions have not stemmed global inequality, 145; and limits of free market for wages, 134; and livable wage, 123
Matsuda, Mari, 21
meat processing workers, 150: deemed "essential" but not paid essential wages, 18, 122; historical employment of immigrants as, 104; immigrants and people of color represented among, 10; International Beef Processors (IBP) appealed to Supreme Court regarding worker compensable activity *(IBP v. Alvarez)*, 104; mandated to work during COVID-19 pandemic, 118, 122; Supreme Court ruled against IBP, 104
Michael's Painting (case): majority of workers signed authorization cards at, 51; National Labor Relations Board (NLRB) ruled that firm must bargain with Painters Union, 51; and undocumented migrants, 54–55;
minimum salary, 11; as replacement of hourly wage, 11, 117
minimum wage: five states with no state law on, 104, 154; importance of, 117, 157; living wage as the, 144; Massachusetts first state to enact (1912), 78, 79; need for a higher, 144; need to remove exemptions for domestic and agricultural workers, 117; as organizing principle, 9; and racial justice, 31; state legislatures preventing localities from raising, 91; states as patchwork of different, 103. *See also* federal minimum wage

National Labor Relations Act of 1935 (NLRA): impact on Black and Mexican laborers, 103; integrated labor rights as civil rights, 41; meant to exclude people of color and women, 16; occupational exclusions, 15, 57

Nevada: Las Vegas taxi drivers, 110–12

New Deal labor laws: altered relations between employers and workers, 3, 9; Commerce Clause and, 79; exclusion of agricultural and domestic workers, 57; and foundations of racism, 15. *See also* Fair Labor Standards Act of 1938 (FLSA); National Labor Relations Act of 1935 (NLRA)

North American Free Trade Agreement (NAFTA): contained eleven protective labor principles, 145, 153; and North American Agreement on Labor Cooperation (NAALC), 146

One Fair Wage (OFW) movement, 65; and racial legacy of wage systems, 65, 134

Patel v. Quality Inn South (case), 56

Peonage Act of 1867, 76

political economy of wages: corporations raise wages to forestall unionization, 123; economic-based discrimination, 2–5

Pope, James Gray: and Thirteenth Amendment as basis for enhanced labor rights, 77

Portal-to-Portal Act of 1947, 103, 104–6. *See also* meat processing workers; warehouse workers

prison and detained labor: GEO Group and CoreCivic litigation, 82–83. *See also* Thirteenth Amendment

race and wage policy. *See* federal minimum wage; minimum wage

racial political economy, 11, 57. *See also* political economy of wages; structural discrimination

Reconstruction, 73, 76–78, 91

Restaurant Opportunity Council (ROC United): and origins of tipping practice in slavery and Jim Crow, 24;

ROC-led struggle to end tipped minimum wage, 87; traces origins of tipped wages to 1938 minimum wage law, 32

Roosevelt, Franklin D. (president): enacted Fair Labor Standards Act of 1938, 33; enacted National Labor Relations Act of 1935, 33; Perkins, Frances (Secretary of Labor), role in establishing minimum wage, 33

service charge system: alternative to direct tipping systems, 71; applies to all service workers in Massachusetts, 71; collective bargaining a better alternative to, 70; covers food and beverage services in Hawai'i, 71; fees should go to employees, 71; limitations of, 71; not the property of employers in Hawai'i, 71; and predictability in compensation, 69; problems in systems run by employers, 70; as race-conscious reform, 134; Union Square Hospitality Group adopted, 132

Service Employees International Union (SEIU): and Fight for $15 strategy, 36; and Justice for Janitors campaign, 151

Santa Monicans Allied for Responsible Tourism (SMART), 29; mobilized for living wage ordinance for hotel industry, 31

sex workers: definition of sex work, 37; industry structured to avoid paying minimum wage to, 38; Las Vegas and vagrancy laws against, 47; misclassification and wage theft, 12, 38. *See also* exotic dancers

Signal International LLC (Allied Signal Shipyard). *See* guest workers

Starbucks: raising of wages at, 102; unionization at, 123

state preemption of local minimum wage laws, 88–91; deployment of Thirteenth Amendment as litigation strategy, 89–90; Eleventh Circuit Court of Appeals and *Lewis* case, 89; and *Lewis v. the Governor of Alabama*, 88–89. *See also* Thirteenth Amendment

states with minimum wage tied to federal wage: problems with, 81

states without minimum wage laws, 85–86; federal-state governmental structure limits enforcement, 154; possible complaint against U.S. for failing to protect workers, 154; prisoners' legal recourse to challenge wage payment, 82. *See also* Thirteenth Amendment

strategies to improve economic lives of workers: address market failures, 122–23; address politics related to minimum wage, 126; enact basic income to supplement minimum wage, 135–36; enact risk premiums for hazardous work, 121–22, 134; end minimum wage exemption for agricultural and domestic workers, 129–30; end tipped wage, 132–34; establish wage boards, 125–26; implement pay transparency, 121; increase minimum wage and enforce payment, 126–28; index the minimum wage, 124–25; link hourly wage in transition to minimum salary, 136–38; raise minimum wage, 123–24; reinterpret Thirteenth Amendment, 135; reward work, 130–31; use presidential extraordinary powers, 128

structural discrimination, 5; defined, 10

subservience thesis, 8

Sure-Tan v. National Labor Relations Board (case): and undocumented workers as employees, 55, 152

Thirteenth Amendment (1865): as basis for right to unionize and minimum wage litigation, 73–74; and challenge to unequal application of minimum wage laws, 9, 74; and court acknowledgment of debt bondage and peonage, 74; and Department of Justice use of to address economic justice, 27; government obligations under, 75–76, 78; and involuntary servitude, 2–3, 71–74, 80; justifies exploitation in prisons, 2–3; possible litigation combining Fourteenth Amendment and, 74, 75–76; and pursuit of economic justice, 27; Thai garment workers case and, 72; universal nature of, 71; workers and rights claims under, 72–73. *See also* gig workers; disabled workers in sheltered workshops; prison and detained labor; state preemption of local minimum wage laws; states without minimum wage laws

tip credit systems: allows employers to avoid paying minimum wage, 68; benefits of ending, 69; *Cezarz v. Wynn* (2021) ruling on management of tip pool, 67; forty-five states allow, 88; Hawai'i increased, 124

tipped minimum wage: and employer flexibility to pay lower wages, 65; as exploitative, 68; increasing minimum wage as solution to, 71

trade agreements: as vehicles for setting and enforcing wage standards, 149. *See also* North American Free Trade Agreement (NAFTA); United States-Mexico-Canada Agreement (USMCA)

trade-wage dichotomy, 144; importance of a wage-setting authority, 150; trade agreements with enforceable minimum wage provisions, 129

Trafficking Victims Protection Act of 2000 (TVPA), 80

Trans-Pacific Partnership (TPP): and minimum wage protections at risk, 148; and political debates in the U.S., 149; regional trade agreement, 144

Trump, Donald J. (president): plan to withdraw from Trans-Pacific Partnership (TPP) negotiations, 150; reversal of enforcement of federal law under, 120

undocumented workers: AFL-CIO supported employer sanction in debates about Immigration Reform and Control Act of 1986, 152; employed at Quality Inn South motel and plaintiffs in *Patel v. Quality Inn South*, 56; employed at Surak Leather Factory and plaintiffs in *Sure-Tan v. NLRB*, 55; estimated 18 percent unionized, 105; excluded from some basic income proposals, 136; lack of bargaining power, 57–58; and legal wage claims, 8, 55; not eligible for back pay under *Hoffman Plastic Compounds v. NLRB*, 55; as plaintiffs in *Depianti v. Jan-Pro*, 59–60; as victims of wage theft, 49; *Sure-Tan* decision determined they were statutory employees, 55; UNITE! (Union of Needletrades, Industrial, and Textile Employees): campaigns against Guess? Inc., 32; prominence of Latino immigrants in campaigns, 32

United States-Mexico-Canada Agreement (USMCA, 2020): enforceability of labor standards remains an issue, 147; and minimum wage standards, 153

Uvawas (El Monte sweatshop case, 1995): *Bureerong v. Uvawas* suit, 80; effort to use Thirteenth Amendment against private employers, 72, 73; *Bureerong* was ultimately settled, 72–73. *See also* Thirteenth Amendment

Voting Rights Act of 1965: and March on Washington (1963); support of labor for, 34

Wage and Hour Division (WHD), Department of Labor (DOL): authority to investigate wage and hour violations, 62; decrease in investigations during Bush administration, 62–63; enforcement issues prioritized by administrators of, 62; exemption for apprentices, trainees, disabled persons, and students, 62; and exemptions to minimum wages, 62; General Accountability Office (GAO) report on, 63

wage justice, 9; exotic dancers and restaurant workers seeking, 3; link to racial justice, 4, 12, 43; and racial history

legacies, 9; and weak enforcement of wage laws, 63

wage reforms: better enforcement of wage and hour law, 4; and construct of hourly wage, 4; relevance of critical race theory to, 5; states' and localities' ability to raise wages above federal minimum, 91

wage theft: exotic dancers/sex workers and, 45, 49; explained, 53; and federal enforcement of labor laws, 63; growth in, 2; guest workers', day laborers', and sex workers' experience of, 12, 58; and immigrants, 62; immigrant sex workers vulnerable to, 63; impact on immigrants and workers of color, 8, 20, 26, 43–44, 157; legally sanctioned, 12; and legal remedies to address, 26; limitation of disparate impact claims, 113; survey of, 96; and threats of violent coercion, 73; by transient businesses, 5; undocumented workers as victims of, 23, 49; and violations of overtime laws, 58

warehouse workers, 106–7, 123. *See also* Amazon corporation

Weil, David: administrator of Wage and Hour Division (WHD) at Department of Labor (DOL), 59, 62; and "fissured workplace," 59, 128; on secondary negative effects of fissuring, 62

Women's Trade Union League (WTUL): and liberal labor legislation, 33

worker misclassification and wage theft: impacts on day laborers, guest workers, and sex workers, 12

worker retention ordinances (WRO): described, 37; Hotel Employees and Restaurant Employees Union Local 11 effort to legislate local working conditions, 37; and Los Angeles City Council, 37. *See also* Durazo, María Elena

Founded in 1893,
UNIVERSITY OF CALIFORNIA PRESS
publishes bold, progressive books and journals
on topics in the arts, humanities, social sciences,
and natural sciences—with a focus on social
justice issues—that inspire thought and action
among readers worldwide.

The UC PRESS FOUNDATION
raises funds to uphold the press's vital role
as an independent, nonprofit publisher, and
receives philanthropic support from a wide
range of individuals and institutions—and from
committed readers like you. To learn more, visit
ucpress.edu/supportus.